THE ART OF NAMING

NEONYM® Creative Guide to Selecting Names and Trademarks

PETER H. KARLEN

METAMARK
BOOKS

BUSINESS/SCIENCE/TECHNOLOGY DIVISION
CHICAGO PUBLIC LIBRARY
400 SOUTH STATE STREET
CHICAGO, IL 60605

THE ART OF NAMING: NEONYM CREATIVE GUIDE TO SELECTING NAMES AND TRADEMARKS

© 2008 Neonym Corporation

All Rights Reserved

Except for a reviewer who may quote brief passages in a review, this book may not be reproduced, adapted or transmitted, in whole or in part, in any form or by any means, graphic, electronic, or mechanical, including without limitation photocopying, recording, taping, or by any information storage retrieval system, without written permission from the copyright owner who may be contacted at www.neonym.com.

The content of this book is subject to the Cautions/Disclaimers in Section II of the Guide.

Published by Metamark Books, La Jolla, California USA

Book and Cover design by Jill Davis Design, Cardiff, California

Photos: © iStockphoto.com, pp. 18, 108, 226, 234, 250, 270; © Jack Davis, pp. 14, 48, 172, 202, 218; © Jill Davis, p. 4; © Carol Sonstein, La Jolla, CA, p. 305.

ISBN 978-0-9820420-0-7

Printed in the United States of America

Contents

Acknowledgements *1*

I INTRODUCTION *2*

Tasting the Trademark... *5*
Marked for Success *5*
Explanation of This Guide *7*
Terminology and Glossaries... *9*
Editorial Viewpoint *10*
Reader Input *10*

II CAUTIONS/DISCLAIMERS *12*

Legal Considerations.. *14*
Marks and Names Mentioned in Text................................... *15*

III METHODS *16*

1 Start Early *18*
2 Patience and Diligence *18*
3 Flexibility *19*
4 Product Qualities.. *19*
5 Company Story *20*
6 Computer Programs Which Generate Names *21*
7 Online Databases *22*
8 Reference Books *22*
9 Name Selection Companies *23*
10 Trademark and Trade Name Searches *23*
11 Online Search Engines *24*
12 "Tweaking" Marks *24*
13 Foreign and International Searches *25*
14 Trial Uses of Mark *26*
15 Focus Groups *26*
16 Intra-Company Selection1 .... *27*
17 Test Marketing *27*
18 Consumer and Employee Participation;
     Naming Contests *28*
19 Consumer Choice *28*
20 Extramural, Outside Feedback *29*
21 Source of Marks; Personnel *29*

22	Buying Someone Else's Mark	30
23	Licensed Marks	31
24	Consent Agreements	31
25	Expired and Cancelled Registrations	32
26	Other Abandoned Marks	32
27	Foreign Marks	33
28	Playing Off Another's Mark	33
29	Inventory of Industry Marks	34
30	Semantic Positioning	34
31	Competitive Analysis	35
32	Inventory of Restrictions	36
33	Choosing the Kind of Mark	37
34	Appropriate Registrations	37
35	Selection Chart	38
36	Foreign Registrations	38
37	Creativity	39
38	Lateral Thinking	40
39	Transmutational Thinking	41
40	Analytic Thinking	42
41	Analogies	42
42	Re-Definition	43
43	Order of Selection	44
44	Post Selection Branding	44

IV GENERAL CONSIDERATIONS 46

45	Similar Marks	48
46	Avoidance of Conflicting Marks	48
47	Selection of Multiple Marks	49
48	Sound of Your Mark	50
49	Audibility	50
50	Phonetic Marks	50
51	Fixed Pronunciation	51
52	Legible Marks	52
53	Easy-To-Pronounce Words	52
54	Best Spelling	53
55	Word Mark Appearance	54
56	Textual Visibility	54
57	Dominance	55
58	Word Order	56
59	Word Division or Combination	58
60	Word Mark Stylization	58
61	Font/Typeface	59
62	Visual and Graphic Possibilities	60

63	Matching Word With Design	61
64	Slogan Possibilities	61
65	Nickname Potential	61
66	Adaptable Marks	62
67	Stimulating and Calming Marks	63
68	Memorable Marks	64
69	Easy-To-Remember Marks	64
70	Humorous Marks	65
71	Metaphors	65
72	Dilution	66
73	Timing Factors	66
74	Long-Lasting Marks	67
75	Time Factors and Connotations	68
76	Social Trends	70
77	Product Expansion and Contraction	70
78	Solidity, Mass, and Inertia	71
79	Velocity; Flexibility	71
80	Good or Pleasant Connotations	72
81	Inappropriate Marks	72
82	Unintended References; Malapropisms	73
83	Metaphoric Consistency	73
84	Advertising Costs	74
85	Internet Usage	75
86	Adjectival Marks	76
87	Business Resources	76
88	Protection Costs	76
89	Word Origins	77
90	Problems In Other Languages	78
91	Global Palatability	78
92	International Use of English Words	78
93	International Adaptability	79
94	International Legal Considerations	81
95	Virtual Worlds	81
96	Words With Many Syllables	82
97	Shorter Marks	82
98	Parsimonious Marks	83
99	Customer Base	84
100	Customer Self-Expression	85
101	Gender Considerations; Masculine/Feminine/Neuter	85
102	Social Status, Vocabulary, and Propriety Levels	86
103	Multi-Level Market Considerations	86
104	Consumer Marks Vs. "Trade" Marks	87
105	Pricing	87
106	User of Mark	88

107	Entire Trademark Program; Trademark Architecture and Nomenclature	89
108	Trademark Families	90
109	Trademark Themes	91
110	Salability	91
111	Plurality of Marks; Multiple Marks for the Same Product	92
112	Multiple Marks for Closely Related Competitive Products	93
113	Relationship of Mark's Owner to Product	94
114	Relationship to Contiguous Marks	94
115	Connections With Other Aspects of Your Business; Telephone Numbers	95
116	Patent Considerations	95
117	Trade Secrets	96
118	Relationship to Your Business	96
119	The Right Impression as to Business Focus and Form	97
120	Business Self-Expression	97
121	Aesthetic Decision	98
122	Resonance	99
123	Marks With Meaning	100
124	Links With Folklore and Cultural Figures	101
125	Spiritual Content	101
126	Magic	102
127	Subconscious, Subliminal Associations	102
128	Alphabetical Position of Mark	103
129	Typing and Keyboard Considerations	103
130	Internet Considerations	104
131	Domain Name Availability	104

V SUBJECT MATTER 106

132	Fanciful, Capricious Marks	108
133	Arbitrary Marks	109
134	Suggestive Marks	109
135	Descriptive Marks	110
136	Inter-Category or Hybrid Marks	111
137	Geographically Descriptive Marks	112
138	Place Names; Toponyms	112
139	Addresses	113
140	Cultural Icons; Landmarks	113
141	Quality Designations	114
142	Generic Designations	114
143	Surnames	115

144	First Names	*116*
145	Middle Names and Nicknames	*116*
146	Full Names	*117*
147	Others' Names	*118*
148	Historic Names	*118*
149	Names From Fiction	*119*
150	Mythological Names	*119*
151	Astronomical Names	*120*
152	Legendary Names	*120*
153	Group Names	*120*
154	Eponyms	*121*
155	Acronyms, Bacronyms, and Initials	*122*
156	Abbreviations	*123*
157	Extractions	*123*
158	Nominatives and Genitives	*124*
159	Plurals and Singulars	*124*
160	Suffixes and Prefixes	*125*
161	First Letters of Marks	*125*
162	Last Letters of Marks	*126*
163	Omitted Letters and Telescoped Marks	*127*
164	Decapitations	*127*
165	Added Letters	*128*
166	Changed Letters	*129*
167	Replaced Letters: Symbols Instead of Letters	*129*
168	Infrequently-Used Letters	*130*
169	Trite Use of Letters; Misspelled Words	*130*
170	Vowel Sounds	*131*
171	Euphony and Cacophony	*131*
172	Rebuses	*132*
173	Add-Ons	*133*
174	Composite Marks	*134*
175	Combined Words	*134*
176	Combination/Blended Words; Portmanteaus	*135*
177	Dual Meaning Composites	*136*
178	Reversed Letters or Words	*136*
179	Backwards/Flipped Letters	*137*
180	Chiasmus	*137*
181	Anagrams	*138*
182	Alphabetic/Numeric Analogs and Transmutations	*139*
183	Palindromes	*139*
184	Numbers, Numeric Devices, Currency Symbols, and Alphanumeric Marks	*140*
185	Other Alphabets and Numerals	*140*
186	Punctuation	*141*

187	Marks With Diacritical Symbols	*141*
188	Upper and Lowercase Lettering	*142*
189	Internet Domain Names	*142*
190	Titles	*143*
191	Classical Roots	*143*
192	Foreign Language Terms	*144*
193	Translations	*145*
194	Anglicized Words and Names	*145*
195	Incongruous Marks; Multi-Language Marks	*146*
196	Colloquialisms, Slang, and Idioms	*146*
197	Obscure Words	*147*
198	Puns On Words	*148*
199	Double Entendre	*148*
200	Parodies	*149*
201	Rhymes and Semi-Rhymes	*150*
202	Alliteration	*150*
203	Rhythmic Marks	*150*
204	Tautonyms; Reduplicated Words	*151*
205	Ricochet Words	*152*
206	Colors In Word Marks	*152*
207	Sounding Like the Product; Onomatopoeia	*153*
208	Product Component Marks	*153*
209	Looking Like the Product	*154*
210	Diminutives	*154*
211	Experiential, Evocative Marks	*154*
212	Reification of Verbs; Agentive Words and Gerunds	*155*
213	Noun Marks	*155*
214	Verb Marks	*156*
215	Pure Adjectives	*156*
216	Adverbs	*157*
217	Other Parts of Speech; Conjunctions, Prepositions, and Articles	*157*
218	Mixed Metaphors; Oxymorons	*158*
219	Metonyms	*159*
220	Homonyms; Soundalikes	*159*
221	Synonyms	*160*
222	Antonyms	*161*
223	Contronyms	*162*
224	Multiple Meanings; Homographs, Heteronyms, and Capitonyms	*162*
225	Body Parts	*164*
226	Animal Marks; Theronyms	*164*
227	Literary or Commonly-Used Expressions	*165*
228	Newly-Devised Slogans and Phrases	*165*

229 Taglines..*166*
230 "Mission" Marks *166*
231 Action Marks *167*
232 Serendipity; Self-Connected Marks....................................*167*
233 Miscellaneous Subject Matter *168*
234 Prescribed Format Marks; Call Letters *168*
235 Miscellaneous State Marks *169*

VI DESIGN MARKS *170*

236 Design Goals *172*
237 Design Factors *173*
238 Design Selection Process *173*
239 Energy Flow and Feng Shui..*173*
240 Visual Activity *174*
241 Symmetry...*174*
242 Anomaly...*175*
243 Balance *175*
244 Orientation *176*
245 Movement and Rotation *177*
246 Gravity...*177*
247 Perceptibility...*177*
248 Density; Concentration *178*
249 Angular vs. Curved *178*
250 Location *179*
251 Size; Scalability...*179*
252 3-D Effects *179*
253 4-D Effects *180*
254 Texture...*180*
255 Reproduction Quality *181*
256 Black-And-White Usage *181*
257 Black-And-White Reproduction...*181*
258 Grayscale Values, Stippling, and Shading *182*
259 Media of Use *182*
260 Electronic Designs *183*
261 Changeable Designs *184*
262 Product/Design Congruence...*184*
263 Form of Expression *185*
264 Simpler Designs *185*
265 Geometric Designs *186*
266 Pictorial Designs...*186*
267 Descriptive Designs *186*
268 Quasi-Functional Designs *187*
269 Copyrightability..*187*

270 Design Subject Matter *188*
271 Character Images *189*
272 Classic Symbols *189*
273 Timeless Designs *190*
274 Everyday Symbols *191*
275 Colors In Designs *191*
276 Appropriate Designs *192*
277 Stylized Words *193*
278 Signatures *193*
279 Hand-Drawn Marks *194*
280 Monograms *194*
281 Designs With Words *195*
282 Single Letters *195*
283 Package Surface Designs *196*
284 Patterns *196*
285 Word Art *197*
286 Natural Shapes *197*
287 Medallions and Seals *198*
288 Stitching Designs *198*
289 Ornamental Designs *198*
290 Cutouts and Brands *199*
291 Other Non-Inked Marks *199*

VII OTHER KINDS OF MARKS AND DEVICES **200**

292 Three-Dimensional Configurations *202*
293 Vehicles *202*
294 Buildings and Structures *203*
295 Clothing *203*
296 Labels, Tags, and Tabs *203*
297 Container Shapes *203*
298 Container Features *204*
299 Pill and Tablet Shapes *204*
300 Holograms *205*
301 Moving Marks *205*
302 Olfactory Marks *205*
303 Flavors *206*
304 Tactile Marks *206*
305 Sound Marks *207*
306 Light Marks *207*
307 Color Marks *208*
308 Color Combinations *208*
309 Liquid and Gel Colors *209*

310	Powder and Particle Colors	*210*
311	Pill and Tablet Colors	*210*
312	Wire, Rope, and Thread Colors	*211*
313	Miscellaneous Ornaments	*211*
314	Product Displays	*211*
315	Living Matter Marks	*212*
316	Trade Dress	*212*
317	Collective Marks	*213*
318	Collective Membership Marks	*213*
319	Certification Marks	*214*
320	Functional Marks	*214*

VIII PROHIBITIONS 216

321	Prohibited Statements	*218*
322	Misdescriptive Marks	*218*
323	Indecent or Scandalous Marks	*219*
324	Misleading or Deceptive Marks	*220*
325	Disparaging Marks	*220*
326	Flags and Insignias	*221*
327	Deceased Presidents	*221*
328	Surname Prohibition	*221*
329	Living Individuals	*222*
330	Deceased Individuals	*222*
331	Copyrighted Images	*222*
332	Foreign Prohibitions	*223*
333	Marks Protected By Statute	*223*

IX TRADEMARK GLOSSARY 224

X LINGUISTIC GLOSSARY 232

XI INDEX OF WORD MARKS 248

XII IMAGES 268

About the Author *305*

ACKNOWLEDGEMENTS

I wish to express my deepest appreciation to the following people whose help and guidance made this book possible. To Carolanne Gano, graphic designer of Sydney, Australia, for her comments and suggestions regarding the Design Marks section. To my wife Lyn Thwaites, Managing Editor of the CLIMATE CHANGE BUSINESS JOURNAL, and former Managing Editor of the NUTRITION BUSINESS JOURNAL and the ENVIRONMENTAL BUSINESS JOURNAL, for her editing and insightful suggestions regarding the content of this Guide. And to Jill Davis who contributed so much to the format, design, and aesthetics of the book.

Also, I wish to acknowledge all our clients who supported us over the years and from whose experiences and challenges we derived much of the knowledge that made this Guide possible.

—*Peter Karlen*

THE IMPORTANCE OF TRADEMARK SELECTION AND NAMING

I Introduction

"In the beginning was the Word."

JOHN 1:1

The average person encounters

as many as 1,000 trademarks every day. Blanketed over the physical and electronic environment, these words and symbols are designed to attract attention and identify products. Your trademark will be one of them. But will it be magnetic and memorable or forgotten in milliseconds?

OUR GOAL IS TO HELP YOU SELECT an outstanding mark that will attract customers and be a standard bearer for your business.

A trademark is a word, name, phrase, symbol, design, configuration, or other device used by one provider to distinguish its goods from those of another. In addition to traditional marks comprised of words (e.g., NIKE), phrases (WE ARE DRIVEN), and flat designs (the AT&T "globe" logo), marks may consist of sounds (the NBC chimes), colors (the brown of UPS delivery trucks), three-dimensional shapes (the MCDONALD'S arches), and even scents (fragrances applied to liquid fuels). A service mark has the same functions but in relation to services. *(See more complete definitions in the Trademark Glossary, Section IX.)*

Trademarks and service marks, often called "brand names" when in word form, not only indicate the origin of products and help advertise them, but also guarantee consistent quality of the products they accompany.

I Introduction

TASTING THE TRADEMARK

Some new business owners believe that once advertised and displayed their products will sell themselves and that marks are not very important. As Shakespeare wrote, "What's in a name? That which we call a rose, by any other name would smell as sweet." Unfortunately, at least in the context of 21st century commerce, the Bard was wrong. New owners soon discover that without distinctive marks or similar devices their products are lost in a whirlwind of competition.

Mark Twain got close to the truth when he said of a cigar smoker, "He goes by the brand, yet imagines he goes by the flavor." Indeed, the new business owner soon discovers a trademark is just as likely to start selling the product as the product itself.

In describing a COKE vs. PEPSI taste test in which test subjects chose COKE when they were aware of product identity but preferred PEPSI in the blind taste test, one writer noted that the unblinded test subjects were actually "tasting the trademark." (See Rebecca Tushnet, "Gone in 60 Milliseconds: Trademark Law and Cognitive Science," 86 TEXAS LAW REVIEW 507 (2008).) Similarly, fast food labeled MCDONALD'S tasted better to children than the same food unlabeled. (See Thomas N. Robinson, et al., "Effects of Fast Food Branding on Young Children's Taste Preferences," 161 ARCHIVES OF PEDIATRICS & ADOLESCENT MEDICINE 792 (2007).)

MARKED FOR SUCCESS

Selecting the right mark and *trade name* is one of the most important tasks in establishing a business. Because the public comes to know you and your products only in relation to the marks and names you use, they often become the principal value of your business. Consider the following financial figures.

The September 1992 Financial World had the following valuations for major brands: MARLBORO $31.2B, KODAK $12.8B, COCA-COLA $24.4B, JOHNSON & JOHNSON $10.8B, and BUDWEISER $10.2B. In the Interbrand 2001 rankings of the "World's Most Valuable Brands" MARLBORO was over $22 billion, COCA-COLA and JOHNSON & JOHNSON rose to over $68 billion, and BUDWEISER and KODAK exceeded $10 billion. By 2007 Interbrand's rankings still showed COCA-COLA at the top, at $65.3 billion, with MICROSOFT and IBM closely following at $58.7 billion and $57.1 billion, respectively, and GE in fourth place at $51.6 billion.

I Introduction

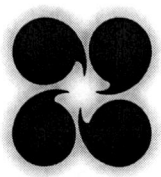

Beware too much committee decision-making which can stall progress and stifle ingenuity....

Brand values estimated by Interbrand and other sources usually denote the total value of the "brand," not merely the value of the trademark (the "brand name"). *(See the definition of brand in the Trademark Glossary, Section IX.)* Yet, because the trademark is the identifying symbol of the brand, without which the brand typically has little value, it comprises a major portion of the brand value.

Imagine trying to buy United Parcel Service of America, Inc. and being told that you could buy all the assets except the UPS and UNITED PARCEL SERVICE trademarks. How much would the company be worth without the marks? Another measure of value apart from sale price is the mark's earning power. That power is measured not only by the mark's ability to affect consumer choices but also by the premium (the additional money) the consumer will spend on the branded product rather than buy a cheaper alternative.

Many people establishing new businesses leave trademark selection until last. They fail to appreciate that the mark is a vessel for the value of their business, and a bad mark is a cracked cup allowing customer goodwill to flow away like water. Some business owners are not even aware of trademark values unless reminded of how pervasive branding is even within their own business. A survey by Roger C. Collins of 180 large North American corporations showed that such businesses often have huge inventories of marks, one or more corporations even claiming 2,500 marks. The median number of brand names was 15, with 30 percent claiming more than 60. A corollary is that many owners are not even aware that devices they use, such as designs, shapes, configurations, and sounds, are eligible for trademark status and protection. Thus, a big opportunity exists to dramatically enhance corporate equity and profits by selecting and protecting a portfolio of good marks.

Many trademark considerations also apply to Internet domain names. Domain names are often vital to business success. Though the domain name will often contain the company's trademark or trade name, as

I Introduction

per **hersheys.com** and **toshiba.com**, for purely online businesses, like **amazon.com** and **monster.com**, the domain name is the enterprise's primary designation. As such, domain names have dramatically increased in value, even spurring active domain name trading and speculation. In 2007 at least 106 domain names were sold for over $100,000, and one, **porn.com**, sold for almost $9.5M. (NYT, 2/1/2008, "Domain-Name Trading Gains Respect," at C-1) Probably most of those 106 names did not comprise famous trademarks or *trade names*. The value of domain names that do contain valuable trademarks or trade names, like **ford.com** or **burgerking.com**, could be tens of millions of dollars.

EXPLANATION OF THIS GUIDE

The scores of factors, considerations, and factual examples appearing henceforth come from years of experience in naming and trademark selection and are designed to enhance your knowledge and creativity in selecting names and marks.

Most topics are illustrated with well- or lesser-known marks, most of which are registered, so you can see how these principles apply to selection of real marks. Trademarks generally appear in all capital letters. Internet domain names appear in bold letters. In selecting marks used to illustrate concepts, the preference is for older "tried and true" marks, though new marks are sprinkled throughout.

The numbered paragraphs referencing designs and other marks that are not alphanumeric refer to specific U.S. Patent & Trademark Office (USPTO) registrations so you can view the cited marks. If you are reading an electronic version of this Guide, for almost all such registrations there is a link from the registration number to the page on which an image of the registered mark appears. Just click the registration number in the text. Most PC and Mac users can also click back from the linked page to the source page. The data for such cited registrations is not complete and is generally not being updated since the only purpose is to show the image or basic registration information for such design or other non-alphanumeric marks. (If you want more complete updated registration data, you must go to the USPTO website at **www.uspto.gov**.) If you are reading a paper version of this work, then, with help from numerical location tabs on the outside of the right hand page, you can find the images for the cited registrations of designs and other non-alphanumeric marks at the end, in ascending order of registration number.

7

I Introduction

Many of the insights and suggestions are not absolutes. Some successful marks violate ordinary rules of trademark selection, something we note in the text.

Though numerous topics are listed, the list is not exhaustive, nor do we cover every factor and consideration. Undoubtedly other factors, considerations, and rules not covered will surface in your selection process. *(See Section II, Cautions/Disclaimers.)*

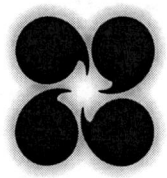

Picking an ordinary word like APPLE, KIWI, or ORANGE is like casting a net into the sea and landing a fish, whereas devising KODAK, EXXON, or QANTAS is more like assembling a jigsaw puzzle.

Also, almost all factors and considerations mentioned are not discussed in ultimate detail since the individual listed topics could be subjects of lengthier discussion. For instance, many topics by themselves are or could be subjects of articles, monographs, and even books. For that reason alone, this Guide by itself cannot equip you to professionally select trademarks and *trade names*. And even though this Guide will help you develop marks and names for your own business, you will still need professional help, especially from a trademark attorney, to select, search, test, and register your mark or name.

Occasionally, a particular concern is addressed in more than one numbered paragraph. Also, sometimes numbered topics overlap with others, with the hope that information categorized one way may strike a chord when categorized another.

The topics are arranged in a logical order, and many topics flow into ones that follow them, so that it makes sense to read the numbered paragraphs in ascending order.

Some of the Methods discussion *(Section III)* contains information already familiar to those with knowledge of naming and trademarks, but the very enumeration of selection techniques will serve as a useful reminder of methods one should keep in mind.

I Introduction

TERMINOLOGY AND GLOSSARIES

Included is a Trademark Glossary *(Section IX)* containing abbreviated definitions for trademark terminology. Words and their derivatives in italics are defined in the Trademark Glossary. To avoid visual clutter, a defined term will be italicized only once in a numbered paragraph, generally when it first appears. In the electronic version of this Guide there is a link between italicized trademark-related terms in the text and their definitions in the Trademark Glossary. Just click the italicized term. Most PC and Mac users can also click back from the linked page to the source page.

Since the terms "goods," "services," and "products" appear too many times to italicize them and link them to a referenced definition, by "goods" we mean physical articles like clothing, electrical devices, furniture, and chemicals; by "services" we mean performance of a duty, function, or activity such a financial, medical, advertising, and transportation services; and by "products" we are generally referring to both goods and services.

Though "trademarks" and "service marks" have separate definitions, where the context permits, "trademark(s)" is sometimes used to denote both trademarks and service marks. As mentioned previously, trademarks that consist of words are also called "brand names," which is why trademark selection is a process of naming, as is *trade name* selection. Thus, in the paragraphs on word marks, the term "mark" is usually equivalent to "brand name." Moreover, many of the considerations used in selecting a brand name apply to trade names and domain names, though one should be careful to note critical differences between brand names, trade names, and domain names and how they are selected.

Also included is a Linguistic Glossary *(Section X)* because the text contains technical linguistic terms like "lexeme," "morpheme," "phoneme," "meronym" and "tautonym" which require working definitions. Unlike the trademark terms defined in the Trademark Glossary, the linguistic terms in the Linguistic Glossary are not italicized in the text. Nonetheless, the reader who encounters an unknown linguistic term should try finding it in the Linguistic Glossary, and if not listed there, then in an online dictionary.

I Introduction

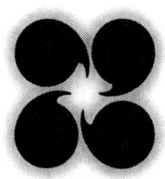

In general, avoid joining a crowd of similar marks. For instance, in book publishing many animal names are already imprint marks, such as PELICAN, PENGUIN, and BANTAM. Why be one more zebra in a herd of zebras?

EDITORIAL VIEWPOINT

We believe that in selecting a trademark the goal should be a mark which not only is commercially powerful but also has the following qualities: aesthetic, inspiring, non-pejorative, intelligent, and memorable. If the device can be imaginative, so much the better, though cute and clever marks often don't succeed if those are their only advantages. A long-lasting mark becomes part of the cultural landscape. Why litter that landscape with an uninspiring or unimaginative mark which only degrades the commercial environment? Besides, if you want to sell quality products, you will prosper more with a quality mark.

READER INPUT

We welcome readers' suggestions for adding new topics (e.g., additional methods, general considerations, or subject matter) when e-mailed to us. If we add any reader-suggested topic to any new version of this work and receive that suggestion more than 10 days before publication of that new version, we will provide a published acknowledgement to the person submitting the new topic, but only if they request acknowledgement in the e-mail containing their submission. We will rewrite text submitted for a new topic, so that any acknowledgement will extend only to the idea for the new topic. Such acknowledgement only applies to new topics and not to suggested changes or corrections to existing topics and items, which we also welcome. The acknowledgement will reflect only an attribution and the person's name and city/town and State of residence, if provided (e.g., "idea submitted by John Doe, Plaintown,

Introduction

NM"). No other consideration or compensation will be given. A suggested new item will be deemed received when we actually first open and view any e-mail transmission, not when it is merely sent to us. Because of spam filters and other factors, no one submitting an idea or suggestion should assume it has been received. Please send ideas and suggestions to Neonym Corporation at **www.neonym.com** via its Contact Us page. Thank you.

WHAT YOU NEED TO KNOW BEFORE READING THIS GUIDE

II Cautions/ Disclaimers

"The beginning of wisdom is to call things by their right names."

CHINESE PROVERB

Please carefully read the following
cautions/disclaimers before using this Guide and keep them in mind when pondering any concept, definition, or statement in the text.

NOT EVERY CONSIDERATION, factor, or kind of name or mark is discussed in this Guide, and numerous considerations and legal requirements, especially those peculiar to certain trades and industries, are <u>not</u> mentioned. And not every selection technique or kind of mark or name mentioned may be suitable for every business or activity.

LEGAL CONSIDERATIONS

The purpose of this NEONYM® naming and trademark selection Guide is <u>not</u> to give legal advice. At each stage the selection, investigation, testing, use, and registration of trademarks, service marks, trade names, and domain names should be done with the help of a qualified trademark attorney. The only purpose here is to make the reader aware of many considerations which may be involved in selection, so when choosing a name or mark the reader will be more resourceful and imaginative.

Also, the focus is selection, <u>not</u> legal protection, and though some factors regarding U.S.A. legal protection are mentioned, many other factors regarding use, registration, usage and registration symbols, prohibitions, and other concerns are <u>not</u> mentioned and must be discussed with your trademark attorney when you embark on a naming or trademark program.

You cannot rely on any legal points or definitions in this work since trademark and unfair competition laws rapidly change and vary from jurisdiction to jurisdiction; moreover, most legal rules regarding trademarks and commercial

II Cautions/Diclaimers

names are subject to exceptions, qualifications, and differing interpretations. Even within a single jurisdiction different judges or trademark examiners can reach different conclusions about the same matter. Thus, no version of this work can be entirely accurate, up-to-date, or complete no matter how recent. Many marks and names believed to be easily protectable have been denied protection, and vice versa. Therefore, no one should act on the information in this Guide but rather act only after seeking professional legal advice. For relatively current information on U.S. trademark law, see updated versions of Title 15, United States Code and updated treatises such as GILSON ON TRADEMARKS and MCCARTHY ON TRADEMARKS.

No attorney-client relationship is established by our transmission or by your receipt or reading of this work, and any communications you send us or we may send you about or arising from this work will not be legally privileged. Furthermore, the information in this Guide is not provided in the course of an attorney-client relationship, does not constitute legal advice, and does not substitute for, nor should be used to contradict, legal advice obtained from an attorney licensed in your State.

MARKS AND NAMES MENTIONED IN TEXT

All commentary on and reference to specific names and marks is based on general knowledge concerning famous names and marks and limited factual investigation regarding other names and marks. Some marks and names mentioned are only hypothetical. Commentary on or reference to any mark or name may be based on recent or older court cases or usage of that name or mark, and may no longer represent the mark's or name's most current usage, strength, or legal status. Some referenced marks are no longer in use. If any errors regarding origins, usage, rendition, characteristics, strength, validity, or qualities of any mark or name appear in the text, upon written request from the mark's/name's owner we will either correct them or delete mention of the mark or name.

You should not rely on such commentary or reference in taking any action, making any decision or forming any opinion in relation to the marks or names mentioned in the text, since the only purpose of mentioning those marks or names is to illustrate concepts.

TECHNIQUES YOU MAY USE TO SELECT A NAME

III Methods

"The nameless is the origin of Heaven and Earth, while naming is the origin of the myriad things."

LAO-TZU

The following are some general

methods for selecting marks, including a number of sources for generating words and names. Not covered are many specific techniques for creating lists of possible marks.

1 START EARLY

TO AVOID HASTY CHOICES, start selection early. You will often need as much time as possible before product introduction in order to launch with a viable, protectable, available mark. For example, it takes quite some time after selecting the mark to know whether it will be registerable. At the U.S. Patent & Trademark Office (USPTO), for instance, an examiner may take six months or more from the application filing date to issue an initial refusal. The application may not be published for opposition until approximately 12 to 18 months after filing (or longer), so until then you may not know about third-party objections.

Ideally, selection should start years before product launch. Even aside from legal requirements and third-party objections, the process itself can be lengthy, e.g., creating lists of candidate marks, performing availability searches, conducting focus groups and market studies, reserving domain names, and preparing logo formats. In fact, the mark should often come at the very beginning of product development. As said, "In the beginning was the Word...." (John 1:1)

2 PATIENCE AND DILIGENCE

Don't rush to select a mark. Having a good mark can "make" your business, whereas a bad one can "break" it. Moreover, if you choose poorly, you may get sued by competitors for trademark infringement and unfair competition.

III **Methods**

State, Federal, and foreign trademark registries are so jam-packed with applications and registrations that it is hard to find available marks, except when one is original and imaginative. This is why it is important to generate numerous marks for evaluation, so you have much to look at and spur your creativity. Often a new business may have to consider five, ten, twenty, or even fifty marks before getting the right match. As Linus Pauling noted, "The best way to have a good idea is to have a lot of ideas."

You may want to keep a centralized list of dozens of marks from which candidates are added and subtracted. Naturally, before embarking on costly trademark searches and other steps like test marketing, you will probably create a short list of five to ten marks. One approach is to rank the listed marks in order of preference, then start your availability searches at the top of the list until you find an available mark.

3 FLEXIBILITY

During selection it's usually best to remain flexible and open-minded. For example, you may not want to become too attached to any mark early in the process. After all, that mark may prove unavailable or blind you to other kinds of marks which might be better. A mark seemingly perfect at first may be unavailable or have other weaknesses, e.g., problem meanings in other languages. *(See Globally Palatable Marks, ¶ 91.)* Also, even an available mark may face later objections from investors and company insiders who can veto it.

The advantage of flexibility is the chance to focus on more than one kind of mark and compare the virtues of each. For instance, flexibility is shown by willingness to consider *fanciful*, *arbitrary*, and *suggestive* marks. As the Chinese proverb says, "Sour, sweet, bitter, pungent, all must be tasted." A spillover of flexibility is that even when focus finally shifts to one kind of mark, or even to a specific mark, what you have learned about the semantic qualities of other kinds of marks will help in tweaking the remaining mark(s). *(See "Tweaking" Marks, ¶ 12.)*

4 PRODUCT QUALITIES

As if explaining to a potential customer, describe your product or service, its functions and characteristics, as well as the markets it will populate; when finished write down this description. Then write down a list of qualities,

III Methods

feelings, associations, and other words and phrases which come to mind from the description. Often the list of generated words and qualities will provide a root word or morpheme which becomes part of the mark. Occasionally, morphemes from two or more words can be pasted together to form a composite mark. *(See Composite Marks, ¶ 174.)* Or the words may generate useful synonyms. *(See Synonyms, ¶ 221.)*

For instance, if selling laundry detergent, useful words and concepts might be "fresh," "clean," "safe," "bright," "white," "fragrant," and "easy"; if offering gas masks, the words and concepts might be "toxic," "noxious," "rescue," "save," "air," "breathe," "life," "pure," "clean," and "hope." Your list should include words and qualities which come quickly "off the top of your head," coupled with those that later come from careful reflection. Frequently the best mark is one that subtly reflects some or many of the qualities you first listed.

Often the final mark does not arise in brainstorming sessions but in moments of quiet reflection. As artist Grant Wood noted, "All the really good ideas I ever had came to me while I was milking a cow."

5 COMPANY STORY

Sometimes a mark will arise from the company "story," especially when the company has a long or intriguing history. The technique is to access, document, memorialize, and review the history for inspiration. After all, a mark rooted in the history of the company or its founders may provide an intimate connection to the past, a connection that can motivate owners and employees and strike the imagination of consumers.

Company founders have used family history to derive marks, e.g., VICTORINOX (Victoria, the founder's mother plus INOX, the international symbol for stainless steel), SARA LEE (a founder's daughter), WENDY'S (Dave Thomas' daughter), and MIRAMAX (Miriam and Max, the founders' parents). BETTY CROCKER came from William Crocker, a company president, and EDSEL was the unusual first name of a Ford Motor Company officer—a good mark coupled with an odd looking

III **Methods**

car. *(See Serendipity; Self-Connected Marks, ¶232.)* Product history has also generated marks, e.g., CANON mimicking the company's first camera product, the Kwannon, and BLAUPUNKT ("blue dot" in German) reflecting the company's early practice of placing blue dots on headphones that passed quality control tests.

Company and founder stories are a common source of marks. Marks having such origins may motivate the company management and workforce. Yet, such origins are typically not trumpeted to the outside world since revealing the mark's origin may submerge other useful meanings the mark may acquire.

6 COMPUTER PROGRAMS WHICH GENERATE NAMES

By spawning long lists of suggestions, special computer programs can generate marks for those finding it hard to devise one. Online or shareware anagram and random word generators may be helpful. Supposedly TAB for diet soft drinks was selected from a randomly generated list of thousands of three-and four-letter English words. Even specialized software is available for generating lists of names for specific purposes. For example, a number of software choices exist for generating nicknames and musical band names. Typically, the software will not yield the very best names, but names generated can be "tweaked" *(See "Tweaking" Marks, ¶12)* or inspire other names.

A problem with using name-generating software is that by merely picking through an "alms-basket of words," you may not be exercising the same thoughtfulness and creativity used in devising words from scratch. Words developed creatively will usually be better than those spawned mechanically, though occasionally one can win the lottery with a software-generated mark, particularly if the software encourages the user to prescribe selection parameters in great detail. Those programs that enable the user to control numerous parameters may partially replicate the pen-and-paper creative process.

The reason computer-generated names so rarely succeed is that you need the lengthy pen-and-paper brainstorming process to develop a strong feeling for what you ultimately want. Just because a program can instantly generate scores of names doesn't mean you can spot a winner amongst them without having experienced the time-consuming creative process.

III Methods

7 ONLINE DATABASES

The Internet abounds with useful databases. Here are a few examples: encyclopedias, thesauruses, the dictionaries (including foreign language and classical language works); Biblical databases like **blueletterbible.com;** Shakespeare databases covering character names, idioms, and invented words; word origin lists; lists of company name origins and product slogans; and lists of unusual kinds of words such as anagrams, tautonyms, ricochet words, and rebuses. Though the USPTO TESS trademark database is usually employed for preliminary availability searches, it is a field for trademark grazing for those who just want to browse. Using the "Structured Form Search (Boolean)" in that USPTO database is useful since that mode easily enables focused browsing, especially for design marks when "Description of Mark" is one of the fields selected. Usually the talisman for one's product is not found in these databases, but they can supply ideas and inspiration.

One caution: unless you have a focus or strategy in poring through long electronic lists, it's easy to get lost in a mist of words, and browsing though disparate lists is often like eating at a smorgasbord and forgetting what everything tasted like.

8 REFERENCE BOOKS

Was Lycos (Latin for "hunting spider") for Worldwide Web search services found in a reference book? (It's not a word on the tip of one's tongue.) One suspects that most marks having obscure meanings were culled from reference books. To stimulate creativity, look in dictionaries, encyclopedias, and thesauruses. Thesauruses and synonym finders are particularly useful because when you have a meaning in mind, you can view numerous words which convey that meaning in various shades. An excellent source showing unusual origins of words and phrases is BREWER'S DICTIONARY OF PHRASE AND FABLE. Similar sources are slang and jargon dictionaries. Brand name and trade directories are also possible sources since they show marks in your field. The Bible, primarily the King James Version, remains an ultimate literary source since its words and ideas are imbued throughout the English language. Shakespeare, the font of English idioms, is also an inspiration. For slogans, collections of idioms and famous quotations are useful. For design marks, public domain clip art in books, on disc, or on the Internet can help you. Sometimes protected images may inspire, but beware focusing on trademarked and copyrighted images because you may be encouraged to copy, even unconsciously.

III **Methods**

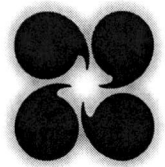

Paper books have one big advantage over computerized sources: serendipity. With two pages of a book in sight, something on the next page may accidentally catch your eye, whereas many computer screens won't show as much content without scrolling. Sitting down with a book also encourages more relaxed and leisurely browsing, conducive to creativity.

9 NAME SELECTION COMPANIES

If stumped in selecting a mark and not working with an imaginative attorney or advertising agency, then consider name selection companies around the United States who, for a fee, can generate marks for you. Because name selection and word creation is an art, there is no substitute for the experience of people whose livelihood is trademarks and trademark selection. Even if the naming company does not generate a great mark, the process of providing information, answering questions, and interacting with naming professionals usually has substantial educational benefits.

Like a yogi posed with his foot in back of the head, the over-tweaked mark may be so contorted that it loses its choice sound, meaning, or appearance.

10 TRADEMARK AND TRADE NAME SEARCHES

Always do an extensive availability search before adopting any mark. This may start with "screening" searches often done online or via computer databases. For USA marks, typically a screening search will cover U.S. State registrations (i.e., Alabama through Wyoming) and Federal applications and registrations at the U.S. Patent and Trademark Office (USPTO). If the screening search is "clean" and discloses no conflicts which would preclude usage, then at minimum a "full" search is usually ordered from a trademark search company, covering, e.g., the same State registrations and Federal applications and registrations but also common law and unregistered marks, trade directories, business names, and Internet domain names.

III Methods

Remember the many ways in which marks uncovered by a search may conflict with your mark, some considerations being the relationship between your products and those connected with the uncovered marks, as well as similarity of sound, appearance, and meaning. A test for "conflict" between marks is whether, given the parties' respective goods and services, the concurrent use of the marks in commerce would likely create public confusion. Even if your products are completely unrelated to those sold in connection with an identical or nearly identical mark used by somebody else, "anti-dilution" statutes may protect the owner of the other mark against use of your mark, particularly if the other mark is "famous."

Please note that search results are not 100% reliable, and occasionally some conflicting marks or names won't appear in the search results. This is because the search databases are often weeks or months out of date, even carefully devised search parameters and strategies won't disclose every conflicting mark, and not every source of conflict is covered by the databases. Generally, the more you spend on searches, the more reliable the results. The selection, ordering, and evaluation of searches should be done with an attorney's participation.

11 ONLINE SEARCH ENGINES

Even before spending money on formal trademark searches, you might run your list of possibilities on Internet search engines. After all, even USPTO examiners use search engines to determine whether marks can be distinctively used. A good initial choice is the "meta" search engine, like that at **dogpile.com**, which provides results from numerous search engines. Sometimes a **google.com** or **yahoo.com** search will show an obvious conflict. If a word you try out is widely used descriptively, or as a mark, trade name, product name, meta tag, or otherwise, the uses may emerge in the search results. Widespread or descriptive usage may lead you to abandon a possible mark before spending further time and money on it.

12 "TWEAKING" MARKS

If the search discloses a conflict with another's mark, rather than discard a good idea you might "tweak" your mark to possibly avoid a conflict. The following techniques are sometimes used: adding a suffix or prefix to the mark or even adding a distinctive new word; changing letters in the mark, especially the first letter of a word; converting a letter into another

III Methods

kind of typographical symbol, e.g., an "S" into a "$"; combining two words into one; subtracting letters, suffixes or prefixes; adding distinctive punctuation marks such as "?" and "!"; adding diacritical marks like the umlaut, tilde, or accent mark; reversing the order of words; using another form of a word (i.e., by shifting to another member of a lexeme); finding a synonym for one or more words in a multi-word mark; or changing the spelling of a word. Of course, where two marks are already confusingly similar, any of these techniques alone is unlikely to succeed, and success can only be made more likely by making two, three, or more of these changes all at once, by which time the newly constructed mark may be undesirable. That is, like a yogi posed with his foot in back of the head, the over-tweaked mark may be so contorted that it loses its choice sound, meaning, or appearance.

Section V on Subject Matter is replete with marks that reflect tweaking via the techniques described previously.

13 FOREIGN AND INTERNATIONAL SEARCHES

If you intend using the mark abroad, you may want to conduct international or foreign trademark searches. A mark cleared for use in the USA may not be available in many foreign countries, which could inhibit your expansion plans and lower the value of your business to buyers who intend full expansion. E.g., ZANTAC was available for use in the UK and USA but not available in France. Fortunately, AZANTAC was available in France so the mark's owner didn't have to make a dramatic adjustment for the French market.

Even if you don't intend foreign usage, international or foreign searches may be desirable because owners of famous foreign marks not registered at the USPTO nor appearing in USA trademark searches may try to stop others from using their marks in the USA.

Many types of foreign searches are available from search companies. For example, a worldwide

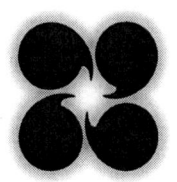

When a mark expresses just the right idea but is unavailable or unsuitable for use, you can transmute it, as an alchemist makes gold from lead.

III Methods

identical screening search may disclose identical registered or published marks throughout the world, and country-by-country availability searches help show whether the mark conflicts with the same or similar marks in each country searched. Additionally, for marks capable of different meanings or connotations in various countries/jurisdictions, you may want to conduct a connotation search to rule out connotations or meanings that might be ridiculous, unpleasant, or legally problematic. Foreign searches tend to be expensive, and before ordering a search one must carefully determine exactly what the search covers.

Many foreign trademark registries make their databases available electronically, online or otherwise, some without charge, but the databases are not equally accessible or useable, and a certain expertise is needed to make the electronic searches effective. As with domestic searches, you need an attorney's advice and participation.

14 TRIAL USES OF MARK

Before searching a mark, see how it looks on materials you would use it on, e.g., for trademarks look at usage on labels, tags, containers, packaging, sales displays, and advertising materials, and for service marks on business cards, letterhead, leaflets, brochures, printed and audiovisual advertisements, and business signs. You might also record audio renditions of the mark to test its sound. Often a mark attractive in the imagination is dull on paper or painful to the ear. Occasionally, the reverse is true: a mark seemingly DOA actually comes to life on screen or paper.

Like focus groups *(¶ 15)* and test marketing *(¶ 17)*, trial uses are like taking a car for a test drive before buying, though many companies don't have the time, money, or desire to test beyond trial uses and ad hoc focus groups.

15 FOCUS GROUPS

Having selected but not tested a mark, what about focus groups? Until you "try" the mark on somebody else, you really don't know if it will succeed. At least consider using focus groups within your own company, or even outside the company among trusted friends and associates. If you want a more objective response from people outside the company and outside your circle of friends and associates, then as much as reasonably possible, focus groups should usually reflect the kinds of people who might be customers and should

III Methods

reproduce the conditions in which the products will appear in the market. Market research firms can help determine initial consumer reactions.

As with any kind of testing or feedback which requires disclosure of the mark, you should consult an attorney to determine whether you should apply for registration before making disclosures, e.g., in order to prevent anyone else from applying first. Also make sure that you have some understanding with the participants, or better yet a written contract, regarding your intellectual property rights and the confidential nature of the trademark development process, about which you should seek legal advice.

16 INTRA-COMPANY SELECTION

After attending to "confidentiality" concerns, you may want to ask various people in your company to participate. A company may not want to restrict selection to its executives working with an advertising agency but may also want various departments to participate, including sales and marketing, art and design, and product development. Participants can be split into working groups based on various criteria, each group perhaps to develop one kind of choices and evaluate trademark lists developed by other groups. In this way talents of more creative and imaginative employees will be mixed with those of the more practical and analytical. However, just because many voices are heard does not mean that they all decide. Rarely will all participants agree on a final choice, so ultimately the company leadership must decide. Beware too much committee decision-making which can stall progress and stifle ingenuity since many committees are like back alleys where ideas are beckoned, then abandoned or smothered.

Sometimes the company may conduct a "contest" by awarding a prize to the person or department which selects the winning entry. *(See Consumer And Employee Participation; Naming Contests, ¶ 18.)* Surprisingly, such contests have produced few famous marks. An example of employee selection is HOSPIRA for hospital products, derived from "hospital," "spirit," and the Latin "spero" which means "I hope."

17 TEST MARKETING

A more uncommon approach is to test market the selected mark or a group of marks in limited territories or markets and then note the results through sales figures or customer surveys. Typically, this process is conducted with

III Methods

the help of market research professionals who can conduct tests with a population demographically similar to the intended market. Naturally, for test-marketed marks you will almost always conduct trademark searches, determine the mark's availability, register domain names, and apply for trademark registration before marketing begins, so that the mark's public use will not result in prior domain name registrations and trademark applications by others who learn of the mark from the testing.

18 CONSUMER AND EMPLOYEE PARTICIPATION; NAMING CONTESTS

Occasionally, companies encourage customers or employees to suggest new product names. The typical method is a contest whereby the winning submission earns a prize. A virtue of this process is that it elicits hundreds or even thousands of ideas from the very persons who consume or produce the product and lack the biases of company owners. Of course, such a contest must be conducted with advice of counsel and in compliance with local and national laws governing contests so the company can avoid legal obligations (other than the prize) to the person submitting the winning entry.

Seldom will such a contest yield a great mark, but at least it may spark consumer interest in a new product, as did the BOEING contest for the model 787 jet which drew approximately 500,000 entries and yielded the DREAMLINER name. Enter "naming contest" on a search engine and you will see some examples like Hormel's famous SPAM, Moog Music Corporation's VOYAGER for synthesizers, THERMOS for vacuum flasks, and Andersen Consulting's ACCENTURE for business management consulting. Supposedly, PENTIUM emerged from a process involving a company contest.

19 CONSUMER CHOICE

When the product is being marketed, occasionally consumers already have their own name for it. If so, why not adopt that crowd pleaser, especially if already recognized and protectable? Hypothetically, if the public is already calling your unusual car the "Hawk" (just like the VW Beetle is called the "Bug"), you might consider that name. Sometimes the consumers' name for the product won't supplant your mark yet may become a trademarked nickname. *(See Nickname Potential, ¶ 65.)* Probably the best example is COKE, adopted by the Coca-Cola Company after it discovered the public's frequent use of COKE in lieu of COCA-COLA.

III Methods

20 EXTRAMURAL, OUTSIDE FEEDBACK

In addition to internal feedback from employees, you might seek input from other persons (not customers) with whom the company has ongoing relations. Where the mark is subject to government agency scrutiny (e.g., FDA approval), prior discussions with the agency may be helpful. When seeking outside funding for product launch, you might encourage comments from the bankers, brokers, and lenders. Occasionally you might even seek advice from community leaders.

Naturally, in working with such persons, you may be concerned about how much information to impart to them. In all these situations it may be impossible, impractical, or impolitic to secure confidentiality agreements, so you should discuss with legal counsel the nature and timing of outside participation.

21 SOURCE OF MARKS; PERSONNEL

One concern is getting the right persons to devise the new mark. If the wrong person is involved you might get a great mark but face claims by the mark's originator. Usually ideas and copyrightable works (like some designs) created by employees within the scope of employment will automatically belong to, or can be used by, the employer; so if your employee creates the mark on assignment you may not be overly concerned about ownership claims. Nonetheless, even employees may claim that their contributions were outside the scope of employment or created on their own time, thus entitling them to ownership or compensation. This is why intellectual property agreements should generally be executed by all company employees participating in devising the mark, particularly a design mark which might be copyrightable. *(See Copyrighability, ¶ 269.)*

Typically ad agencies and name selection companies hired to develop a mark won't make ownership claims; but, again, to avoid the unusual claim written understandings are recommended.

With copyrightable designs and other copyrightable content, using non-employee contributors presents concerns. Even if you secure a written copyright transfer, under current law, by giving advance written notice the transferor can possibly revoke the transfer during a five-year period beginning 35 years after execution of the transfer. (See 17 U.S.C. Section 203.) And work-made-for-hire agreements may not apply to designs created by independent contractors.

III Methods

> "Naming is a process of linguistic distillation. Unlike the literary author, the trademark professional doesn't use thousands of words but rather reflects brand concepts, values, and goals, often with only a single word."
>
> PETER KARLEN

All things being equal, fewer problems arise when using employee talent and attorney-drafted written agreements with all contributors. Such agreements may not only help avoid title and compensation claims but can also be used to preserve the confidentiality of the development process. Because the hiring party's bargaining power is usually greatest before hiring, agreements should be attorney-drafted and typically signed before the contributor starts work on the project. Contracts tendered to people already hired are less likely to be accepted "as is" or at all.

22 BUYING SOMEONE ELSE'S MARK

You can buy someone else's mark. Why spend weeks or months creating a sculpture if you can buy one from an artist? Many marks already registered may be available for purchase. A widely-used, valuable mark will, of course, cost more. But you may also be able to pick up a bargain: registered marks barely in use can sometimes be purchased for relatively small sums, e.g., $2,000 – $10,000. Buying a mark requires a formal transaction and attorney-drafted written instruments, almost always involving acquisition of business good will associated with the mark and recording the assignment at applicable trademark registries. Because buying a registered mark entails special risks, you should involve a trademark attorney in all aspects of the transaction.

Where the purchase doesn't involve taking over the seller's business but merely getting the mark and a pro forma conveyance of good will, many prospective buyers are not enthusiastic. Many

III Methods

people like to create their own marks and don't relish wearing somebody else's old trousers. Yet, sometimes the mark for sale is the perfect mark, even if someone else devised it. And buying a long registered mark can have big advantages. For instance, registration costs may be saved, and because the mark is already registered, the buyer doesn't have to go through the registration process and face examiner refusals or third party oppositions, unless the buyer wants to register the mark in more jurisdictions or for more products. Moreover, existing registrations maintained for long periods may be somewhat immune from third party challenges, though only your attorney can tell you how strong the registration is.

23 LICENSED MARKS

Many well-known marks are available for licensing. The obvious advantage of licensing a well-known mark is that you may achieve almost instant recognition with reduced advertising costs. For instance, manufacturers of children's products often license names from children's cartoons or movies, e.g., FLINTSTONES, POKEMON, and BUGS BUNNY used for vitamins. Also, note the innumerable movie character marks used on premiums offered at fast food outlets. Licensing is even sometimes possible when doing a "takeoff" on someone else's mark; e.g., Paul Newman's FIG NEWMANS is licensed by Nabisco Brands Co. which controls FIG NEWTONS. Nonetheless, licensing has drawbacks. Royalty payments can be a continuing drain, and many inconveniences come with licensing agreements such as licensor inspections and quality control rights as well as restrictions on using the mark.

To protect your investment, great care must be exercised in negotiating and drafting the licensing agreement to ensure inter alia that the licensor owns the rights it is granting, you can assign your rights, and the licensor cannot terminate the license except for good cause. Moreover, whenever possible and desirable, you will ask for appropriate exclusivity. As with outright purchases, you need legal counsel to help with the agreement.

24 CONSENT AGREEMENTS

In addition to purchases and licenses, another avenue exists for using someone else's mark. On occasion, a company which won't sell or license its mark will give consent for a non-conflicting use, often via a co-existence arrangement. For instance, if the company knows it will be hard to stop

III **Methods**

your use for unrelated products, a co-existence agreement will have two advantages for that company. First, it will limit your use of the mark (e.g., to specified products) and thus curb your expansion, and, second, it may relieve that company of policing obligations and potential liabilities emanating from a license agreement. Most co-existence arrangements are secured without payment to the other party. A co-existence arrangement can be very tempting if you love your new mark. But you must consider the restrictions imposed by such an arrangement and determine whether it would be better to abandon the new mark and find an unencumbered one.

25 EXPIRED AND CANCELLED REGISTRATIONS

Look at expired and cancelled trademark registrations. You can peruse tens of thousands of such registrations. Many of these orphaned marks have long since been abandoned by their owners, and there are some gems. If you like such a mark, and searches show no conflicts with other marks, you must check whether the mark has truly been abandoned, legally speaking, in order to be available for use. *(See Other Abandoned Marks, ¶ 26.)* To ensure that a mark has been abandoned, you must conduct a thorough investigation, usually with an attorney and private investigator, and often involving direct inquiries with the mark's former owners.

Often old marks associated with bygone products are still alive and well, e.g., as of the writing of this text EDSEL is still used by Ford Motor Company and WURLITZER is still registered for radios. If the mark you thought abandoned is still registered or used, you might seek a license.

26 OTHER ABANDONED MARKS

When a mark has been abandoned, it may be available for use. A mark is "abandoned," whether registered or not, when its use has stopped with the intent not to resume. Typically, intent not to resume may be inferred from the circumstances. Under Federal statute (in effect when this work was first published) non-use for three consecutive years is prima facie evidence of abandonment, and a mark will only be deemed "used" when the use is bona fide and made in the ordinary course of trade and not made merely to reserve a right in the mark. When the owner of record does not confess abandonment it is often impossible to be sure that the mark is available. For registered marks, one technique to test abandonment is to file a cancellation petition at the trademark registry and seek a ruling that the mark has been abandoned. You will need a trademark attorney's help to determine abandonment or file a cancellation petition.

27 FOREIGN MARKS

When abroad you might encounter an attractive foreign mark never used in the USA. For U.S. usage such a mark might be a candidate if (1) it is not a famous mark, (2) its foreign owners do not intend expansion into the USA, and (3) you have no intention of expanding into the foreign owners' territory of use. Various laws prevent piracy of famous marks even in countries where the mark has not been used. These laws allow internationally famous marks to expand worldwide without interference by trademark pirates who register famous marks in countries into which the owners have not yet expanded. Moreover, even if the mark is not famous but the owners reputedly intend expansion into the USA, adoption is risky because it may attract legal proceedings and is otherwise morally questionable. If risks are unreasonable, you might seek a usage license. As in all situations when you contemplate using another's mark, you need legal advice.

28 PLAYING OFF ANOTHER'S MARK

One way to generate a noticeable mark is to play off another's successful mark or name. Specific techniques and variations include, e.g., analogies *(¶ 41)*, parodies *(¶ 200)*, reversals *(¶ 178)*, anagrams *(¶ 181)*, synonyms *(¶ 221)*, homonyms *(¶ 220)*, rebuses *(¶ 172)*, and even antonyms *(¶ 222)*. Naturally, if you come too close to the other mark or name you risk a claim for infringement, unfair competition, or dilution, depending on the degree of closeness, your product's relationship to those of the other owner, and the strength and fame of the other mark. E.g., HERE'S JOHNNY for portable toilets elicited a suit by Johnny Carson, VICTOR'S LITTLE SECRET for adult paraphernalia drew fire from the owners of VICTORIA'S SECRET, LOUIS VUITTON was parodied by CHEWY VUITON dog toys, and the owners of JORDACHE were not pleased by LARDACHE used on jeans connected with porcine imagery. Because the law of trademark parody is more gray than black and white, don't parody or adapt another's mark without first getting legal advice.

III Methods

29 INVENTORY OF INDUSTRY MARKS

Before even generating possible marks, create a list of successful (and perhaps even unsuccessful) marks in your industry. Such an inventory not only shows what kinds of marks have been successful – not that you must join a crowd of similar marks – but also enables you to position your mark in relation to other industry marks and properly reflect your company's business personality. Remember, your mark has much of its meaning in relation to the universe of all other trademarks, particularly those in your industry. Also, a thorough inventory will tell you what words are not available, and may save the time and expense of researching marks that never should have been considered.

For instance, for insurance frequently used are geographical terms (such as WAUSAU, ALLSTATE), names indicating trustworthiness (PRUDENTIAL, RELIANCE), and names harking back to old cooperatives (FARMERS, STATE FARM). For newspapers, subject matter is more diverse but still within distinct categories, e.g., investigative (EXAMINER, ENQUIRER), protective (GUARDIAN, SENTINEL), postal (POST, MAIL), informative (HERALD, TRIBUNE), temporal (TIMES, CHRONICLE), communal (UNION, CONSTITUTION), celestial (SUN, MERCURY), terrestrial (GLOBE, WORLD), communicative (TELEGRAPH, DISPATCH), and, of course, journalistic (NEWS, JOURNAL). Though you may not want to join an established category, severe departures from trademark themes common in an industry may not be successful even if memorable. For instance, for insurance, house marks consisting of first names, trendy slogans, or animal names might not succeed.

30 SEMANTIC POSITIONING

After inventorying successful marks in your trade, profession, or industry to see what kinds are viable, you can test your initial selections against successful marks. This test helps determine whether your selection semantically compares well with already-successful marks. For instance, if launching a new heavy duty pickup truck you might compare your candidate mark against DODGE RAM, FORD F-150, and CHEVROLET SILVERADO to see whether your mark semantically conveys similar feelings of strength, power, speed, and reliability. You wouldn't want a mark semantically "weaker" in relation to those essential product qualities.

III Methods

When establishing a niche in an already established market, you want to semantically position your mark into that niche, whether the niche lies at the end or middle of the product spectrum. For instance, if launching a new sneaker brand, you should consider the broad spectrum of existing brand names, ranging from the fanciful KEDS and ADIDAS; the arbitrary CONVERSE and SKECHERS (derived from a street slang word for a person who can't sit still); the suggestive PUMA and REEBOK (from "rhebok," an African antelope); and the almost descriptive NEW BALANCE and CREATIVE RECREATION.

Semantic positioning is obviously important when entering a mature market, when it's important to create a mark that helps establish a niche or compete in broad market segments. But such positioning is also important when being the first to offer a new kind of product. In the latter situation, you may want words, taglines, or slogans that connote your first entry into the market, or product marks like VELCRO and CROAKIES that, without becoming generic, are widely identified with the product, thus leaving little room for competitors.

Semantic positioning is arguably one of the most important considerations in naming. In many situations it may be the most important.

A mark rooted in the history of the company or its founders may provide an intimate connection to the past, a connection that can motivate owners and employees and strike the imagination of consumers.

31 COMPETITIVE ANALYSIS

For marks in competitive markets, one of the most important selection tasks is competitive analysis. Even if you know the semantics you wish the mark to convey *(Semantic Positioning, ¶ 30)*, from a business perspective you still must test those semantics against actual or projected market conditions, as indicated in connection with many of the General Considerations explored in Section IV. For example, considering specific competitors, will the word mark's semantics give you an advantage in

III Methods

relation to your actual or projected (1) product line, (2) market segments, and (3) territories? Do you have adequate resources to sufficiently promote and legally protect the mark in a highly competitive environment? Can your mark survive in a national market for all its products, or must you begin as a niche or regional player? A formal competitive analysis may give answers. In this analysis you might chart your chief competitors, their competing marks, ad budgets and monetary support for their marks, customer bases, revenues, outlets, goodwill, etc. Having that information, knowing your mark's semantic position, and considering the nature of your mark, you can make an educated guess as to whether your mark will be DOA, comatose, lethargic, or a healthy survivor.

Selecting a mark for a competitive market is like choosing a seed for a garden. Determining the mark's survivability and its suitability for particular products, demographics, and territories is like determining sufficient space, water, soil, and light to grow a new seed amongst mature plants. Although successful large businesses typically grow out of strong, distinctive brand names, great brand names do not always generate successful businesses. Sometimes the nascent trademark is not supported by adequate advertising or promotion and cannot emerge from the shadows of its competitors, much like the seedling of a great tree cannot emerge from the undergrowth when planted in barren soil or without adequate light or water. (Mark 4:14-20)

32 INVENTORY OF RESTRICTIONS

Before starting, save time by inventorying all trademark restrictions and prohibitions in your industry. For instance, in the nutrition industry, marks that promise certain health benefits may be subject to FDA enforcement actions. *(See Prohibited Statements, ¶321.)* Marks for pharmaceuticals must be more dissimilar to each other than in other industries in order to prevent mistakes in dispensing drugs. *(See Similar Marks, ¶45.)* Regulations in other industries might affect misleading marks. Furthermore, if intending use in many jurisdictions, you should research regulations in all those jurisdictions. E.g., when expanding into the European Union you should consider its stringent regulations in many industries. In general, see Prohibitions, Section VIII. Clearly, you will need attorney help to determine restrictions and prohibitions.

III **Methods**

33 CHOOSING THE KIND OF MARK

A logical early step in selection is to list in order of preference all kinds of subject matter you might consider, as well as undesirable subject matter. That is, you should establish the basic parameters, allowing for flexibility. By going through the headings in the section on Subject Matter, Section V, or in similar lists, you can determine desirable and undesirable subject matter. If you are not sure what kind of mark will work, you might try several kinds, e.g., a "portmanteau" *(¶ 176)*, a "ricochet" *(¶ 205)*, a mythological name *(¶ 150)*, an animal name ("theronym") *(¶ 226)*, or a foreign word *(¶ 192)*. Though a particular product or industry might attract only a few kinds of marks, like a magnet attracting only iron filings, you might test unconventional kinds of marks before letting yourself be captured by the magnet's pull. Surprisingly, the winning mark is often quite dissimilar from the kind of mark you first envisioned.

If you have ample time to select, one technique is to develop successive lists of marks each embodying candidates of one kind. By reviewing each list separately, you can compare apples to apples, oranges to oranges and then compare the winning entry on each list to those on other lists, much like a dog show where the working, terrier, toy, and other category winners compete for "best in show."

34 APPROPRIATE REGISTRATIONS

Depending on your expansion plans, once you have selected the mark and done appropriate availability and connotation searches, you will need to protect the mark through registrations at the State, Federal, and sometimes even international levels. With an attorney's help, almost always you should apply for registration soon after analyzing the search results and making final selection decisions because search results can go out of date quickly, and if you delay someone else may apply for registration of the same or similar mark during the delay. Under USPTO rules and those of many foreign registries, the earlier-filed application for the same or similar mark is considered first and may block later-filed applications. In many foreign jurisdictions early filing is very important since ownership may be given to the first to file, not the first to use the mark.

With your attorney you will have to carefully identify the products for which applications are filed, considering all the jurisdictions in which you

III Methods

will be applying. Selecting the right products is often almost as difficult as selecting the right mark. And when your business will be conducted through different legal entities, with your attorney's help you must decide which entity will own and register the mark.

35 SELECTION CHART

One way of roughly comparing candidate marks against each other is to create a rating chart. The left column may list your company's 10 most important considerations, perhaps in order of importance. The second column may be 1–10 weightings for each consideration. The next column could then be the mark's 1–10 scores for each consideration. So the final column would be the products of the weightings multiplied by the scores. The sum total of these products would be the mark's final score. That mark with the highest total score wins. Following is a sample chart with hypothetical considerations, weightings, and scores.

CONSIDERATION	WEIGHTING	SCORE	PRODUCT
Adaptability	10	3	30
Social and Propriety Level	9	7	63
Legal Strength	9	5	45
Memorability	7	8	56
Global Palatability	7	2	14
Internet Usage	6	2	12
Visual Possibilities	5	6	30
Self-Expressiveness	4	7	28
Protection Costs	3	4	12
Nickname Potential	2	7	14
		TOTAL	**304**

36 FOREIGN REGISTRATIONS

When the mark is not reserved abroad through registration, any plans to expand internationally may be frustrated. Some businesses may even eschew marks not available for registration in certain foreign countries/

jurisdictions. Treaty arrangements with many foreign countries allow you to gain a priority filing date for a trademark application based on an earlier application in another treaty country. For instance, at the time of first publishing this information, if you applied for a USPTO registration, you might have had up to six months from the USA filing date to apply in various treaty countries, where your application may have got priority based on your earlier U.S. filing date. *(Dated Statutory reference; see Section II, Cautions/Disclaimers.)*

Also, now that the USA is a party to the Madrid Protocol, qualified USPTO filings can be used to gain registration in multiple member countries. An *international registration* at WIPO (World Intellectual Property Organization) via the Madrid Protocol is often the quickest and most efficient way to gain and maintain registrations around the world, though the Madrid process has its perils, as your attorney can explain. An attorney's participation in a Madrid application is even more important than in a domestic one, and since the Madrid application will be examined in each designated country/jurisdiction, your attorney will have to use foreign associates to deal with issues that arise in various countries/jurisdictions.

37 CREATIVITY

Seldom does the "perfect" mark pop into one's head right away. Mozart, a genius capable of composing musical works in his head, said he "composed as a sow piddles." But very few people are capable of streaming trademarks in that way. Rather, selection is an arduous process, involving days, weeks, and even months of brainstorming. Though brainstorming heats the cauldron of creativity, often the final mark does not arise in brainstorming sessions but in moments of quiet reflection, early morning or late night. As artist Grant Wood noted, "All the really good ideas I ever had came to me while I was milking a cow."

Because *arbitrary, suggestive,* and *descriptive* word marks (but not *fanciful* marks) are ordinary extant words, selecting those kinds of marks is not so much "invention" as "discovery." That is, picking an ordinary word like APPLE, KIWI, or ORANGE is like casting a net into the sea and landing a fish, whereas devising KODAK, EXXON, or QANTAS is more like assembling a jigsaw puzzle.

One way to enhance creativity is to imagine that you are not just a "creator" but also a "receptor." This means accepting that the best choice might

III **Methods**

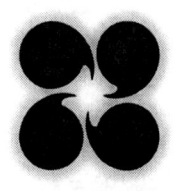

JORDACHE for trendy, European-style clothing, reflects the three founders, Joe, Avi, and Ralph NakASH; the three-person "Jordache" tennis game; the clothing's panache; and "jour d'acheter," meaning "day of buying" in French.

not come from grasping and clawing but rather from readying yourself to receive the result. As Michaelangelo claimed, he did not make the shapes of his sculptures; rather the shapes were already in the stone. He merely freed them from their marble prisons. Analogously, with marks comprised of existing words, the words are already leaping about in the language, waiting to be seized by the imaginative namer. With fanciful marks like PROZAC, KODAK, and NVIDIA, the process often seems rather analytical. I.e., it seems like the mark was created by piecing together and tweaking various elements. And certainly tweaking is part of the process. E.g., LEXUS was the result of morphing ALEXIS, and KODAK could also have been spelled CODAC, CODAK, CODACK, KODAC, KODACK, or KOEDAK; that is, in creating fanciful marks many variations are usually considered. But frequently, even with fanciful selections, one experiences "Eureka" when the mark emerges without being pieced together, and only upon reflection does one realize that the mark's pieces each have meaning. So the brainstorming/Eureka process is like casting puzzle pieces on the floor, only to wake next morning and find they have been mysteriously put together.

38 LATERAL THINKING

Imagination is vital to good selection, and a key technique is the same lateral thinking used to solve riddles or generate clever jokes. The "lateral thinker" constantly looks for translations, metaphors, metonyms, homonyms, synonyms, eponyms, puns, and like devices. This form of thinking often involves connecting the seemingly unconnected. One concern is whether the imaginatively-devised mark is so obscure that there is no discernible semantic connection, even metaphorical, between mark and product. (Though semantic connections need not be obvious, at least

III Methods

a slender semantic thread should connect mark and product.) For instance, LYCOS, an ingenious mark for a Worldwide Web search service, is derived from "Lykos," meaning "hunting spider" in Latin, not an obvious connection but not too obscure either. In contrast, L'EGGS for women's hosiery sold in egg-shaped containers is an obviously clever mark referencing body parts and container shapes and connoting the elegance of French fashion.

Sometimes one looks for a golden mean in making a lateral connection between mark and product. For instance, hardly any lateral thinking is reflected in a *descriptive mark* like TASTY for foods. At the other extreme, how many people could decipher the thinking behind EXXON, legally a strong mark, said to have been constructed from ON connoting energy (as in neutron and electron) and EX symbolizing experimental? The golden mean of lateral thinking could be STARBUCKS, named after Starbuck, the ship's first mate in Melville's MOBY DICK, also reflected in the mermaid logo.

39 TRANSMUTATIONAL THINKING

One important technique, reflected throughout this Guide, is transmutational thinking, a form of lateral thinking. This thinking is used to devise marks based on subject matter such as rebuses, translations, synonyms, and homonyms. When a mark expresses just the right idea but is unavailable or unsuitable for use, you can transmute it, as an alchemist makes gold from lead. E.g., many surname marks not available or not ideal succeed when translated. For instance, after carmaker Horch could no longer use his German surname, meaning "hark" or "listen," he translated it into the Latin AUDI. Similarly, tire distributor Shojiro Ishibashi translated his Japanese surname into BRIDGESTONE, though a more exact translation would be "stone bridge." In the health food industry GARDEN OF LIFE, used for Biblically inspired products, has thrived even though EDEN for similar products already existed. Marks can be transmuted within a language via synonyms or without the language via translations, but also sometimes from word to symbol. For instance, STAR can be turned into *, and HASH or POUND into #.

Transmutational thinking not only involves lateral translation but also vertical adjustment, e.g., via hyponyms/hypernyms and meronyms/haplonyms, much like choosing one box in a set of nested Chinese boxes. For example, in choosing a floral name for a product a meronymous range (i.e., from whole to part) might be BOUQUET, FLOWER, and PETAL

III **Methods**

or a hyponymous range (i.e., from broader class to narrower) might be FLOWER, ROSE, and TEA ROSE. As with Chinese boxes, sometimes the "smallest" variety is the most refined and distinctive and therefore the most valuable.

However, because confusion is judged not only in relation to sound and appearance but also meaning, transmutation does not always avoid conflicts with other marks. To avoid confusion the transmutation should be disguised or non-obvious. Few would suspect that AUDI and HORCH mean the same thing in different languages, especially since Latin is not a living language. And though GARDEN OF LIFE connotes EDEN and touts Biblical themes, its three-word construction provides sufficient distance from EDEN.

40 ANALYTIC THINKING

Lateral thinking *(¶ 38)*, which involves shifting the frame of reference, is complemented by analytic thinking which entails analysis and piecing together of the mark's components. Composite marks *(¶ 174)* are largely a product of analytic thinking, though sometimes a spark of imagination reflects lateral thinking. Hypothetically, POLLONAISE for a French restaurant serving primarily chicken, with classical background music, would be, in part, a product of analytic thinking, e.g., POLLO for chicken, NAISE being a French suffix, and the entire word spelled almost like the classical music form "polonaise." The same with COMPILEX used for a computerized personal injury law database, COMP suggesting "computer," PI denoting "personal injury," LEX meaning "law," and COMPILE suggesting the database. Compare JORDACHE for trendy, European-style clothing, reflecting the three founders, Joe, Avi, and Ralph NakASH; the three-person "Jordache" tennis game; and the clothing's panache. (JORDACHE also evokes "jour d'acheter, meaning "day of buying" in French.)

41 ANALOGIES

To "slipstream" another company's successful mark without incurring the risks of a pun *(¶ 198)* or parody *(¶ 200)*, you might consider a choice analogous to the successful mark, i.e., one that emulates that mark in a parallel or skewed fashion. For example, the FOR DUMMIES series of books which features works like WINDOWS FOR DUMMIES was followed by the competitive COMPLETE IDIOT'S GUIDE series. Somewhat predictably, MR. COFFEE for coffee found a companion in MRS. TEA for tea. Was DAIRY

III **Methods**

QUEEN an inspiration for BURGER KING, or AUNT JEMIMA for UNCLE BEN'S? This technique can be used by a competitor or by any company trying to develop a common theme for its own related products.

Though your mark may not be a pun or parody in relation to the other company's mark you have slipstreamed, you may still generate opposition or liability if the "analogy" is likely to cause public confusion. Remember that "likelihood of public confusion" arises not only from similarity of sound and appearance but also from similarity of meaning. *(See Avoidance of Conflicting Marks, ¶ 46.)* Thus, as with all choices which play off another's mark, you need legal advice.

42 RE-DEFINITION

When entering a mature market, your mark may only thrive if it can redefine the product. For example, the nutrition and natural products industry is saturated with marks that connote natural ingredients and vitamin/mineral/herbal origins, so some companies launching new products choose fanciful marks that sound pharmaceutical, such as LEPTOPRIN for a vitamin/herbal supplement, PAVAXIN for a vitamin/mineral supplement, and VIRUPEL for a herbal/nutraceutical supplement. (Cf. ZICAM for a homeopathic zinc gluconate cold remedy which can be characterized almost as pharmaceutical.) These marks immediately distinguish their products from a host of competing product names containing well-worn industry words such as NATURE, NATURAL, and HEALTH and quasi-descriptive morphemes which disclose vitamin/mineral/herbal ingredients. The pharmaceutical connotation for vitamin products and other dietary supplements is one that arguably suggests more potency, science, testing, and credibility.

Perhaps redefinition's most powerful effect is where the mark connotes that the product is first in its field. That effect can occasionally be achieved by using words like FIRST and ORIGINAL, but, as with marks containing the words FIRST NATIONAL which once had a powerful meaning, the effect is usually weak. It's easier to develop a slogan that descriptively redefines the product and proclaims its novelty.

The aim of this kind of branding is to connote a new or different kind of product in order to distinguish it from competitive products, without stretching the imagination too far. Such branding sometimes resembles janitors calling themselves "maintenance engineers," a true ID for some

III Methods

janitors, an exaggeration for others. Redefinition is quite important for credibility when dealing with a crowded market having some products of questionable efficacy or quality.

43 ORDER OF SELECTION

If you have already committed to packaging, imagery, or *trade dress*, then the *word mark* must sometimes follow suit. But when starting from scratch, carefully consider the order of selection. Consider the relative emotional, sensory, conceptual, and aesthetic importance of the various marks and identifying devices (e.g., logos, words, *slogans, taglines, trade names,* and packaging).

For instance, advertising agencies sometimes offer clients a list of possible word marks already in stylized formats so the client is comparing logos to each other, not pure words. However, often the better approach is to start with words and then, if two or more candidates are short listed, compare them in stylized formats. After all, in most dimensions the word is more important than the *design*. For example, the word, not the design, passes by word-of-mouth via radio and news reports; the design can only be seen, not heard. Though the design may be the best visual marker on goods, business signs, etc., usually the word behind the design connects to the consumer to indicate source and quality. (With certain goods sold only on a store shelf, the design may be more important.)

When developing multiple marks in a "trademark architecture" *(¶ 107)*, including house and product marks, slogans and taglines, where does one start? Where the company is initially based on a single product, like VELCRO hook and loop fastener, perhaps one starts with the product mark. Conversely, where the company will offer a variety of products, maybe the house mark and marks for product lines should come first.

44 POST SELECTION BRANDING

The selected "final" word is usually only the beginning of a long *branding* process. Almost always, the surviving choice is never perceived without misgivings after other candidates are cast overboard. But this uncertainty is justified because virtually no mark is perfect for a product or business. As Yogi Berra observed, "If the world were perfect, it wouldn't be." Much like a wild horse that must be broken in before saddled, the imperfect choice is

III Methods

gradually transformed via branding efforts in order to become the "perfect" moniker for the product or business. E.g., with goods, all the accoutrements of the word, including complementary *designs*, labels, tags, containers, packaging, and displays reveal more qualities of the word, as do the brand *taglines, slogans,* themes, and stories. This branding process is typically ongoing and ceaseless, so the word is constantly unfolding itself.

Though this Guide mentions some aspects of branding, especially in discussing many different kinds of marks and branding devices, the reader should consult other works on brand development.

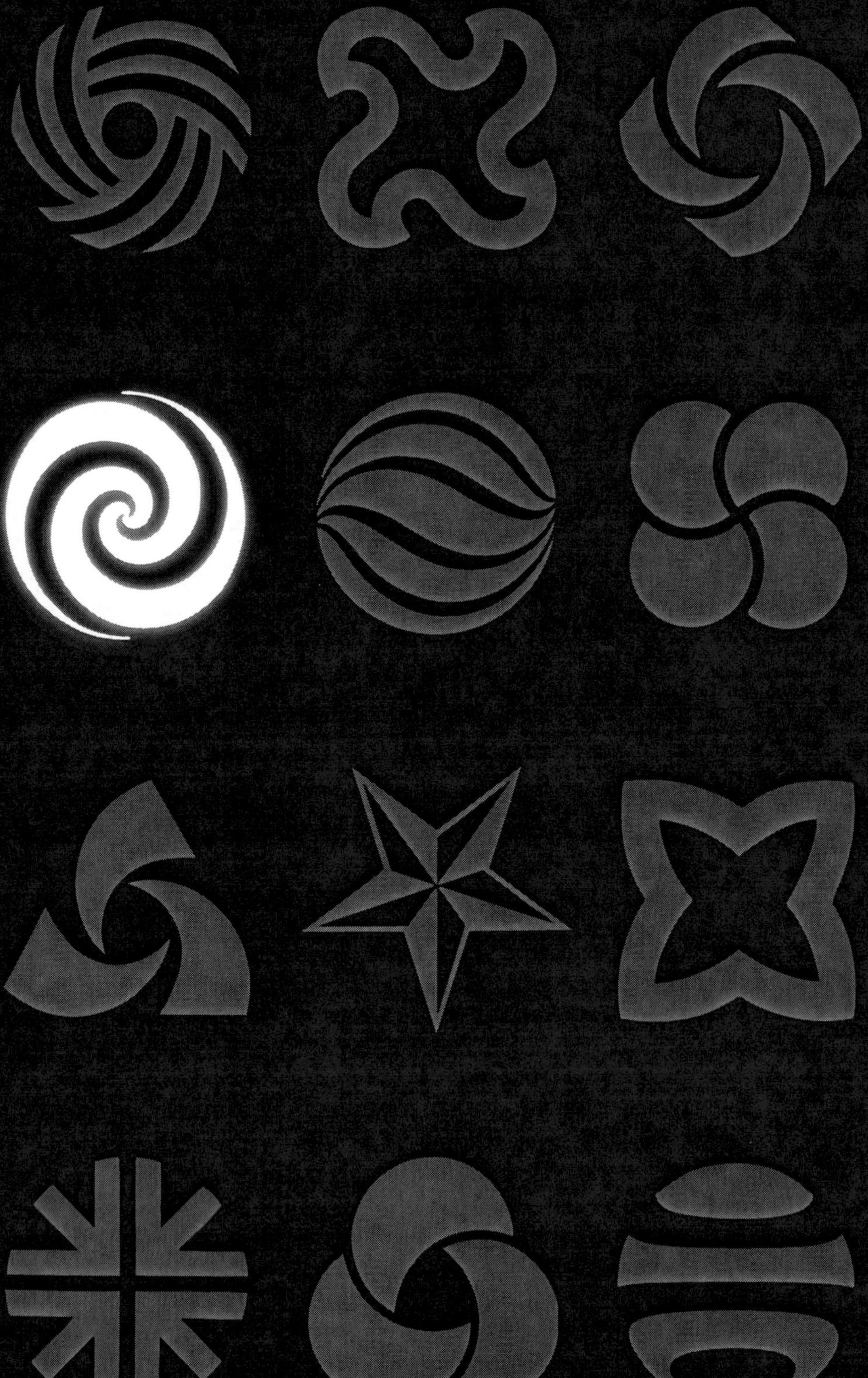

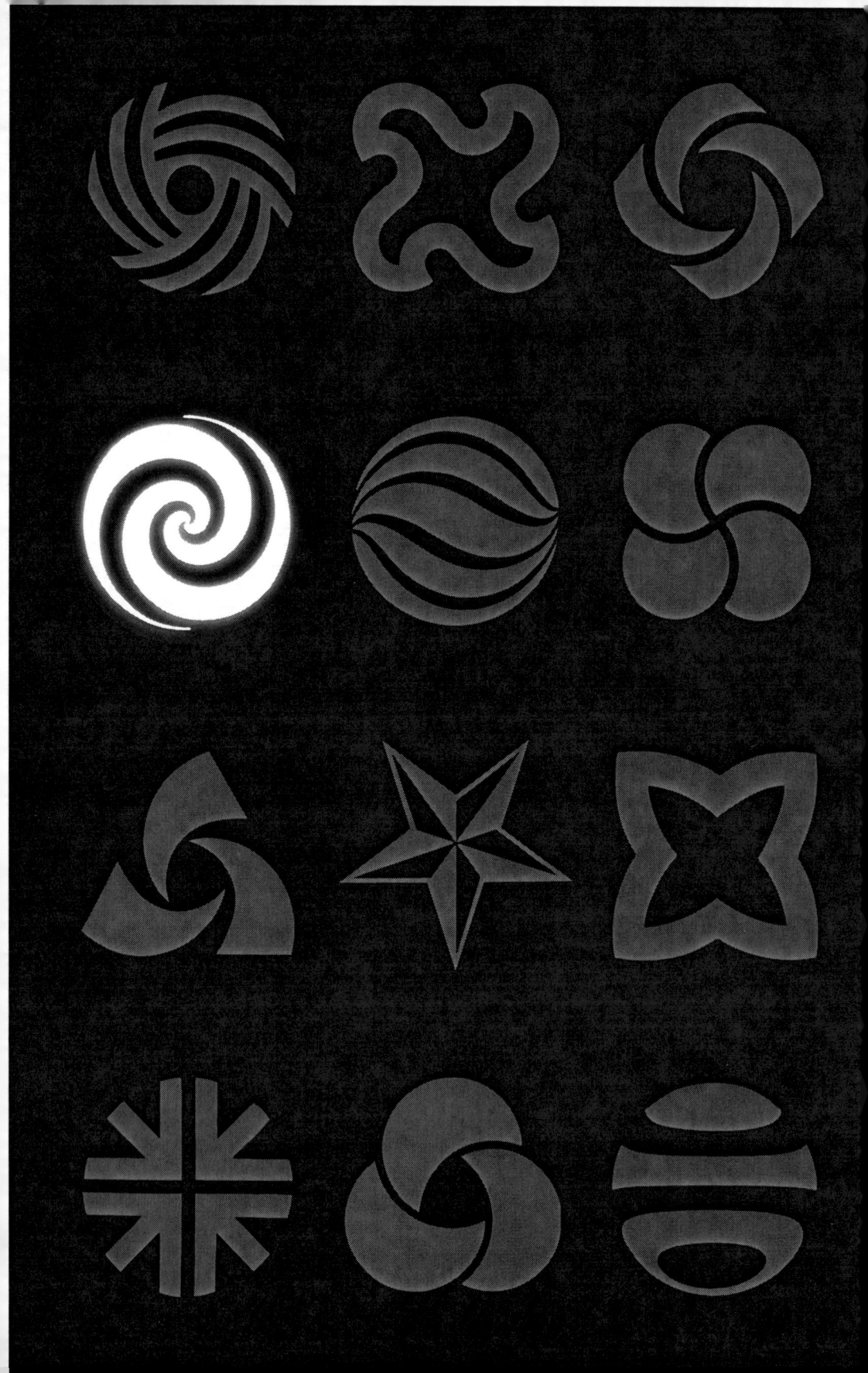

IMPORTANT FACTORS YOU MAY CONSIDER

IV General Considerations

"If names are not correct, language will not be in accordance with the truth of things."

CONFUCIUS

The following selected general

considerations are important in trademark selection. Most or almost all these considerations will play a role in selecting marks, particularly word marks.

45 SIMILAR MARKS

IN GENERAL, AVOID JOINING A CROWD of similar marks. For instance, in book publishing many animal names are already imprint marks, such as PELICAN, PENGUIN, and BANTAM. Why be one more zebra in a herd of zebras or one more iron filling around a magnet? You probably won't stand out, and you might only create public confusion, resulting perhaps in legal claims against you.

As another example, many computer businesses select marks with unoriginal components such as TECH, MICRO, and DATA, so they get lost in a blizzard of similar marks. In fact, the estimate is over 175,000 business names with MICRO in them. Naturally, some marks like MICROSOFT can still stand out because of market share, high quality products, and early market entry.

In some industries it is more important to stay away from other marks. For instance, to prevent accidental mistakes in dispensing drugs, pharmaceutical marks must usually be more dissimilar from each other.

46 AVOIDANCE OF CONFLICTING MARKS

As indicated earlier *(Trademark and Trade Name Searches, ¶ 10)*, conflicts may arise from similarity of sound, appearance, or meaning. In sound COPPER TAN was once held similar to COPPERTONE and EX BIER similar to BECK's BEER. (The Vatican, though, has never objected to PAYPAL.) In particular, beware the oronym, a word or word combination sounding just

IV General Considerations

like another having a different meaning, e.g., BEEFEATER sounds just like "bee feeder," and ARM & HAMMER is a dead ringer for Armand Hammer, the name of a famous industrialist. In meaning, TORNADO was once held similar to CYCLONE, and similarity in meaning can even cross languages so that LIGHTNIN' was arguably similar to BLITZ (German for "lightning", as in Blitzkrieg ("lightning war")). Moreover, similarity in meaning can even cross barriers between word and image. A *design mark* depicting a key was held confusingly similar to the *word mark* KEY, both used for publications. Though similarity in appearance generally pits one design mark versus another, word marks can have similar appearance. For instance, THE GREATEST SNOW ON EARTH looks like THE GREATEST SHOW ON EARTH, or WHERE THERE'S LIFE...THERE'S BUGS is similar to WHERE THERE'S LIFE...THERE'S BUD.

However, likelihood of confusion depends not only on similarity between the marks but also between the products sold with the respective marks and on strength of the other marks similar to the one you are considering. Remember, only a qualified attorney can properly evaluate your search results and judge similarity. All doubts should usually be resolved in favor of caution; after all, regardless of whether you are right in asserting that your new mark is not confusingly similar, USPTO or court proceedings can be costly, cloud your rights in the mark, and delay registration for years.

47 SELECTION OF MULTIPLE MARKS

If you fear that your first choice may be refused by the USPTO or opposed by a third party, to improve your odds you might select one or two additional marks so that you can apply to register the alternative marks at the same time. Generally, it's prudent to make the second or third choices quite different from the first choice and not merely variations. After all, if the first choice encounters examiner or third-party objections, these obstacles may also apply to variations. E.g., a third party already challenging your first choice will usually notice any variations on that choice, so a variation that might have passed unnoticed may now face opposition.

In some cases you might even use two or more marks simultaneously, either separately (e.g., a product sold under two different marks) or together (e.g., a product label showing both marks). Again, more marks can mean better odds and more flexibility.

IV General Considerations

48 SOUND OF YOUR MARK

Consider how your mark sounds. You may be happy with your *word mark's* looks and connotations, but have you considered how it sounds over the phone or in radio advertisements? Try it out. Long, multi-syllabic, non-phonetic, *fanciful* marks may not be good choices because of sound recognition problems. In particular, with fanciful marks one should remember that confusion can arise because of sounds of certain letters; e.g., "M" can be confused with "N," "D" with "T," "P" with "B," and "S" with "Z." And, of course, a number of letters and letter combinations can spawn identical soundalikes, e.g., "C," "K," and "QUE"; "S" and "C" when followed by "E," "I" or "Y"; "I" and "Y"; and "CU," "QU," and "KW." Also, to avoid confusion and embarrassment, always determine whether you mark is an oronym (a soundalike) of another word or word combination in the same way that ICE CREAM is an oronym of "I scream" or the trademark BEEFEATER is an oronym of "bee feeder."

49 AUDIBILITY

Related to sound considerations like recognizability and letters with similar sounds is "audible distinctiveness." When used in ordinary speech (e.g., in a sentence or phrase) will the mark stand out? Marks with visual or semantic distinctiveness will not necessarily catch the listener's ear. For instance, EXXON and JANTZEN may be visually striking but not necessarily as audibly distinctive as COKE, SPRITE, and PEPSI. All things being equal, long vowel sounds tend to be more ear-catching than short ones; e.g., compare JELL-O to the hypothetical JELLA, GOOGLE to GOGGLE, VELCRO to VELCRA, and JEEP to JEP. Lesser-used consonant sounds may be more auditorily distinctive, e.g., the "Y" in YAMAHA and YAHOO!, the "SH" in TOSHIBA, the "SN" in SNICKERS, and the "TW" in TWIX.

Don't forget that a *word mark* is often communicated and remembered as much by sound as by sight (e.g., on radio, in audiovisual formats, and by word of mouth), so that audibility should be considered as much as visibility.

50 PHONETIC MARKS

Whenever possible, use phonetic words because, if the public can't readily pronounce the mark, you create confusion. As Mark Twain once quipped, "Names are not always what they seem. The common Welsh name BZJXXLLWCP is pronounced Jackson."

IV General Considerations

When consumers are unsure how to pronounce your mark, you may have to launch a costly advertising campaign to educate them, or else indicate pronunciation when depicting the mark, e.g. HÄAGEN-DAZS, with an umlaut, for ice cream. Moreover, product recommendations often travel by word of mouth, so that new customers who "hear" about your product by name will find it more quickly on the shelf or over the Internet if they can spell what they heard. In this regard, remember that certain letters have similar sounds and can be confused with each other, especially when placed in certain parts of a word, e.g., "B" and "P," "M" and "N," "D" and "T," and "K" and "C." Depending on the position of the potentially confusing letter, you may want to avoid using it, particularly as first letter of a word mark.

A mark phonetic in one language may be hard to pronounce in another, a consideration for marks used internationally. To clear uncertainty about pronunciation you can sometimes specify the preferred pronunciation when registering the mark. E.g., see U.S. Reg. No. 2,558,555 for M@DNOYZ for which the specified pronunciation is MADNOISE, and U.S. Reg. No. 305,349 (expired) for PINAUD which specified PENO as the correct pronunciation. *(Cf. Fixed Pronunciation, ¶ 51.)*

51 FIXED PRONUNCIATION

Generally you want a mark that will be pronounced the same way by most speakers. Ambiguity in pronunciation not only can make the mark harder to establish but also increases the risk of confusion with other marks. For instance, in judging similarity between your new mark and marks already registered, the USPTO will assume all reasonable pronunciations of your mark and of the registered marks. As an example, GENETEK could be pronounced either as GENE-TEK, two syllables with the first embodying the long E sound, or as GEN-E-TEK, three syllables all embodying the short E sound. Even GEN-E-TEK has two plausible variations: GEN-e-tek (stress on the first syllable) and gen-E-tek which sounds like "genetic." Conversely, this factor may be favorable after your mark is registered since later applicants for similar marks may have their choices evaluated against all reasonable pronunciations of your mark and theirs.

As mentioned *(Phonetic Marks, ¶ 50)*, it is sometimes possible to specify pronunciation in the USPTO application, but that does not mean that alternative pronunciations will be disregarded in judging similarity.

IV General Considerations

Even if pronunciation in English-speaking countries is uniform (e.g., where the mark is comprised of a real word), one should beware different pronunciations in other countries. A reverse example is ADIDAS, pronounced largely as a-DI-das in the USA and UK but originally pronounced in Germany and elsewhere as A-di-Das after the company founder Adi Dassler.

Fixed pronunciation may be especially important for *fanciful marks* because they are frequently transliterated sound-for-sound into other languages and alphabets. Also the fanciful mark's connotation may be diluted if the "wrong" pronunciation coexists with the "right."

Of course, where the mark is subject to multiple pronunciations, the user can vigorously advertise the desired pronunciation, which may cure the problem. Sometimes the user may even want to use pronunciation symbols, like those used in dictionaries, to indicate correct pronunciation.

52 LEGIBLE MARKS

Consider how legible the mark is to the different kinds of potential customers. Even if phonetic, a long or multi-syllabic mark, or a mark comprised of clumps of consonants or vowels, may be difficult to discern at first glance, especially if the wrong typeface is used. For instance, SALVATORE FERRAGAMO and ABRACADABRA are phonetic but not "quick reads." You might need an extra blink of the eye to take in compacted, clustered consonants, as in SCHLAGE and GROLSCH. Legibility might matter for some marks which must thrive on the Internet, where instant recognition is a factor and milliseconds count. See Rebecca Tushnet's article, "Gone in 60 Milliseconds: Trademark Law and Cognitive Science," 86 TEXAS LAW REVIEW 507 (2008).

One palliative for a hard-to-read mark is to adjust the font in which it typically appears, so the mark becomes easier to read. This means selecting the right font, deciding on capitalization, kerning and boldfacing the letters (or not), and otherwise adjusting individual letters. Yet, remember that one cannot typically control how your *word mark* may appear when used by non-licensed third parties.

53 EASY-TO-PRONOUNCE WORDS

Easy-to-pronounce marks are usually best, so avoid pronunciation problems, if possible. As mentioned elsewhere *(Phonetic Marks, ¶50 and Words*

IV General Considerations

With Many Syllables, ¶96), non-phonetic spellings and long words can be awkward, but there are numerous other considerations. For instance, certain trigraphs and other consonant clusters like THW, SCHL, and SHV are not easily pronounced by all. Or using the same sound in two parts of a word, e.g., via "consonance," can result in problems, especially with letters like "R" and "L". For example, the medial "R" in "February" is often not pronounced; the same is true of "forward," often pronounced as "foward." Also note "slalom." A two-word mark in which the first word's last sound is the same as the second word's last sound may also be awkward, e.g., hypothetically BARBARA ARDEN, POCONO OVAL, or BLACK CRACKER. Another concern is assonance in some multi-word marks like HARMON/KARDON, each word beginning or ending with similar but not identical sounds, a semi-rhyme reminiscent of tongue twisters like "she sells sea shells by the seashore."

54 BEST SPELLING

Choose spelling which will have the best connotations. Ponder the following choices, on the left "what is," on the right "what could have been":

SONY	SONI
KODAK	CODAC
PROZAC	PROSAK
NYQUIL	NIKWIL

SONY is clearly better than SONI. The "Y" is clearly stronger than the "I", giving the mark a more distinctive appearance. As a word, SONY gives a stronger impression than SONI and is somehow more Western and dynamic. The "K's" in KODAK are clearly stronger and more distinctive than the "C's" in CODAC, whereas a "K" in PROZAC would have been too strong for a calm-inducing drug. Remember that you frequently have a number of choices for spelling fanciful marks. For instance, a sibilant sound can be made with an "S," "C," "Z," "PS," or even "X"; "C," "QU," and "K" are often sound equivalents; so are "Y" and "I."

Though spelling choices remain for most fanciful marks, more limited choices should apply to *arbitrary, suggestive,* and *descriptive marks* consisting of real words. Common misspellings like KWIK for QUICK and TUFF for

IV General Considerations

TOUGH usually don't make the mark more distinctive. Many misspellings of real words can cause confusion or double-takes without adding to distinctiveness. Yet, misspelling real words can succeed in various situations. For instance, misspelling can be effective when the original word is relatively unknown and the misspelling yields a word that appears fanciful, as with GOOGLE, derived from the mathematical term GOOGOL (10 to the 100th power). Occasionally, changing the spelling of a real word can avoid confusion with another mark containing that word. (Because confusion is judged in relation to sound, appearance, and meaning, don't count on avoiding confusion by changing a real word's spelling.) If artful and unusual, sometimes even a simple misspelling of an ordinary word can thrive, as with SKIL for tools.

55 WORD MARK APPEARANCE

Choice of letters not only affects a mark's semantics but also its appearance. The following spelling differences arguably affect appearance more than meaning:

EXXON	EXON
QUALCOMM	QUALCOM
3M	MMM
JETTA	JETA

The famous marks on the left appear stronger and more distinctive than their hypothetical alternatives on the right. Though a *word mark* doesn't have any fixed graphic appearance since it may appear in various fonts, you must still consider appearance in relation to the most frequent forms in which the word might be used, e.g., all capital letters, initial capital letter, and sometimes all lower case (e.g., **adidas**).

56 TEXTUAL VISIBILITY

The more visible a word, even without regard to stylization *(¶ 60)*, the better, especially when the mark must compete for attention side-by-side with other marks, e.g., on supermarket shelves or Internet shopping sites. We discuss various aspects of a mark's appearance, including length *(¶ 97)*, spelling *(¶ 54)*, and initial lettering *(¶ 161)*. Together these and similar characteristics determine a mark's textual visibility.

IV General Considerations

The more unusual the first letter of the mark (e.g., X, K, J, Z, and Y), typically the more visible; e.g., an initial letter like X is often more noticeable than an O. Also, the more unusual a particular letter as the mark's last letter, the more visible the mark as in MICHELOB, COMPAQ, and IMPROV. A word utilizing a K rather than a C for the same sound is more noticeable (as per KODAK vs. CODAC), and so is a word which doubles a consonant, e.g., like EXXON vs. EXON or QUALCOMM vs. QUALCOM.

Regarding length, a longer word is often more visibly noticeable than a very short one even though shorter words have so many other advantages. There is probably an ideal length for maximum visibility, depending on the textual medium in which the mark is primarily exposed to the public. A long mark may actually be less visible on business signage than a short one, but in onscreen text a three-letter mark will usually be less visible than a six-letter one.

> "Names are not always what they seem. The common Welsh name BZJXXLLWCP is pronounced Jackson."
>
> MARK TWAIN

57 DOMINANCE

In devising a multi-word mark, consider which word will/should be dominant and where it should be placed. The dominant word is typically the most distinctive component of the mark. For instance, with DAIRY QUEEN, QUEEN is dominant since DAIRY is arguably descriptive. With other marks, particularly embodying already-existing sayings or terminology, it's harder to tell; e.g., with BANANA REPUBLIC for clothing, which word is dominant?

Usually a word becomes more important or dominant when placed first. Compare:

THE REPUBLIC OF TEA	TEA REPUBLIC
SIMON & SCHUSTER	SCHUSTER & SIMON
PLANET HOLLYWOOD	HOLLYWOOD PLANET

IV General Considerations

Dominance is important in a few ways. First, in judging potential confusion with other marks, your mark's dominant component may be the critical factor. That is, the dominant word in your mark is more likely to create similarity with another's mark. One technique, therefore, is to rearrange the mark to make the similar word less dominant. Second, dominance has a role in strengthening a mark. Making the most distinctive word more dominant can strengthen a mark.

58 WORD ORDER

Word order can be important because it affects meaning, rhythm, and dominance, among other factors. For example, with rhythm, when the mark consists of two names, the one with more syllables more often appears first. E.g., compare the rhythmic effects of the following:

MERCEDES BENZ	BENZ MERCEDES
PACKARD BELL	BELL PACKARD
MONTGOMERY WARD	WARD MONTGOMERY
PRENTICE-HALL	HALL-PRENTICE
HARCOURT BRACE	BRACE HARCOURT

However, where the two names are separated by "and," the rhythm and word order often changes and the name with fewer syllables may appear first, e.g., compare:

SMITH & WESSON	WESSON & SMITH
MARKS & SPENCERS	SPENCERS & MARKS
BLACK & DECKER	DECKER & BLACK
TOM & JERRY	JERRY & TOM
ABBOTT & COSTELLO	COSTELLO & ABBOTT
GILBERT & SULLIVAN	SULLIVAN & GILBERT

IV General Considerations

Changing word order can move a mark away from the *descriptive* toward the distinctive. Compare:

CLUB MED	MED CLUB
SAKS FIFTH AVENUE	FIFTH AVENUE SAKS
TEAM FROG	FROG TEAM

Changing word order allows you to place the more distinctive word first and thus make the mark stronger. Compare:

ABERCROMBIE & FITCH	FITCH & ABERCROMBIE
LOCKHEED MARTIN	MARTIN LOCKHEED
JUSTERNINI & BROOKS	BROOKS & JUSTERNINI

In most languages word order has no symmetry, as far as meaning is concerned. HARD ROCK is not equivalent to ROCK HARD nor COLD STONE synonymous with STONE COLD. But even if some equivalent meaning can be achieved in reversing word order, especially by adding or subtracting a preposition between the words, the semantics almost always will be different. Compare:

DAIRY QUEEN	QUEEN OF DAIRY
BURGER KING	KING OF BURGERS
MASTERMIND	MINDMASTER

In devising marks consisting of surnames, one should usually avoid a word order which makes the mark seem like a single proper name. Compare:

SMITH BARNEY	BARNEY SMITH
LOCKHEED MARTIN	MARTIN LOCKHEED
NEIMAN MARCUS	MARCUS NEIMAN
MCDONELL DOUGLAS	DOUGLAS MCDONELL

IV **General Considerations**

Finally, with two words having equal number of syllables, the first consonant and vowel sound may dictate word order, assuming semantic factors, which ordinarily have priority, don't dictate the reverse. E.g., in most cases where semantics do not dictate placement, the word with the shorter vowel sound will come first, as with ricochet words *(¶ 205)*. Note HARRY AND DAVID'S and even NEIMAN MARCUS, where the AR sound is only slightly longer than the EI sound. In contrast, the stronger, more plosive consonant may demand first placement. Compare BILL AND WILL vs. WILL AND BILL. Arguably BILL should come first. Of course, there are exceptions to these prevailing word orders, especially when flow of sound will control. MAC & JAC is easier to say than JAC & MAC because the "N" sound in & is slightly awkward when immediately followed by the "M" sound in MAC.

59 WORD DIVISION OR COMBINATION

When the mark consists of two words, one can often choose between combining or separating them as with K MART vs. KMART or DIE HARD vs. DIEHARD. A middle ground, seldom ideal, is the hyphenated mark, e.g., BAND-AID and SLIM-FAST. The combined one-word mark may be harder to read, but if this combination does not exist as a dictionary word, it is often the stronger choice. Marginally this one-word combination form is less likely deemed *descriptive* or confusingly similar to another mark than the two-word construction, as shown here.

SAFE WAY	SAFEWAY
TRAVEL LODGE	TRAVELODGE
GOOD YEAR	GOODYEAR
PALM OLIVE	PALMOLIVE

As mentioned *(Upper And Lowercase Lettering, ¶ 188)*, another modality is the one-word construction with the second component capitalized, as with **VirusScan** and **MasterCard**.

60 WORD MARK STYLIZATION

Stylization as well as spelling affects strength of a mark. Most famous *word marks* (e.g., SUPERMAN, IBM, and KLEENEX) are used in stylized form,

IV **General Considerations**

with stylization accentuating a word mark's mood and meaning. *(See Stylized Words, ¶ 277.)* Thus, when attaining a short list of possible marks, try them in various typefaces. Because some marks cannot be effectively stylized for all products, you may have to discard them. For stylization the first letter of a word mark is often very important, especially when that letter is capitalized and the others not, as in the stylized versions of WOOLITE (U.S. Reg. No. 1,732,360), KLEENEX (U.S. Reg. No. 1,785,525), and HOOVER (U.S. Reg. No. 652,995). The choices are legion: custom or existing font, serif or sans serif, bold or light, italics or reverse italics, shaded or not, or anything in between. *(See Font/Typeface, ¶ 61.)*

Yet, don't be hypnotized by a striking stylization. Just because a candidate mark appears irresistible when stylized doesn't mean you should embrace that mark. Remember that a word mark will be used by third parties in ordinary typeface and that sound and meaning are typically more important than appearance. Thus, to fairly judge, one technique is to compare the candidates when all shown in the same font—apples to apples, oranges to oranges. Only if two or more candidates still remain neck and neck should you compare them in their ideal stylized forms.

61 FONT/TYPEFACE

Even a strong *word mark* can be crippled by choosing the wrong font. The right font can enhance the word's metaphoric associations and may even add new dimensions. To achieve optimal results, the hand-lettered custom font is often best since the artist can make each letter of the mark complement the others and express the *brand* identity. Notable examples of custom font marks are logos for CANON (U.S. Reg. No. 1,090,231), DIXIE (U.S. Reg. No. 1,112,247), IBM (U.S. Reg. No. 1,205,090), NEIMAN-MARCUS (U.S. Reg. No. 601,864), and SEARS (U.S. Reg. No. 1,529,006).

If you don't aspire to a custom font but will choose an established one, then consider the following. Beware possible legal issues, especially copyright claims by typeface designers, and get appropriate written permissions when necessary. Choose a font from the right historical period, culture, and country of origin and one readable in all sizes in which it will be used. Generally don't electronically distort an existing font (e.g., condense or expand) because letters originally designed to complement each other in relation to shape, interior space, height, width, weight, and kerning (spacing between characters) may not do so when distorted.

IV General Considerations

Factors considered in selecting or designing fonts are stroke weight, weighted or unweighted stems, cap height, x-height, descender line, horizontal or vertical serif features (or none), and kerning. Each variable helps determine the font's personality and ability to reflect your brand identity. Your designer can illustrate and review these factors with you. For illustrated texts on these font issues, see, e.g., Doyald Young's books FONTS AND LOGOS and LOGO TYPES & LETTER FORMS. (His name is Doyald.)

62 VISUAL AND GRAPHIC POSSIBILITIES

Consider names having visual and graphic possibilities. A mark consisting of the name of an animal, plant, boat, or body part can be illustrated in visual terms, so you can generate a logo or *design* to accompany the *word mark*. Compare JAGUAR, TACO BELL, JACK IN THE BOX, SHELL, CHEVRON, POLO, ARM & HAMMER, and HANG TEN. Also note MITSUBISHI, meaning three diamonds (i.e., diamond shapes) in Japanese, hence the three-rhombi logo (as in U.S. Reg. No. 2,783,750) and the DIAMANTE model name. Moreover, consider SUBARU, Japanese for the Pleiades star cluster mimicked by the company logo in U.S. Reg. No. 2,431,546. Both the word and the design become stronger marks when so closely related, particularly where the word mark is arbitrary like SHELL or APPLE.

Words directly and easily turned into images are typically concrete nouns like APPLE and JAGUAR. Fully abstract nouns like HONESTY, COURAGE, and PRAISE can only be represented in metonymic or metaphoric images, i.e., images of worldly manifestations of that noun (e.g., with COURAGE an image of a lion, a courageous act, or a projectile piercing a thick barrier). A prime example is UBUNTU for computer software, from an African word meaning "humanity to others" or "I am what I am because of who we all are," symbolized by a somewhat abstract design mark that looks like three people of different races in a circle, holding hands. See U.S. Reg. No. 3,271,576 and the colored version of that design on the UBUNTU website. Less abstract nouns can be shown by images of the noun's concrete components (e.g., with POLO, the horses and players). Yet, even many concrete nouns cannot readily generate distinctive images. For instance, many amorphously shaped vegetables, like lettuces and cucumbers, seldom generate trademarked images.

IV General Considerations

63 MATCHING WORD WITH DESIGN

As mentioned in Visual And Graphic Possibilities *(¶ 62)*, selecting a word with graphic potential is a plus, and where the word expresses the *design*, and vice versa, the resonance between them may enhance the strength of each. Sometimes the effect is even more powerful when the word and corresponding design only suggest each other as with HANG TEN and its design. (See U.S. Reg. No. 877,451 for the HANG TEN design.) Occasionally, it's possible to replicate in a design the peculiar characteristic of the word since many word devices can be reflected in designs. For example, the word qualities or subject matter on the left correspond to those for designs on the right:

> palindrome *(¶ 183)* symmetry *(¶ 241)*
>
> homonym *(¶ 220)* visual ambiguity *(¶ 240)*
>
> solidity *(¶ 78)* density *(¶ 248)*

64 SLOGAN POSSIBILITIES

Consider marks that might yield memorable slogans such as "Fill it to the rim with BRIM," "Raise your hands if you're SURE," "It's not just a deal, it's a DELL!," "With a name like SMUCKERS, it has to be good," and "B of A: Banking on America." Sometimes the slogan becomes an excellent mnemonic device for making the mark unforgettable. The best marks to include in slogans will be *arbitrary* and *suggestive* ones. Because such slogans are usually *descriptive*, one may weaken a suggestive mark by including it in a slogan which pushes the mark toward descriptiveness. Slogans can be memorable and effective if techniques such as rhyme, rhythm, alliteration, pun, or double entendre are used. And the slogan itself may sometimes become a protectable mark *(Newly Devised Slogans And Phrases, ¶ 228)*.

65 NICKNAME POTENTIAL

Even a good mark can be made more effective by developing a complementary nickname, and marks can be selected based on their ability to spawn nicknames. Some well-known nicknames are BUD for BUDWEISER, COKE for COCA-COLA, HOG for large Harley-Davidson motorcycles, CHEVY for CHEVROLET, and HO-JO for HOWARD JOHNSON. One approach is to look

IV General Considerations

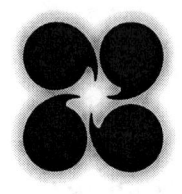

> "Fashion is something that goes in one year and out the other." So you want a mark which can persist with the cool breeze of the past at its back and the hot breath of the future in its face.

for marks whose first syllable or first morpheme has an interesting meaning perhaps related to the product; e.g., COC(A-COLA) and BUD(WEISER) fit that model. If your mark is pregnant with nicknames, you may not have to give them life; often consumers will "midwive" the nickname, as with HOG and CHEVY.

66 ADAPTABLE MARKS

Because the usual goal is to select a long-lasting mark *(Long-Lasting Marks, ¶74)*, the mark's ability to adapt to changing commercial environments can be important. Multi-syllabic tongue twisters, phrases or multiple words are not often very adaptable, e.g., in relation to add-ons, slogan possibilities, and adjectival use. Similarly, a *design mark* may be more valuable if potentially usable in black-and-white as well as in various color schemes. Examples of testing a mark's adaptability are ABERCROMBIE & FITCH, originally associated with fishing and hunting gear, then with high-quality conservative clothing and luxury items but later applied to trendier youth clothing and accessories, and BANANA REPUBLIC, once linked to fashionable "safari" clothing, now adapted to dressier, more urban fashion. If the mark is not adaptable and you anticipate waves of changing products to be sold under the mark, you will be "putting new wine in an old bottle."

The more adaptable mark usually has more metaphoric potential, i.e., the ability to make more connections. The ABERCROMBIE & FITCH product change was almost 180 degrees, yet the mark was rich and unusual enough, especially the distinctive ABERCROMBIE component, to make the transition. However, could BANANA REPUBLIC, connoting mostly a South American country, accommodate such a change?

IV General Considerations

Consider that GUCCI was first used for saddles, HASBRO for school supplies, NOKIA for rubber boots, NINTENDO for playing cards, DUPONT for gunpowder, and TIFFANY for stationery.

67 STIMULATING AND CALMING MARKS

Many strong marks convey subliminal or sometimes obvious visceral messages, encouraging consumers to buy the product. Some messages are stimulating, some calming. Good examples of stimulating are ZEST for soap bars, PEPSI for sodas, CARNIVAL for cruises, and CHEERIOS for breakfast cereal. All these marks are energetic and enlivening and have a direct or metaphoric relationship to the product.

To devise a stimulating mark one must search for things, ideas, feelings, and sounds that inspire, exhilarate, electrify, intoxicate, provoke, rouse, or thrill. Most of these marks will be *suggestive*, if not of the product then of feelings associated with the product or its use. CHEERIOS is a particular triumph, containing not only the happy CHEER and even the descriptive "OS," but also the old-fashioned British goodbye, CHEERIO. PEPSI is also masterful, supposedly originating from "pepsin," the digestive aid, but also containing the stimulating PEP, the affirmative SI, and the energetic Greek letter PSI.

In contrast to stimulating marks, some marks should be calming, e.g., marks for products associated with quiet, sleep, and relaxation. Calming effects are achieved semantically with words or morphemes such as LAX (as in OCULAX), DOZ(E) (as in SANDOZ), NI/NY and QUIL (as in NYQUIL, a joinder of "night" and "tranquil"); with vowels, especially the long "A" sound of "father" (as in at least one "A" in AMANA); and with consonants expressing unfocused energy, such as "M," "N," "L," and "W." As a test, which is more calming for sleep products: ROZEREM, LUNESTA, or AMBIEN? Probably AMBIEN wins, starting with a vowel, having consonants all expressing unfocused energy, and containing the word BIEN connoting "well." LUNESTA would rate second, starting with the calming L, containing the LUNE morpheme connoting the moon, and ending with the calming "A," though also containing a stimulating "T." ROZEREM would come third, starting with the energetic "R" and comprised of ROZE (connoting past tense of "rise") and REM (abbreviation for "rapid eye movement"), though containing the "Z" associated with sleep and ending in the calming "EM."

IV General Considerations

68 MEMORABLE MARKS

A good mark stays in the customer's mind and gains recognition after widespread use. In some ways a mark can be described as a "commercial mantra" and should function as such. Cf. memorable marks like SMUCKERS for jams and jellies, RED HOTS for candy, BANANA REPUBLIC for clothes, and BAZOOKA for chewing gum. Of course, not all "memorable" marks are easy to remember because there is a distinction between initially sticking to memory on first contact and staying in memory once remembered, the same distinction between a quick drying glue and a slower drying one which creates a stronger bond. An unusual and striking mark may not stay in long term memory, especially if it doesn't resonate with many associations. For instance, SMUCKERS, from the Smucker surname, for jams, jellies, and other food products, is very distinctive yet lacking in associations. To make that name stick required top notch *branding*, exemplified by the slogan "With a name like SMUCKERS, it has to be good." In contrast, RED HOTS for stinging red cinnamon-flavored sweets, though quasi-descriptive, could immediately stick in a child's memory.

As Jerry Yang said, "It is a pretty recognizable brand name. Originally it was "Jerry's Guide to the World Wide Web," but we settled on 'Yahoo.'"

69 EASY-TO-REMEMBER MARKS

No matter how clever or distinctive, a hard-to-remember mark can be ineffective. Marks may be difficult to remember, even if striking, when too long and convoluted or when very unusual and capricious without linguistic connections.

As known by memory trainers, something is best memorized when easily associated with other subject matter; i.e., the more "attachment hooks" the word has, the more it sticks, like VELCRO tape.

The more overtly clever or subconsciously powerful, the more the word will stick. Similarly, advertising slogans or themes which draw attention to aspects of the mark can fix it in memory. E.g., note "Fill it to the rim with BRIM" for coffee, and "SERUTAN is 'natures' spelled backwards" for nutritional supplements.

Of course, just because your mark sticks to memory like a burr to a sweater doesn't mean success. Meaning and metaphor, even if obscure, are usually more important than memory. As Adlai Stevenson said, "Words calculated to catch everyone may catch no one."

IV General Considerations

70 HUMOROUS MARKS

Humor, especially when clever, can make a mark easily known, though relatively few famous marks are humorous. DOGPILE, YAHOO!, and GOOGLE for online search services are memorable and humorous. Specific kinds of humor in marks are puns *(Puns on Words, ¶ 198 and Parodies, ¶ 200)*, expressions used out of context like PLAY IT AGAIN SAM for used sports equipment *(Literary Or Commonly Used Expressions, ¶ 227)*, silly-sounding words like GOOGLE (derived from "googol" meaning "10" to the hundredth power or "1" followed by one hundred zeros; hinting at "googly," an off-breaking ball in cricket; or reminiscent of Barney Google), words relating to dirt like DOGPILE or to excretions like DOG FARTS *(Good Or Pleasant Connotations, ¶ 80)*, obvious anagrams of slang words like FCUK (standing for French Connection United Kingdom), or words with some sexual connotations like RAMSES for condoms. RAMSES is one of the cleverest marks since it has at least five different connotations, i.e., a powerful Egyptian pharaoh (some believe it was Ramses II who said "no" to "Let my people go;" Exodus 5:1-2), something thrust forward, the ram as symbol of virility, "rammish" meaning "sexual," and the original source of modern condoms, sheep's intestine. More obscurely amusing is that Ramses II, an inspiration for the mark, was reputed to have had over 100 children.

71 METAPHORS

Metaphors are essential considerations. Marks incorporating metaphors, especially *suggestive marks,* can be good choices. Examples are FRUIT OF THE LOOM for clothing, CHICKEN OF THE SEA for canned tuna, CREAM OF WHEAT for hot cereal, CHOCK FULL O'NUTS for coffee, MOUNTAIN DEW for soda, TIDE for laundry detergent, TIME for news magazines, and VISA for credit card services. Poetic, metaphysical, spiritual, or romantic metaphors are often successful. Consider PRANA, meaning "breath of life" in Sanskrit, as originally applied to climbing clothing and accessories.

Some marks even have multiple metaphoric associations. For instance, APPLE for computer products (including the APPLE logo which shows the bite off the apple) may be metaphorically associated with Adam and Eve's "apple of knowledge," the apple given by Paris to Aphrodite in Greek mythology, an apple given to the teacher, and the apple as symbol of health, wholeness or object of desire ("apple of my eye"). As shown *(Mixed Metaphors; Oxymorons, ¶ 218)*, marks can also be constructed out of mixed

IV General Considerations

metaphors, and metonyms can be useful devices *(Metonyms, ¶219)*. For insights on how metaphor is embedded in language see METAPHORS WE LIVE BY by G. Lakoff and M. Johnson.

72 DILUTION

A mark is selected for its strength and distinctiveness, now and in the future. But a mark now unique may not remain so, and, therefore, you must gauge how likely it is that your mark may be *diluted* by other marks. "Dilution" occurs when others use the same or very similar marks even for unrelated products, so that the public may no longer perceive that your mark indicates a single source for all products linked to that mark. Thus a famous mark like ROLEX or SARA LEE would be diluted if someone not its owner used it for garden tools or other unrelated products.

Many of the same considerations governing legal protection costs *(¶88)* apply in determining likelihood of dilution. Common words not used *arbitrarily,* and even *fanciful* words likely to be surrounded by soundalikes, may be prone to future dilution. Thus, for fanciful marks, if your availability search, designed to elicit soundalikes, reveals numerous soundalikes, even for unrelated products, your candidate mark may be susceptible to dilution. E.g., the fanciful mark JETTA could be shadowed by soundalikes like JEDDA, JESTA, JEDI, and JET.

73 TIMING FACTORS

Not every mark is chosen for immediate use. With "intent-to-use" (ITU) registration applications common around the globe, a mark can be chosen for future use and selection made by imagining future market conditions when use will start. ITU applications in the USA can mature into registrations after the mark is used in "commerce," but such applications can often be extended for years before an Allegation/Statement of Use must be filed. In many jurisdictions registration can be secured without usage, though it will often be vulnerable to cancellation for failure to use the mark within limited periods following registration. Delayed usage sometimes allows selection and registration applications for multiple candidate marks or marks which might only survive under future market conditions.

Some marks and names may actually have predetermined, limited lives, especially those for products with time limits on utility, legality, or salability, such as computer chips which rapidly become obsolete along

IV General Considerations

with their names as well as goods which won't comply with scheduled government regulations within a few years of launch. To take maximum advantage of their limited lives, such marks should usually be chosen and submitted for registration well before product launch. Though it may be tempting to economize on selecting, searching, and protecting "nonce" marks (i.e., marks like TORINO 2006, coined for a particular occasion or short-term usage), if product success depends on a mark that fails because you didn't do your homework, the damage can be serious since there is little time to recover. Because timing decisions usually entail legal factors, always consult an attorney.

74 LONG-LASTING MARKS

Unless your product is a "gimmick," you generally want a mark which promises long-lasting use and significance. For most industries trendy, fashionable marks are not usually recommended but rather marks which can be rooted in the cultural soil and grow over time. As they say, "fashion is something that goes in one year and out the other." So you want a mark which can persist with the cool breeze of the past at its back and the hot breath of the future in its face.

Long-lasting marks are particularly important for patented products. Though the patent will expire after a period of years, a mark for a patented product may be so dominant during the patent term that the owner continues to enjoy almost a monopoly even after the patent expires. For instance, the patent on VELCRO hook-and-loop fastening has long expired, so anybody can sell hook-and-loop fasteners; however, only the makers of the VELCRO-brand product continue to control that mark, and their market position remains dominant since the product is known almost exclusively by its trademarked name. The same is somewhat true for pharmaceuticals even with generics available, e.g., VALIUM, LIBRIUM, and BENADRYL. With patented products care must be taken to avoid the mark becoming the unprotectable generic name of the product, as with former marks such as TELEPHONE, KEROSENE, and ESCALATOR. *(See Patent Considerations, ¶ 116.)*

The *fanciful mark* is often best for long-term survival. This is because meanings and connotations of real words can change over time, thus making the mark obsolete, unfashionable, unsuitable or dull, something less likely with a fanciful mark having no explicit meaning.

IV General Considerations

Consider DENNY'S, from the nickname for Dennis, in turn derived from Dionysus, the Greek god of food, drink, and merriment. Perhaps the originators of DENNY'S were unaware of its Greek origin since all they desired was a replacement for DANNY'S, their previous mark.

Also, avoid marks having built-in technological obsolescence. If WIRED, for cutting-edge magazines about high-tech, were not such a high-energy word having anagramic possibilities and multiple meanings *(¶ 181)*, could it become "tired" in a "wireless" age (unless perhaps associated with neural implants)? AIRBUS may suffice in an age of subsonic aircraft, but how will its land-crawling connotation, emanating from BUS, fare with supersonic aircraft? The TUBE in YOUTUBE might seem obsolete as cathode ray TV tubes head for extinction, yet the mark also touts the YOU TOO connotation. Also note TAB, once a cutting edge mark for sodas, especially upon the introduction of can-opening tabs. As paradox master Oscar Wilde noted, "It is only the modern that becomes old fashioned."

75 TIME FACTORS AND CONNOTATIONS

Consider a mark's temporal content, particularly in relation to *arbitrary* and *suggestive* marks. That is, you should consider whether the mark is connected to the past, harkens to the future, or lives in the ever-present now. Obviously, atavistic marks like ROMAN MEAL, connoting an association with ancient Rome, can thrive at least as long as the connotation has not disappeared. E.g., the concept of Roman civilization may weaken over time as relatively fewer people learn about ancient Rome. Because of market niche and effective advertising, MIDAS, associated with Greek mythology, has thrived even though the purchasing public is ever less familiar with the ancient king with the golden touch. Cf. QUILL for office supplies. Thus, with an atavistic mark the owner must consider how

IV General Considerations

long the connection to the past will be meaningful to customers, and the owner may create new metaphoric associations if the old ones fade away.

With the future so rapidly upon us as a fierce wind on the face, creating marks with futurity in them is more difficult. For instance, with "future" marks the question is, how long will the terminology be consistent with new technological developments and "lingo," and how long before usage catches up with language? As examples, terms like AI ("artificial intelligence"), DUST ("smart dust"), WARP, and BOTS (associated with "nanobots") may seem somewhat futuristic but may actually be or become passé. Interesting examples of obsolete high-tech terminology can be found in WIRED Magazine's ratings of words as "Expired," "Tired," and "Wired." As Yogi Berra once observed, "The future ain't what it used to be," so if selecting a futuristic mark, remember that even the concept of futurity may rapidly change. A futuristic mark is often more of a gamble than an atavistic one.

The timeless or time-neutral mark is one that may survive for a long period. For example, words of Greek origin are such candidates because of the universality of Greek thought. Note XEROX, HYPERION, PENTIUM, and NIKE, which, though superficially harking back to ancient Greek civilization, reside in the temporal present. These marks are like "petronyms" (words set in stone) or "frozen" words whose strength and meaning are not quickly thawed by time.

With *fanciful marks* one can sometimes inject temporal connotations with letters alone. In some contexts the letters A, B, D, G, H, O, W, and Y may be slightly past-oriented while E, I, N, and Z are more futuristic. Perhaps it's no coincidence that the Internet age is characterized by so many "I" and "E" marks like Apple, Inc.'s *family* of "I" marks such as iPOD and iPHONE and marks like eBAY and eHARMONY. Vowels alone may emanate temporal feelings, going from present to past as they move from the front of the mouth to the throat: witness present to past in "ring," "rang," and "rung" (ranging from the short "I" sound made at the front of the mouth to the short "U" sound deep in the throat). Clearly, typeface selection can also influence time perception: sans serif fonts usually more future-oriented, serif fonts more past.

The mark's temporal associations may lend themselves to certain kinds of products. For instance, "future" marks often go with high-tech electronic

IV General Considerations

products, "past" marks may complement staple food products, and time-neutral marks are frequently good for banking and insurance services.

76 SOCIAL TRENDS

One cannot ignore significant social trends. For example, the USA population is growing older, more ethnic, and less educated, at least in the humanities. As a result, easy-to-read phonetic marks *(¶ 50)* may be more viable for this older, more diverse, less sophisticated audience. Similarly, nostalgic, memory-evoking marks may appeal more to an older population. And there may be more tolerance for ethnically-diverse terminology. Naturally, analyzing social factors becomes more complicated whenever the mark will be used internationally, especially because of demographic variations; e.g., some countries have graying populations while others flaunt the bloom of youth.

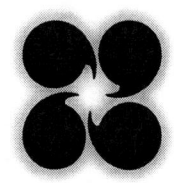

> "Each generation wants new symbols, new people, new names. They want to divorce themselves from their predecessors."
>
> JIM MORRISON

77 PRODUCT EXPANSION AND CONTRACTION

Consider not only existing and planned products to be sold with the mark but also other products you might consider. For instance, a mark perfect for children's products may not suit a new line of related adult products. An example is MAUI, a great mark for swimwear and warm water sportswear but not easily expandable for cold weather products; the converse is POLARTEC, a premier mark for cold weather fleece. Thus, if you select a product mark suitable only for a limited market, you might consider various devices to enter other markets with related products. E.g., the mark might be part of a *family of marks (¶ 108)*, each used in a different market or for a different product. Conversely, if a product's market is likely to become more specialized or limited, the mark might initially be slanted toward or adaptable for that limited market.

IV General Considerations

78 SOLIDITY, MASS, AND INERTIA

An important aesthetic consideration is "solidity." The more solid the mark, the more the impression of business and product stability, though softer, more ephemeral-sounding marks may be good for computer and electronic products. The mark having more "mass" is also sometimes characterized by "inertia," i.e., resistance to change, and may not be suitable for fast changing industries. Perhaps some of the usage dichotomies for solid versus less solid marks are hardware/software, masculine/feminine, and material/spiritual.

Markers for solidity are beginning consonants like B, D, K, and G; more gossamer sounds come from beginning consonants like N, M, L, and S and all vowels. Compare BLOCKBUSTER and BLACK & DECKER with AVAYA and MYLANTA. Remember that consonants represent "contained" energy while vowels are expressed with a free flow of energy, something you can test with your mouth while making letter sounds. *(See Vowel Sounds, ¶ 170.)*

In relation to non-*fanciful marks*, nouns are typically more solid than adjectives, adverbs, verbs, and words from other parts of speech. *(See Noun Marks, ¶ 213; Verb Marks, ¶ 214; Pure Adjectives, ¶ 215; Adverbs, ¶ 216; and Marks From Other Parts of Speech, ¶ 217.)* Even concrete nouns like DOG, PEANUT, and BUGGY tend to be more "solid" than abstract nouns like CUSTOM, FARCE, and VISION.

79 VELOCITY; FLEXIBILITY

In contrast to solidity, mass, and inertia *(¶ 78)*, a mark may express "velocity" or flexibility. Thus, a more solid mark is less likely to connote speed, change, and flexibility in the function or delivery of products. If beginning letters B, D, G, and K are markers for solidity, then velocity and flexibility may be associated with beginning sounds of F, S, V, Z, and C (not the hard C in CAT but the soft one in CIRRHUS). For instance, note the marks CELERON, CISCO, ZENITH, and VISINE. Sometimes an ending sound may also help, as the ON sound in SEMPRON or CELERON, connoting the speed of a subatomic particle. All things being equal, the shorter mark is faster. Also, the shorter the vowel sound, the faster. GLIB is faster than GLOB, and FAD faster than FADE. Which delivery mark is "faster," FEDEX or DHL? DHL is shorter but its "D" sound is more inertial than the FEDEX "F," and the lingering "L" at the end also slows the mark. Similarly, AMD is shorter than INTEL but INTEL faster because of the long "A" sound, the inertial D, and

IV General Considerations

the separate pronunciation of all three letters. A caution is that velocity and change do not always connote reliability.

80 GOOD OR PLEASANT CONNOTATIONS

Generally avoid marks having unpleasant connotations, and adopt ones with pleasant connotations such as CELESTIAL SEASONINGS for herbal teas, FRUIT OF THE LOOM for undergarments, GOOD GUYS for electronic products, GOOD HUMOR for ice cream, and SAFEWAY for supermarket products. This maxim refers not only to words in their entireties but even to roots or sounds of words. Naturally, exceptions exist, especially for unusual products or products marketed unusually. And what may be jarring may also be memorable. In Denmark a mark translated as DOG FARTS was successful for children's candies since it was so humorous and cutting-edge. Cf. U.S. Reg. No. 2,480,765 for STINKY FEET, covering cookies and candy. MONSTER.COM for job search services has been successful, too. BIC for pens was adapted from the founder's name, Marcel Bich, but would BICH have been more distinctive or successful?

81 INAPPROPRIATE MARKS

Avoid inappropriate marks, e.g., marks believed by some to be indecent, insulting, racist, sexist, chauvinistic, or pejorative. *(See Disparaging Marks, ¶ 325.)* Thus, before launching a major product line, consider not only the mark's meaning in foreign languages but also its connotations among various groups and subcultures in your own country. Though the AUNT JEMIMA design mark for pancake mixes, frozen waffles, and syrups, and Native American names for sports teams such as BRAVES, CHIEFS, and REDSKINS, are strong, popular, well-established marks, at the start of the new millennium one might hesitate to adopt similar new marks. As an example of possible problems, Native American groups commenced cancellation proceedings against U.S. Reg. Nos. 986,668, 978,824, and other REDSKINS registrations, contending the marks were disparaging. As of the date of writing this section, those cases were still pending. Also the USPTO partially denied registration of SQUAW because the mark applied to certain products was held disparaging to Native Americans.

As shown by the Native American cases, one must be wary of inadvertently offending others. What is innocuous to some may seem deeply insulting to others. Registration might be denied or other obstacles encountered

IV General Considerations

even if the intention is benign and the aggrieved institution, group, or subculture small. Avoiding such problems is sometimes only a matter of searching a word in a dictionary, thesaurus, and encyclopedia and then getting a legal opinion if there is any doubt.

82 UNINTENDED REFERENCES; MALAPROPISMS

In addition to avoiding ludicrous meanings in other languages *(¶ 90)*, you may want to avoid awkward references in English or funny translations into English. Fortunately for the makers of MYLANTA stomach remedies, nobody conjures up MY LANT when using the product ("lant" being stale urine used for wool scouring). Similarly, though TAG means "day" in German, no one perceives MAYTAG as "mayday," the international distress signal (derived from the French "m'aider") that would not suit appliances known for reliability. To avoid a funny mark one technique is to scan a dictionary, preferably an electronic one, for words that match in sound or spelling the candidate mark or any of its components. This means using a "complete" dictionary like the Oxford English Dictionary, the Chambers Dictionary (also British), or an online source such as the OneLook Dictionary Search at **onelook.com.** What could be worse than to launch a ludicrous mark? If you like a potentially ludicrous mark so much that you don't want to give it up, try a big focus group to see whether anyone sees the gaffe. The more obscure the funny reference, the more likely it can pass without notice.

By the way, when creating acronymic marks *(¶ 155)*, beware unintended rebuses *(¶ 172)*. Fortunately for the owner of DKNY, few perceive it as "decay New York."

83 METAPHORIC CONSISTENCY

Throughout, this Guide is concerned with marks appropriate to their subject matter in relation to issues such as Global Palatability *(¶ 91)*, Malaproprisms *(¶ 82)*, and Mixed Metaphors; Oxymorons *(¶ 218)*. It's easy to spot an oxymoron, and most malaproprisms soon get a laugh, but what about subtle inconsistencies? For instance, the artist Rembrandt was known for his dark palette and works like "The Night Watch." Yet, REMBRANDT is now a brand name for whitening toothpaste. The artist metaphor works, but does it matter that the artwork doesn't connote bright white? Midas was the king with the golden touch, so should MIDAS car repair shops

IV General Considerations

use only gold colored replacement parts? Mercury is a liquid metal which one can never grasp; a hot, fast moving planet; a messenger god; and the source of the adjective "mercurial." Somehow MERCURY succeeds for insurance services, in contrast to most insurance marks which connote solidity and stolidity, like PRUDENTIAL, MUTUAL OF OMAHA, and OLD REPUBLIC. TROJAN is successful for condoms even though men leapt out of the Trojan Horse after it was welcomed into Troy, and RAMSES, also for condoms, was supposedly inspired by the great pharaoh Ramses II who reputedly had over 100 children.

All the marks mentioned in this section are strong and unaffected by such subtle concerns. But to avoid similar non-obvious contradictions you need to go beyond a connotation search designed to find obvious silly meanings in other languages and malapropisms in your own. That means finding all possible associations the mark may have and whether any are subtly inconsistent with your business or products. This consideration especially applies to names from history, mythology, and legend which are rife with associations.

If subtle incongruency does concern you, consider whether the mark's other connotations are so strong that they bury the incongruency. For instance, TROJAN is so strongly associated with Hector and his masculine warrior comrades that it would seldom conjure "Beware of Greeks bearing gifts." Or consider whether you can turn weakness into strength, as per the MERCURY advertising campaign which humorously stressed that the company was not an alien force from another planet.

84 ADVERTISING COSTS

Related to protection costs *(¶ 88)* and dilution considerations *(¶ 72)* are advertising costs. A common belief is that marks approaching the *descriptive* are more easily accepted and recognized by consumers and less costly to advertise. Perhaps that kind of mark succeeds initially when a product is first released and the quasi-descriptive mark is easily connected to the product. However, descriptive marks are harder to protect, and as time passes and competitive products enter the market with similar kinds of weak marks, advertising costs can skyrocket in order to keep the mark distinctive. In the long run, advertising costs for *fanciful* and *arbitrary* marks may be much less.

IV General Considerations

Because fanciful and arbitrary marks can be analogized to delicate seeds of strong plants, to survive as seedlings in a competitive garden they may initially need more water and light in the form of advertising dollars, but once established they grow taller and stronger.

85 INTERNET USAGE

When your mark is a *house mark* or signifies an entire business or one of its divisions, you may want to reserve the mark for Internet usage. For instance, big automobile manufacturers have reserved their more important house marks on the Worldwide Web, e.g., **toyota.com, bmw.com,** and **ford.com.** It's also usually desirable to reserve domain names reflecting product marks.

If a new mark is not available for Internet usage, which can be determined by search, you may not want to adopt it. Please note that standards for Internet name availability are different than those applied by Federal and State trademark registries. Two virtually identical domain names separately owned can often co-exist even in the same top level domain, whereas trademark registration of both names might be impossible, especially at the USPTO. Thus, even when a domain name may be technically available on the Web, that doesn't mean the corresponding trademark should be adopted if someone else has a very similar domain name, especially when associated with similar products. Conversely, because unused, little used, and unrelatedly used domain names exist in the millions, just because there is a registration of a similar domain name doesn't always mean you should shun the corresponding trademark. Hypothetically, if PEANUT were your prospective mark for hairspray, just because someone else had peanut.com for raisins but peanut.net were available for registration, you might want to chance the PEANUT mark. Naturally, you should have legal counsel review potential conflicts with domain names.

By the way, in the early stages of selection when you have a short list of acceptable candidates, you may want to register appropriate domain names for all marks on the list, especially if available at a reasonable price. Whether you reserve only the .com versions or go for other top level domains is a matter of cost and strategy, to be discussed with your attorney. *(See also Internet Considerations, ¶ 130.)*

IV General Considerations

86 ADJECTIVAL MARKS

Select a mark best used as an adjective. This is because marks used in text, particularly in relation to the products to which they apply, should be used adjectivally in relation to those products. For instance, proper trademark usage is "drink SANKA brand coffee" or "drink SANKA coffee" but not "drink SANKA." A mark should almost never be used as a noun or verb. Using marks as nouns can make them unprotectably *generic* for the product with which they are associated, e.g., ASPIRIN and KEROSENE. Phrases, unless used as taglines or slogans, sometimes don't make good marks since they are difficult to use adjectivally in relation to products. Also, multi-word marks starting with THE are less suitable for adjectival use.

87 BUSINESS RESOURCES

The kind of mark selected may sometimes depend on the company's monetary, distribution, and publicity resources. In the long run, a small company may find it harder to finance and protect a weaker, more *descriptive mark,* whereas a big corporation can often protect that same mark from challenges and make it distinctive through heavy advertising. Similarly, in the short run a small company may be unable to sufficiently promote a *fanciful mark* and achieve enough market penetration for the mark to survive. Moreover, a wealthy company may sometimes choose a mark more likely to face challenges because the company believes it can "buy" its way out of trouble via litigation or a license.

Yet, if the small company has a strong patent on the product, the monopoly during the patent term may enable the company to make even a weaker mark distinctive, while not letting the mark become *generic* for the patented product. *(See Patent Considerations, ¶ 116.)*

88 PROTECTION COSTS

Small businesses particularly should consider potential costs of defending their marks. Even when the selected mark is not surrounded by competing marks of similar sound, appearance, or meaning, that situation can change if the mark is susceptible to infringement by similar marks. For instance, when you select a *fanciful* mark like JETTA you may confront numerous soundalikes, e.g., hypothetically META, BETA, HEDDA, FETA, and JEDI. However, if you pick an *arbitrary* mark like PLATYPUS or KIWI, enforcement

IV General Considerations

problems are often reduced because these words may have no precise synonyms, homonyms, or homographs; nothing familiar even rhymes with PLATYPUS, and the rhymes with KIWI, like PEEWEE, might be relatively small concerns. Therefore, to reduce protection costs you might lean toward arbitrary or *suggestive* marks or perhaps unusual, multisyllabic fanciful marks not likely to face soundalikes.

89 WORD ORIGINS

One should consider the word mark's language of origin. English words have many origins including, e.g., Greek, Latin, French, and Germanic languages. Greek is a good source of words/names connoting ideas, abstract concepts, and spirituality, yielding marks such as XEROX and LOGITECH. Latin is a language of law and social order, spawning marks like PRO FORMA for business forms and NON SEQUITUR for a comic strip. As a language of aesthetics and romance, French inspires marks like ESPRIT DE CORP for women's clothing and L'OREAL for cosmetics.

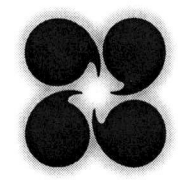

Marks developed for virtual world usage should clearly be compatible with the governing rules, aesthetics, and cultures of the virtual worlds they inhabit.

In devising a new word one should carefully consider whether to mix components from different languages, as with MICRO (Greek) SOFT (Old English); PIZZA (Italian) HUT (German), RADIO (Latin) SHACK (American), and HAND (Old English) SPRING (German) VISOR (French). Even if the languages are closely related, the mixed effect is noticeable, as with LE (French) NOVO (Latin). As with mixed names and metaphors, and other mixed content, such "mixed marks" can sometimes be striking yet also jarring, strange, or ineffective. As one might say about creators of badly mixed marks: "They have been at a great feast of languages, and stolen the scraps." ("Love's Labour's Lost," Act V, Scene I). *(See also **Incongruous Marks; Multi-Language Marks**, ¶ 195 and **Mixed Metaphors; Oxymorons**, ¶ 218.)*

IV General Considerations

90 PROBLEMS IN OTHER LANGUAGES

Shun marks which may have problems in foreign countries because of unfortunate translations. For example, some thought NOVA was unusual for cars in Spanish-speaking countries because "no va" means "it doesn't go," though sales were apparently not affected. The same was true with DRECK for leather preservatives since it means "dirt" in German. Another problem in German was faced by MIST STICK for curling irons since MIST is slang for manure. However, B.U.M. for sportswear did well in English-speaking countries even though in the UK it could connote one's bottom and in the USA a hobo. What would a Spanish-speaking person associate with MIDOL, since "mi dolor" in Spanish means "my pain"? Thus, even with what are believed to be *fanciful* marks, check whether they have meanings or connotations in any language. One way of checking is to enter the proposed mark as a search term on Google, Yahoo! or a "meta" search engine like **dogpile.com** and see what comes up. Better yet, trademark "connotation" searches are available from trademark search services.

91 GLOBAL PALATABILITY

Select a mark which not only avoids problems in certain languages but is usable throughout the world or at least in a great number of countries, regardless of language or culture. Remember, an English word or phrase may not be suitable for countries where English is not widely used. Examples of marks suitable for wide usage across language barriers are CASIO, KODAK, ACURA, SONY, NOKIA, and COCA-COLA. Such palatable marks are usually phonetic, easy to read, and easy to pronounce. Note that some sounds are seldom or never used in certain foreign languages, e.g., the "R" sound in various Chinese dialects and the "L" sound in Japanese. The same not only applies to the sounds of individual letters but also to sound patterns represented by two or more conjoined letters. HWYLEAWR ("goodbye" in Welsh) and LYZWIARSTWO ("skating" in Polish) may seem strange to English speakers; similarly many sound patterns of English words may be tongue twisters to Welsh and Polish speakers.

92 INTERNATIONAL USE OF ENGLISH WORDS

For international use not only must an English *word mark* be globally palatable *(¶91)* (i.e., avoid unfavorable or bizarre meanings in other

IV General Considerations

languages), but one must consider its "translatability." That is, though you might avoid a mark which unintentionally insults, have you chosen an *arbitrary* or *suggestive* mark whose English meaning cannot be expressed in another language?

Eskimos have a number words to designate different kinds of snow, which have no English equivalents. Similarly, English has hundreds of thousands of words more than any other language, many of which words have no equivalents in other languages. Thus, if you pick an English word having strong semantic connections to the products, will it have those meanings, or any meanings, when translated? For instance, abstract English nouns, verbs, and adjectives such as "homily," "synthesize," and "nascent" may have no precise equivalents in many other languages. Similarly, WIDGET, GROOVY, and NERD may sound "neat" in English but have no meaning or one-word equivalents in most other languages.

In countries where no translation exists for your arbitrary or suggestive English word mark, the mark may be considered *fanciful*, which may not be a fatal flaw but is a factor to consider, especially when the mark's meaning is a critical element of marketing.

93 INTERNATIONAL ADAPTABILITY

In selecting a globally palatable mark *(¶91)*, one should consider its adaptability. After all, a mark may have different pronunciations and connotations in various cultures. That is, some marks used globally actually become homographs *(¶224)*, words with the same spelling but with different sounds or connotations. For instance, ADIDAS in Continental Europe is generally pronounced with stress on the first syllable as Á-di-Das, in homage to the company founder Adolf "Adi" Dassler. But in the UK and USA it's pronounced a-Di-das with stress on the second syllable and is more a "noun mark" *(¶213)*. If BAYER were given its German pronunciation it would sound like BUYER, and BRAUN in German would sound like BROWN rather than BRAWN, so that the owners of these marks are fortunate that the German pronunciations were not generally adopted in English speaking countries.

If the mark will likely acquire different pronunciations in various countries, one must not only consider the suitability of these pronunciations but also evaluate the mark's availability in a particular jurisdiction relative to the

IV General Considerations

meaning and pronunciation it may have there. Note, e.g., that IBM in a Spanish speaking country sounds like EBAY + EMMAY.

Of course, a possible remedy is to control pronunciation by establishing strict usage guidelines and perhaps even specifying pronunciation in registration applications, the risk being that the specified pronunciation may not be optimal in every country. Though some trademark registries may accept the pronunciation you specify, particularly when the mark is considered a "foreign" word or pronunciation is uncertain, other registries may reject such specification.

Another consideration is transliteration. In countries not using the Roman alphabet, e.g., in Russia, Asia or the Middle East, buyers and sellers often want trademarks to appear in their alphabet or script. To achieve transliteration, the mark must be translated into another alphabet or script, either phonetically, conceptually, or both. With phonetic transliteration the goal is to reproduce the mark's sounds via the foreign alphabet or script, with the hope that the sounds don't have an inappropriate meaning. E.g., SONY in Chinese is transliterated into characters that sound like "suo ni," which mean "cable" ("suo") "nun" ("ni"), not a snazzy meaning for electronic products but not ludicrous either.

With conceptual transliteration the aim is merely to convey the mark's meaning. E.g., SHELL in Chinese characters is "bei ke" which means "shell," though sounding more like the "BK" abbreviation for BURGER KING. When both phonetic and conceptual aspects are transliterated, the object is to reflect the essence of both sound and meaning, often without precisely achieving either. E.g., COCA-COLA is transliterated into Chinese characters as "ke kou ke le," which means "tasty and happiness producing."

For marks used worldwide, the problems of transliteration are daunting. To minimize complications, one technique is to design a mark easily transliterated conceptually, which avoids the risks of phonetic transliteration. For instance, hypothetically, if your mark were 9CATS or RED CIRCLE, you might expect fewer problems by seeking only conceptual transliteration because most languages could simply express these concepts. But just because the mark can be conceptually transliterated doesn't mean it will have the right connotation. E.g., hypothetically 9CATS might evoke superstitious feelings someplace, a factor often uncovered only by a connotation search.

IV General Considerations

94 INTERNATIONAL LEGAL CONSIDERATIONS

Owners considering international use should beware foreign laws because a mark acceptable in one's own country may not be usable or registrable in other countries. For instance, the considerations mentioned in Subject Matter (Section V) may not always equally apply in certain foreign jurisdictions. A good mark in the USA may elsewhere be considered unprotectably *descriptive*, misdescriptive, non-distinctive, indecent, or confusingly similar to another mark. Sometimes even subject matter accepted in the USA enjoys no legal protection in a foreign country, for example, marks for alcoholic beverages in countries where drinking alcohol is prohibited. *(See Foreign Prohibitions, ¶ 332.)* When a mark well-established in one country is unavailable in another, in the other country you may have to use a different mark for the same products, not always a great inconvenience but one which may detract from the established mark's fame. Cf. ZANTAC used in the USA and the UK but sold as AZANTAC in France.

95 VIRTUAL WORLDS

Consider trademarks developed for or emerging from virtual worlds. Virtual world ("V-W") characters have their own needs to buy and sell virtual products, and virtual worlds are being invaded by real world trademarks. E.g., ADIDAS, AMERICAN APPAREL, IBM, and NISSAN virtual products are available to V-W characters in the SECOND LIFE environment. Also, it won't be long before marks developed for V-W usage emerge into the real world. (Perhaps there will even be V-W trademark registries.) Marks developed for V-W usage should clearly be compatible with the governing rules, aesthetics, and cultures of the virtual worlds they inhabit. I.e., creating a V-W mark is analogous to creating a mark for a foreign country, which may mean immersing oneself in that country's language and culture, though in the case of virtual worlds, one studies the lingo, character monikers, nicknames, nomenclature, culture, and artificial surroundings. Even if a mark is developed specifically for V-W usage, it should usually also have potential for real world usage.

Because V-W goods are typically not tangible, legal protection of V-W marks via real world registration may extend first to services. E.g., if your mark is for V-W shoes, a real world registration might instead cover entertainment services in the nature of commerce in virtual world shoes.

IV General Considerations

(In preparing your trademark registration application, you will need an attorney to properly identify the claimed products.) As with Tom Stoppard's "Rosencrantz and Guildenstern are Dead" whose characters wormhole in and out of Shakespeare's "Hamlet" and their own separate drama, there's no reason why trademarks can't migrate from one fictional world to another, even without use on real world goods. Because V-W trademark issues are novel, you must get legal advice on how to migrate marks between these universes and register V-W marks in real world registries as well as register real world marks for virtual products.

To keep informed about V-W naming you can consult not only real world trademark registry databases but also V-W search engines.

96 WORDS WITH MANY SYLLABLES

Whenever possible, avoid unfamiliar words with many syllables. Though many good marks are comprised of long words, generally speaking even those words are only two or three syllables because of the sound problem with multi-syllabic words. Length does not mean strength, and powerful one-syllable marks abound such as BIC, JOY, GAP, JEEP, KIX, and HEAD. Remember, the consumer must favorably react to your mark, often in a split second. (See Rebecca Tushnet's article, "Gone in 60 Milliseconds: Trademark Law and Cognitive Science," 86 TEXAS LAW REVIEW 507 (2008).) You don't want this thought process to be complicated, especially if developing a *fanciful* mark. Naturally, well advertised multi-syllabic marks can stand out, though relatively uncommon, e.g., ORVILLE REDENBACHER, MITSUBISHI, and SALVATORE FERRAGAMO. These successful daddylonglegs are typically unusual or colorful, and thus worth remembering.

97 SHORTER MARKS

Shorter marks are often better than longer ones and can also save money, particularly over time. As Mark Twain said, "I never write 'metropolis' for seven cents because I can get the same price for 'city'." For example, IHOP rather than International House of Pancakes and UPS rather than United Parcel Service can foster substantial savings in signage, advertising costs, and even employee time. A shorter mark also means less typing and fewer errors for any customer contacting a website named after the mark. Of course, a 7-letter mark is ideal for use in a toll-free telephone number. And one-, two-, and three-letter marks, unless initials of longer words, like DQ,

IV General Considerations

BK, AAA, IBM, and BMW, can be weak and more easily confused with similar marks. So, e.g., if you fancy having a three-letter mark that is not a word nor obviously initials, then to achieve distinctiveness you might want an unusual letter mix like QVC, UBS, OXO, and DHL.

98 PARSIMONIOUS MARKS

In the section on shorter marks *(¶ 97)* we note brevity's practical advantages, for instance, monetary savings on signage and easier data entry. But a more important consideration pervades this entire Guide, as reflected in various paragraphs such as Nickname Potential *(¶ 65)*, Easy-To-Remember Marks *(¶ 69)*, Words With Many Syllables *(¶ 96)*, and Simpler Designs *(¶ 264)*. That consideration is "parsimony," the notion that a mark should embody the least expression necessary to convey meaning and metaphor because by omitting unnecessary expression the mark leaves more to the imagination. Not only is "brevity the soul of wit," but what is not directly expressed often makes the mark pregnant with positive meaning. We should not forget that one origin of trademarks was actual "branding," i.e., the burning of an emblem, and though to be recognizable that emblem had to be distinctive, it was also typically no more complicated than necessary for both practical and aesthetic reasons.

> **"It is a pretty recognizable brand name. Originally it was 'Jerry's Guide to the World Wide Web,' but we settled on 'Yahoo.'"**
>
> JERRY YANG

We note relatively few famous marks (other than *taglines* and *slogans*) having three or more words (excluding articles like "A" and "THE" and prepositions like "FOR" and "BY"). And for longer marks, and even mid-sized ones, the trend is toward abbreviations and nicknames. LEVI STRAUSS is now probably more widely known as LEVI'S; SEARS ROEBUCK is now SEARS; GEORGIO ARMANI is referred to as ARMANI; KENTUCKY FRIED CHICKEN is KFC; INTERNATIONAL HOUSE OF PANCAKES is IHOP; and more people ask for COKE and PEPSI than for COCA-COLA and PEPSI COLA. Similarly with images, the trend is toward simplicity and abstraction, especially with *house marks*, so that the mark becomes more

IV General Considerations

iconic. Witness, for example, the evolution of the U.S. Postal Service's eagle designs (U.S. Reg. Nos. 1,917,921 and 2,494,399) and the DUTCH BOY depictions (U.S. Reg. Nos. 383,644 and 1,161,535).

With parsimonious expression, the gap between "what is" and "what isn't" expressed leaves room for "what could be," which brings us to parsimony's classic expression, the GAP itself. GAP is not only short but attracts one's interest as to what is doesn't accompany. Could GAP have come from GENERATION GAP, an expression of the brand's devotion to young people's clothes? Or does GAP merely connote a physical space in between other retail outlets?

As said throughout this Guide, one consideration in adopting longer marks is the potential to evolve through shortening, e.g., into abbreviations, single words, or nicknames. So if a longer expression must be adopted, preference should extend to the mark that can later be shortened.

99 CUSTOMER BASE

An obvious consideration is customer demographics, e.g., in relation to age, sex, and region. Men's products usually get masculine marks, while women's products get feminine ones. *(See Gender Considerations, ¶ 101.)* Marks are also adjusted for age levels, like KIX, SNAP CRACKLE POP, and SUGAR BEAR for child-oriented breakfast cereals. Of course, occasionally exceptions survive or even thrive, e.g., male names like VIDAL SASSOON and PAUL MITCHELL for female beauty products. However, even a mark which breathes the product's essence may fail if the special connection between mark and product is not established with a narrow, unique or peculiar customer base.

On a more sophisticated level, relevant demographic considerations even have a temporal element. For instance, household cleaning products are more likely first selected by wives than by husbands, though once selected are purchased by both; the reverse with fuel products. Also, one could imagine high tech games being first selected by children before being bought by their parents. In other words, for many products the mark should first appeal to "filter" groups who pass product information to others.

IV General Considerations

100 CUSTOMER SELF-EXPRESSION

Never forget how customers will feel about being seen with a product bearing your mark and how that mark allows customers to express their personalities. A fancy mark, like one from a culture revered for producing the kind of product you sell, may give the customer a sense of privilege and sophistication, especially with personal items like clothing, jewelry, and accessories that more obviously reflect the bearer's taste and cultivation. To use a FABER-CASTELL or VISCONTI pen at a business meeting is a different experience than employing a BIC or UNI-BALL instrument even if the handwriting produced were indistinguishable. A rumor was that even the Pope wears PRADA. Thus, to appeal to taste, pride, and sophistication, the chosen mark should reflect those feelings and attitudes. A mark that appeals to such sensibilities makes the product not only worth buying but worth going to buy. Of course, except for the most haughty, customers in a supermarket checkout line don't flaunt the brand of their bathroom tissue, so this factor is usually not as important for ordinary supermarket fare.

101 GENDER CONSIDERATIONS; MASCULINE/FEMININE/NEUTER

Sometimes you should consider the mark's "gender," especially in relation to the products. For instance, when goods are "feminine" or purchased by women, does one ever select a masculine mark? This is not only a "customer base" consideration *(¶99)* but also a deeper linguistic concern because in many languages nouns pertaining to products are divided into masculine and feminine, and sometimes neuter. All the Romance languages (e.g., French, Italian, and Spanish) divide nouns into masculine and feminine, and Latin from which they originated also uses the neuter. E.g., Spanish uses the masculine "el coche" (car) (or in Mexico "el carro"), and the feminine "la barca" (boat). Moreover, even though English nouns are seldom inflected to show gender, many things have gender, as revealed in pronoun usage. For example, instead of "it" for a ship we often say "she," and when we refer in general to a persons in certain occupations, we often say "he" as we would with a janitor.

Therefore, it is often incongruous, especially for audiences accustomed to nouns being either masculine or feminine, to pick masculine marks for feminine products and vice versa. For these reasons a neuter mark like PENTIUM is proper for "neuter" computer chips, while VICTORIA'S

IV General Considerations

SECRET is good for "feminine" lingerie, and NAUTILUS (meaning "sailor" in Latin) is appropriate for "masculine" weight training machines. Of course, choosing a masculine mark for a feminine product may be better than the converse, since, anecdotally, men are less likely to favor a feminine brand than women a masculine. And, obviously, where one sex provides products to the other, a mark reflecting the providing gender is viable, as per SEBASTIAN and GRAHAM WEBB for women's hair products.

Sometimes the product or business may demand a gender mark which is overtly or subtlely "politically correct." VIRAGO, a strong mark for women's books, is overtly suitable, whereas a relatively rare matronym (like ANSON, son of Ann, or TILLOTSON, derived from a diminutive of Matilda) instead of a more common patronym (like MCDONALD'S or ALBERTSONS) for women's products may be more subtle.

102 SOCIAL STATUS, VOCABULARY, AND PROPRIETY LEVELS

The mark should reflect the right social status, vocabulary, and propriety level for the products. Insurance, banking, legal, and medical services are commonly associated with "dignified" marks, e.g., for insurance PRUDENTIAL, RELIANCE, and TRAVELERS. Fast food, sporting events, and laundry detergents often come with more "imaginative" marks, e.g., for fast food JACK IN THE BOX, BOB'S BIG BOY, and IN-N-OUT BURGER. If you sell the same kinds of goods but in different grades, then each market tier can have its own mark, e.g., HOME DEPOT/HOME EXPO and OLD NAVY/GAP/BANANA REPUBLIC.

A central theme of this Guide is connotative and metaphoric consistency. *(See Metaphoric Consistency, ¶83.)* Violate metaphoric conventions in relation to class, social status, and propriety at your peril. A mark's misleading impression means expensive remedial advertising either to clear the wrong impression or carve an unusual niche.

103 MULTI-LEVEL MARKET CONSIDERATIONS

A mark effective for one class of customers may be less so for others. This is true both for vertically arranged customers as well as horizontally arranged markets. For instance, the vertical market for pharmaceuticals often includes distributors, hospital administrators, pharmacies, doctors, and ultimately patients. A pharmaceutical marketed directly to the public,

IV General Considerations

even if a prescription product, will typically have a mark that patients can relate to, such as AMBIEN for sleep medications (suggestive of "ambience" or "morning well-being," i.e., AM plus BIEN) and ROGAINE for hair growth preparations (suggesting "gained" rows of hair); but certain drugs with which the public has no contact through public advertising (e.g., various chemotherapy products for cancer) may have marks, like DAUNOXOME and PACITAXELINE, that are directed to physicians and other health care providers. Looking at horizontal markets, a mark suitable for urban populations might not appeal to country folks.

104 CONSUMER MARKS VS. "TRADE" MARKS

A key market consideration is whether you are developing a consumer mark or a mark only used in the trade. Consumer marks, i.e., those used on products sold to the general public, are typically more "friendly" and easy-to-use. Marks used only in the trade, i.e., B-2-B marks, can be more arcane and technical, a distinction illustrated by pharmaceutical marks like DISALCID and PHENTERCOT for products primarily sold to and through physicians and FLOMAX and FLONASE for products publicly advertised.

Typically, consumer marks are more valuable than B-2-B marks, and anytime one uses a mark on products sold to the trade, extending that mark to consumer products should also be explored. This principle particularly applies to a "trade" product redistributed to the public in its original or manufactured form. For instance, with a mark used for raw materials, you might explore how the mark can be developed and used on finished products sold by your trade customers. Certainly the "intel inside" campaign makes INTEL both a trade and consumer mark. POLARTEC is a mark known in the trade but also appears on manufactured items sold by distributors and manufacturers.

Unlike consumer marks which may not disclose what company offers the product, B-2-B marks often reflect the company name or some aspect of the company since the trade customer is dealing directly with the company.

105 PRICING

An obvious consideration is your product's price point. Marks reflecting more sophistication often accompany higher prices, and vice versa. Some marks glow gold, while others glow silver, bronze, or even lead. HOME DEPOT is bronze, while its more fancy HOME EXPO sister store is silver.

IV General Considerations

Excluding acronyms, luxury seems to start at five letters, as in PRADA, GUCCI, FENDI, ROLEX, LEXUS, and ACURA.

RALPH LAUREN and POLO reflect pricier clothes than does OLD NAVY; the same with BIC and UNI-BALL compared to VISCONTI and BENTLEY for pens. ACCORD sounds more upscale than CIVIC; the same with AVALON versus CAMRY.

The principal clue to price is obviously direct meaning: compare EXPO to DEPOT. Also, connotation does the job: compare the European, sophisticated-sounding VISCONTI to the more commercial UNIBALL and the mystical sounding AVALON (the legendary isle) to the more mundane CAMRY (an anagram of "my car"). But perhaps even with purely *fanciful marks* the clues are discernable. All things being equal, the tendency is, the longer the word and its vowel sounds, the bigger the price. Though BIC might adorn a few high end products, it was never intended as a luxury brand name. In fact, it's hard to find luxury brands among the large number of famous three-letter marks (excluding acronyms). Excluding acronyms, luxury seems to start at five letters, as per PRADA, GUCCI, FENDI, ROLEX, LEXUS, and ACURA. Never forget that for cheap consumer products you may not want a "luxury" name, or when selling expensive but "rough and ready products" like HUMMER cars, you don't want to rush to your French dictionaries.

106 USER OF MARK

The selection process is usually aimed at marks your company will use on products, but there are exceptions. Sometimes a company might never directly use its mark because the mark is for use by others. Different selection considerations may apply when others will use the mark.

Marks not directly used by their owners include, e.g., licensed and franchised marks where the owner itself sells no products and operates no franchises. Certification marks like Underwriters Laboratory's UL are not used by their owners on products but only by licensees whose products are certified.

IV General Considerations

When selecting a mark which only (or primarily) others will use, particularly large numbers of licensees, a key consideration is "permanency." *(See Long-Lasting Marks, ¶ 74.)* To reflect new market conditions it is much easier to change a mark or adopt a new one when your company is the sole user. Changing a mark used by hundreds of licensees or franchisees can be very difficult. Another reason to get a viable mark when selecting for others' use is to avoid conflicts with other marks. After all, if the mark you select is attacked after you license it to numerous licensees, you may be liable to licensees who depend on the licensed mark. And if your licensees operate in foreign countries not using the Roman alphabet, then you might prefer a mark that transliterates easily. Thus you should exercise more care in selecting a mark to be used by others.

107 ENTIRE TRADEMARK PROGRAM; TRADEMARK ARCHITECTURE AND NOMENCLATURE

For all your marks build a trademark program with the appropriate "architecture." For instance, you may want a *house mark* for the full range of company products. Then you might want a product series mark for an entire line of products, and perhaps separate marks for each single product. As an example, NABISCO is the house mark for Nabisco Brands Co. The red triangle with the white "antenna" used on the corner of the NABISCO packages is used in connection with packaging for a wide range of products. And Nabisco Brands also uses individual product marks such as RITZ for crackers. Similarly, MICROSOFT is a trademark for a line of computer products, but Microsoft Corporation uses individual product marks as well, e.g., WINDOWS, WORD, EXCEL, ENCARTA, and POWERPOINT.

Unless a house mark is used with all your products, the consumer will not perceive them as coming from one source, except if some other "unifying" device is employed such as a common *trade dress*.

To semantically and competitively position your house and product marks, you develop supportive *taglines (¶ 229)* and *slogans (¶ 228)*. In order of development, the company/product logos and trade dresses *(¶ 316)* might come next, followed by a host of miscellaneous branding devices such as medallions and seals *(¶ 287)*, vehicle designs *(¶ 293)*, uniform designs and colors *(¶ 295)*, building or structure designs *(¶ 294)*, packaging designs *(¶ 283)*, container shapes and features *(¶ 297)*, and product shapes and ornaments *(¶ 292)*. If your house mark were the arch's cornerstone,

IV General Considerations

and the product marks its other stones, then the taglines, slogans, trade dresses, logos, and other miscellaneous devices would be the mortar and paste. The rarely achieved goal is a unified, harmonious structure without semantic and metaphoric contradictions, each element supporting and complementing the others.

As with a physical structure, temporal considerations are relevant in devising a trademark architecture. For example, with products that might be updated, refined, or produced in variations, the trademark owner must be prepared to develop congruent names not only for new products but also for older, superseded ones. Like a skin shed from a snake, an older product may need a new identify if the new one keeps the old name. Developing "retronyms" for old products, like COCA-COLA CLASSIC and G1 TRANSFORMERS, is part of maintaining a trademark architecture. Creating such retronyms usually just requires adding an adjective like PLAIN, CLASSIC or ORIGINAL, but when a unique product later spawns a very distinctive cousin, a more imaginative retronym may be needed. (However, rarely will the retronym have no resemblance to the original mark since such a total transformation can cause confusion and require a costly rebranding.)

A stable, manageable, and meaningful trademark architecture is frequently the product of a thoughtful trademark nomenclature, i.e., a pre-arranged naming system. Such a nomenclature may be based on trademark families or themes, and may include naming schemes for retronyms as products become outdated. A trademark nomenclature not only provides predictability but may also save time, money, and effort in naming new products and renaming old ones. Naturally, like the Japanese corporation which developed a 500-year business plan, the company which devises a highly articulated nomenclature with numerous protocols may find its usefulness short-lived, especially in rapidly changing trades and industries.

108 TRADEMARK FAMILIES

When marketing a substantial number of related products, you may want a common characteristic for the various product marks in your product line. Often this common element is *arbitrary* or *suggestive* and capable of being recognized and protected on its own. For instance, under the TWINLAB *house mark* for nutritional supplements, the distributor developed a "FUEL" line of products so that a great number of its product marks end with FUEL, e.g., the amino acid product has been sold under AMINO FUEL and

IV General Considerations

the phosphates product under PHOS FUEL. This usage can create a "family of marks." A common element for a line of products might be the first or last syllable of a word, or an entire word in a multi-word mark.

When a properly-devised common element becomes well known, it may enjoy legal protection and may distinguish even new products having the element attached to their marks. Sometimes the common element alone can also be used and registered as a mark, which strengthens the trademark position of the "family." Examples of common "family" elements are MC associated with various McDONALD'S products, MAC associated with the MACINTOSH line of APPLE computer products, and CITI associated with various CITIBANK financial services marks. The family's strength is often enhanced by registering the various family marks, creating public awareness of the family, and using the family marks together.

109 TRADEMARK THEMES

Marks for related products can have a common theme even without having a common element such as a characteristic suffix or prefix. Automobile marks are good illustrations. INFINITI models have had three-character alphanumeric designations, e.g. J30, I30, Q30, and QX4; BMW cars have been distinguished by three digits in the model numbers, e.g., 318, 323, 328, 528, and 540; HONDA models are distinguished by *arbitrary* real words, e.g., ACCORD, PRELUDE, and CIVIC; and Chrysler sport utility cars have been associated with American Western names, such as LAREDO, CHEROKEE, and WRANGLER. (Note that not all model numbers or designations are perceived or protected as trademarks.)

Unlike the mark connected to a *family of marks* by a common element (e.g., a "MC" element related to McDonalds Corporation fast food), a mark within a group of marks having a common theme will not automatically be associated by consumers with the rest of the group marks. Nonetheless, by using a common theme, the producer has created a mood or feeling associated with all related products.

110 SALABILITY

Consider the mark's future salability and sale value. A mark perfect for your needs may not appeal to bigger companies which might acquire your business. For instance, though successful, your mark might only

IV General Considerations

have regional qualities or reflect your unusual personality or business style, thus having reduced value to national or international acquirers. One way to roughly judge salability is to create a selection chart for your industry like the one outlined in the Selection Chart *(¶ 35)*, but rather than choosing and weighting selection factors according to your own perspectives, do so from those of a typical acquirer. Obviously, salability is a major consideration for marks in fast changing industries with frequent mergers and acquisitions. To maximize salability you need to work with a trademark attorney to broadly search and register your mark.

For companies routinely creating and selling *brands*, salability may be affected by trademark architecture *(¶ 107)*. If you create an integrated trademark program, e.g., involving a *family of marks*, it may be hard to extract one for sale, leaving a smile with a missing tooth. For instance, Apple, Inc. has tried to build a family of "I" marks, the most famous being iPOD. Would there be confusion if Apple Inc. sold one of its "I" marks to another company? Therefore, if you want flexibility to sell a newly developed mark, then consider how well you should integrate that mark into the company's trademark program.

¶ 111 PLURALITY OF MARKS; MULTIPLE MARKS FOR THE SAME PRODUCT

Some companies use more than one mark for the same product, a strategy which allows penetration into different markets and territories. For instance, a higher priced, expensively packaged product may be marketed under a more sophisticated mark, whereas the same product less attractively packaged and lower priced may be sold under another mark. One mark may be more suitable for a particular region, another for the rest of the country. This kind of brand segmentation is common among hotel businesses. E.g., the parent MARRIOTT brand has brothers and sisters named RESIDENCE INN, RENAISSANCE HOTELS & RESORTS, COURTYARD, SPRINGHILL SUITES, TOWNEPLACE SUITES, and RITZ-CARLTON, all to meet different needs at different prices. Multiple marks for one product can also be a must where the product serves multiple purposes, e.g., bupropion hydrochloride sold as ZYBAN for stopping smoking and as WELLBUTRIN for treating depression.

Even if the products serve much the same purpose but are sold differently, separate marks may be recommended. For example, the same compound sold as a dietary supplement and a prescription drug (perhaps at a higher dosage)

IV General Considerations

should probably have two unrelated marks since customers might not pay more for a prescription drug believing they could get the same product at a health food store. However, sometimes using more than one mark for the same product may cause legal problems and public confusion, so prior review by an attorney is a must.

112 MULTIPLE MARKS FOR CLOSELY RELATED COMPETITIVE PRODUCTS

Occasionally, a company and its affiliates apply multiple marks not to identical products but to closely related ones. The motive is typically to create unique identities even for product lines that may compete against each other. For instance, the three companies which separately own GAP, BANANA REPUBLIC, and OLD NAVY all have similar names, have resided at the same address, and are probably under common control. To some extent these brands compete against each other, but each has its own market niche. Similarly, Anheuser-Busch owns the BUDWEISER, MICHELOB, and BUSCH alcoholic beverage marks which compete against each other, and one can probably assume that each brand of beverage is separately brewed. Compare the Walt Disney Company motion picture brands, e.g., DISNEY for family and children's fare, TOUCHSTONE for adult themes, and MIRAMAX for sophisticated and foreign films.

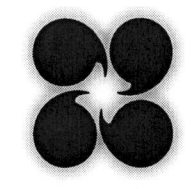

A word mark is somewhat like a "commercial mantra" which becomes imbued in the consciousness of users and customers and shapes how the company and its workforce perceive themselves.

The principal advantage of owning a group of competitive brands is the ability to sell products in different market niches which cannot be reached by all brands in the group. Another advantage is the ability to learn, from marketing each brand, valuable comparative market information which can be applied to the others. And with the ability to cover multiple market segments, one can pressure competitors.

IV General Considerations

113 RELATIONSHIP OF MARK'S OWNER TO PRODUCT

Your relationship to products sold with the mark (e.g., as manufacturer, distributor, or ingredient supplier) may influence selection, especially where the mark is used on one product only or indicates the source of only one component, ingredient, or function in relation to numerous products. As mentioned previously *(Plurality of Marks, ¶ 111)*, two or more marks can appear on the same product even if separately owned by different companies, e.g., as the result of co-branding. The manufacturer and distributor may each have their own separate mark; licensor and licensee marks may both appear; and different suppliers may have their own ingredient and component marks on the same label or packaging.

Thus, as an example, often an ingredient mark or a mark for a product sold only wholesale should reflect B-2-B considerations since the direct customers are businesses. That is, the mark might be more sophisticated and congruous with trade jargon. However, note that many ingredient marks like GORE-TEX, INTEL INSIDE, and NUTRASWEET are also consumer marks frequently promoted with *"look for" advertising*, so even if you sell only to the trade you might devise "consumer friendly" ingredient marks if your business customers will be using those marks on consumer packaging.

114 RELATIONSHIP TO CONTIGUOUS MARKS

Not only can the same product be sold under different marks *(Plurality of Marks, ¶ 111)*, but frequently multiple marks appear together on the same product. Sometimes the mark you select will often or always be used with one or more other marks owned by you or by others. For example, when selecting a product mark that will always appear with your house mark (as RITZ for crackers always appears with NABISCO), good trademark architecture favors some metaphoric relationship between the *house* and *product marks*. *(See Entire Trademark Program; Trademark Architecture, ¶ 107.)* The same applies when your mark will always appear with someone else's mark, e.g., when your *ingredient mark* always appears with another's product mark. An ingredient mark harshly incongruous with the product mark may not be suitable, especially since potential buyers of your ingredient may not purchase it if you insist on having your ingredient mark on their product packaging.

IV General Considerations

115 CONNECTIONS WITH OTHER ASPECTS OF YOUR BUSINESS; TELEPHONE NUMBERS

You may want to connect the mark with other aspects of your business. Sometimes a good mark can even be generated from your telephone number, using the alphabetical keypad. You can often register your telephone number as a mark and under certain circumstances your Worldwide Web domain name. *(See Internet Domain Names, ¶189.)* However, telephone numbers and domain names must be used in a trademark sense to be registerable since without such proper usage they fail to be designations of source or origin. Sometimes an acronym mark can become part of your telephone number as with United Parcel Service's 1-800-PICK-UPS. Cf. 1-800-HOLIDAY for HOLIDAY INN services and 1-800-GO-FEDEX. Seven-letter marks are often useful as telephone numbers. *(Cf. Serendipity: Self-Connected Marks, ¶232 and Typing And Keyboard Considerations, ¶129.)* Before the electronic age business locations made their way into marks, as per SAKS FIFTH AVENUE and the street number 4711, a practice less common today.

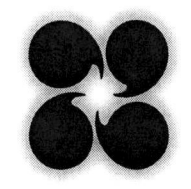

Though legal and practical considerations abound, the aesthetic issues often predominate. Choosing a mark is less a science than an art.

116 PATENT CONSIDERATIONS

Patent protection may affect trademark selection. For a newly patented product (or one for which patent protection is sought), avoid names more likely to become *generic* and thus unprotectable. This is because during the term of patent protection, when your company has a monopoly on making and selling the patented product, the product mark can more easily become the very name of the product rather than identify the product's source. With plant variety patents the problem is sometimes acute because the trademark can easily become a generic plant variety name.

For patented products, *arbitrary marks* are least likely to become generic because the arbitrary mark already has a built-in semantic barrier between

IV General Considerations

itself and the product. For example, KIWI, an arbitrary mark for shoe polish, is unlikely ever to stand generically for the product, nor APPLE for computers, nor even BAZOOKA for bubble gum. *Fanciful marks* like ASPIRIN, NYLON, and YO-YO, which have little or no semantic connection to the product, can occasionally become generic. The marks most likely to be used generically by the public are *suggestive marks* like KLEENEX, FRIGIDAIRE, and THERMOS because they are already semantically close to the product.

117 TRADE SECRETS

Because trade secret protection can give the company a de facto monopoly on products derived from the trade secret, much of what we say regarding patents *(¶116)* applies to trade secrets. E.g., for trade secret products one should avoid marks more likely to become *generic*, a consideration possibly more critical than for patented products.

With the patent, which lasts for a term prescribed by statute, one can plan for the day when the patent will expire and when it may be necessary to argue that the product mark is not generic. But with trade secrets there is no fixed term. The trade secret can persist indefinitely and disappear at a moment's notice because of independent discovery or reverse engineering. (Though patents can also be lost before expiration via court challenges, at least it usually takes many months or years before a final court decree.) Thus, when the trade secret product mark is becoming generic, it may be hard to rescue if the trade secret is suddenly lost or difficult to reclaim even if the trade secret is resurrected through a court proceeding.

118 RELATIONSHIP TO YOUR BUSINESS

The mark, especially a *house mark,* should properly reflect your business in terms of scale, geography, and operations. You generally don't want a mark incorporating words like UNIVERSAL, COSMIC, or WORLDWIDE when only running a local operation in a rural town. The reverse is also true: you often don't want a local geographic designation, e.g., a small town name, when expanding into national and international markets. Cf. DAEWOO which can mean "great universe" in Korean and SANYO meaning "three oceans" in Japanese, supposedly connoting the founder's desire to build a business spanning the Atlantic, Pacific, and Indian oceans. However, where the public will accept a product emanating from and named after one small locality, and the locality name is protectable, then the local name can be a good

IV General Considerations

choice. Consider various names for bottled water such as EVIAN, VICHY, and BETHESDA SPRING. *(See Place Names; Toponyms, ¶ 138.)*

Not only does geographic scale matter but also non-geographic size. MICROSOFT, comprised of two computer-related words MICRO and SOFT, would seem a logical choice for a new computer company, though each component is widely used. However, once MICROSOFT achieved near-hegemony as a result of strong products, management, and support, the company was perhaps no longer MICRO nor SOFT. And strangely, this discrepancy in scale between the mark and the company's preeminence may have contributed to opposition encountered by Microsoft Corporation.

119 THE RIGHT IMPRESSION AS TO BUSINESS FOCUS AND FORM

The name should give consumers the right impression about the business' focus and form. For instance, in naming a non-profit organization, you can choose from basic words such as INSTITUTE, FOUNDATION, CENTER, SOCIETY, and ASSOCIATION. Each of these names gives a different impression, e.g., CENTER connotes a place to which people come, a focal point; FOUNDATION hints at an organization established by a few wealthy founders; and ASSOCIATION implies a broadly based organization, usually with a membership. ASSOCIATION and SOCIETY connote amorphous, participatory entities, while INSTITUTE and FOUNDATION are seemingly more focused and elite. (A compromise might be CLUB, as in SIERRA CLUB, which connotes participation but also exclusivity.) To use ASSOCIATION for a small non-membership organization can be misleading, as can using LTD. in a general partnership's name.

Similar considerations apply to names for business conclaves. For instance, FORUM implies an open meeting with active participation; COUNCIL suggests a closed meeting of select members; SUMMIT promises even a more elite meeting; and CONFERENCE connotes a large conclave with open as well as restricted meetings. So CONFERENCE might be inappropriate for a small elite meeting, and SUMMIT not right for a large open conclave.

120 BUSINESS SELF-EXPRESSION

A mark is somewhat like a "commercial mantra" which becomes imbued in the consciousness of users and customers. A *word mark* and accompanying

IV General Considerations

graphics and *trade dress* not only give consumers an impression of the business and its products but also shape how the company and its workforce perceive themselves. Therefore, a company's entire trademark package should reflect how the company wants to perceive itself. Adopting a trademark program should be part of developing a business "personality" which reflects the company's aspirations and work force. Of course, this lofty role of trademarks is primarily confined to *house marks* since many *product marks* are transitory or selected only for immediate consumer appeal.

Though the origins of even obscure trademarks can often be independently deduced or found on the Web, the typical practice is not to widely publicize a mark's origins, much like a guru not disclosing all the secrets of a mantra. This practice avoids focusing attention on one meaning, to let the mark evoke a broader spectrum of associations. E.g., NIKE's owners don't tout the Greek goddess, and Mitsubishi Corporation doesn't advertise that MITSUBISHI means three diamonds (i.e., diamond shapes) in Japanese. Yet, company employees typically know about the mark's origins and original significance, something they carry with them at work. So an important consideration is how the mark's original significance will attract, motivate, and maintain a work force.

Thus, words exuding dignity, energy, strength, intelligence, and other positive attributes are more likely to motivate employees. As a guess, it may be easier to rouse employee loyalty to a family surname mark with a history like DISNEY, JOHNSON & JOHNSON, and FORD rather than to a more abstract mark like IBM, XEROX, and QVC.

121 AESTHETIC DECISION

Selecting a mark is largely an aesthetic exercise, meaning that the choice is largely subjective. For example, with a *design*, its primary and secondary characteristics are more objective than the tertiary aesthetic characteristics. Such more objective "primary" characteristics could be the design's size, density, and shape. The "secondary" characteristics, slightly less objective, could be balance, movement, and ambiguity. But the critical characteristics at the "tertiary" aesthetic level are ones much less objective, e.g., the design's harmony, grace, sublimity, mystery, gaiety, or coherence.

Though legal and practical considerations abound, the aesthetic issues often predominate, e.g., issues relating to meaning, metaphor, colors, and designs to be used with a *word mark*, and level of discourse at which

IV General Considerations

the mark is designed to communicate. In short, choosing a mark is less a science than an art.

122 RESONANCE

A constant theme in trademark selection is resonance. Can the mark resonate in the public consciousness like a commercial "mantra"? To do so, it must strike deep chords in relation to meaning and sometimes even emotion. A mark having multiple meanings, each somehow related to the product, can resonate. One might describe such a mark as a "pteronym" (a winged word), i.e., a flexible, mobile, multi-dimensional word. An example is RAMSES *(Humorous Marks, ¶ 70)*. CINGULAR (merged into AT&T) for a wireless telephone service also resonates. It not only connotes "singular" referring to the unique nature of the services but also the integrated nature of those services. Moreover, in Latin, from which CINGULAR is derived, "cingula" means a belt or girdle, and "cingulum" is a zone on the earth, each connoting the circular terrestrial nature of the CINGULAR network service.

Resonance can be achieved even when only part of the mark has multiple meanings, some of which can metaphorically connect to the product. An example is the BAY component of eBAY. BAY has numerous possible meanings, e.g., a broad inlet from the sea; an indentation or recess in a range of mountains or hills; a kind of tree or shrub with edible leaves; a recessed or enclosed area as per a bay window; a compartment or area in a ship, aircraft or motor vehicle; an area marked off for a particular purpose like a loading bay; a place on a computer for insertion of a device like a drive bay; the color of a horse; the bark or howl of an animal; or "cornered" in the idiomatic expression "at bay." *(See Multiple Meanings; Homographs, etc., ¶ 224.)* Toponymically, eBay may also connote the East Bay in Northern California, close to where the company was founded. Probably the storage or loading bay associations would be the strongest, though the connection with a body of water may also be a factor as with AMAZON.COM. Also note OXO, not only a palindrome but also a reference to oxtail, a possible ingredient of bouillon cubes; a reminder of Noughts and Crosses aka Tic Tac Toe; a chemistry reference; and even a slight resemblance to a pair of eyeglasses.

Resonance can exist even when multiple meanings are obscure or when one meaning is publicly known while the rest are submerged or hardly known. Strangely, meanings rarely used or known by few can be powerful.

IV General Considerations

A good analogy is a homeopathic solution which after repeated shakings and dilutions becomes more potent even though containing only a few molecules of the original "active ingredient." It is beyond the scope of this Guide to explain the power of obscure meanings, but this phenomenon is readily observed in trademark lore.

123 MARKS WITH MEANING

Always consider whether your mark has meaning. Clearly, all marks consisting of words in a widely used language have some meaning, even if not directly relating to the products. That is, *descriptive, suggestive,* and *arbitrary marks* by their very nature have meaning. Purely *fanciful marks* **(Fanciful, Capricious Marks,** ¶ *132),* consisting of "words" which do not exist in any language, should still give the consumer some feeling about the product. Of course, in certain industries fanciful marks with virtually no meaning can survive, particularly in the pharmaceutical industry where many drug names seem to be drawn out of a hat. Nonetheless, even with pharmaceutical names, the better names have some inkling of meaning. For instance, VIAGRA (for a male potency drug) at least rhymes with NIAGARA, hinting at Niagara Falls, the honeymoon haven. VIAGRA also has a hint of VIRILE, meaning "manly" and echoes AGRA, where the Taj Mahal is located. Perhaps VIA + GRA is a reference to "the way to gratification" in the same way that SANKA (SAN + KA) ("sans" = "without" in French) is a clever expression of "without caffeine." PROZAC for antidepressants brings to mind "prose," indicating a flow of text or flow of life, and perhaps "prosaic" which connotes, if not anything happy, at least something ordinary or uneventful, which is better than depressing. If the "Z" in PROZAC is just a connector, then the mark also suggests PRO (Latin for "in favor of") AC ("activity"), as in "proactive." (Such arcane meanings are capable of affecting public perceptions even if the designers of these marks had not intended nor perceived them, although the designers would probably have perceived them.)

Another "meaning-ful" mark is JABRA for telephone headsets, brilliant because (1) it suggests talking, as per "jabber"; (2) starts with the lesser used letter "J" **(Infrequently-Used Letters,** ¶ *168);* (3) has BR as the last consonant sounds, connoting an external protrusion as in "branch," "bristle," and "brim"; and (4) ends with the feminine "A," which is good for small electronic devices **(Last Letters of Marks,** ¶ *162).* In short, with fanciful marks you might seek a mark "that teems with hidden meaning."

IV General Considerations

124 LINKS WITH FOLKLORE AND CULTURAL FIGURES

Marks may be more memorable if linked to cultural icons and folklore even when the consumer makes the connection "subconsciously." For instance, perhaps McDonald's is strengthened by connection to the nursery song "Old MacDonald Had a Farm." Similarly, JACK IN THE BOX may be helped by subtle connections to "Jack and the Bean Stalk" and "Jack and Jill." Even GREEN GIANT may be unconsciously connected to "Jack and the Bean Stalk" and other fairy tales involving giants. Did the owners of DAIRY QUEEN ever contemplate the "fairy queen" of folklore, music, and literature, or did they only connect to a dairy land beauty queen? Especially with goods sold to or for children, these connections can be meaningful and effective.

When business genius Ray Kroc bought the fast food business from the McDonald brothers, he probably wasn't thinking about children's songs but rather about the brothers' success in mechanizing food service. Yet MCDONALD'S succeeds where other names (e.g., MCPHERSON'S) might have failed because the metaphoric tail often wags the business model dog. And it's not hard to dip into the folklore reservoir whose menagerie of animals and characters populate everyone's memories. For inspiration you need only peruse lists of well-known rhymes, verses, folktales, and children's songs.

As mentioned previously *(Resonance, ¶ 122)*, obscure meanings can be mysteriously powerful. This is true not only for a word's or expression's dictionary meanings but also for its significance within the contexts of folklore, legend, and literature.

125 SPIRITUAL CONTENT

Many customers are drawn to a mark's spiritual or religious content. Naturally, sales of fast food and car parts probably aren't spurred by "spirituality," but surprisingly such content is attractive for most products. Some examples are FIDELITY (from "fidelitas" in Latin meaning "faith"), LUCENT (from "lux" in Latin meaning light), AMWAY (perhaps from "(I) am (the) way"; John 14:6), PETERBILT (Peter, "the rock upon which my church is built"; Matthew 6:18), FRUIT OF THE LOOM (from "fruit of the [thy] womb"; Psalms 127:3 and Luke 1:42), ORACLE (a person or shrine in ancient Greece through which a deity spoke), BRAHMA (in Hinduism, the

IV General Considerations

> "Words without thoughts never to heaven go."
>
> SHAKESPEARE

Absolute), MAZDA (the Zoroastrian "wise one"), and SATURN (the Roman god of seedtime and harvest). TRINITY for bottled water is a perfect example because of Biblical and religious allusions to wine and water, walking on water, baptizing in water, and holy water. BABELFISH, the name of AltaVista's translation service, may have come from the fictional creature in THE HITCHHIKER'S GUIDE TO THE GALAXY and bespeaks a "talking fish," but obviously it also reflects the Old Testament's Tower of Babel and less obviously the New Testament's fish symbolism.

126 MAGIC

The dimension of magic and myth is a source of trademark success, whether the mark be tied to legend or literature. A conscious connection may not even exist, but cultural resonance may still succeed. For instance, in the fast food industry pre-eminent marks have this connection: DAIRY QUEEN (Fairie Queene), BURGER KING (burgher king), JACK IN THE BOX (also with resonance to all the "Jack" tales like "Jack and the Bean Stalk" and "Jack and Jill"), and maybe even WENDY'S (reminiscent of Peter Pan's friend and of the mystical Welsh name Gwendolen, meaning "white"). Proctor & Gamble's FAIRY mark excels for dishwashing liquid and related products, justifying its appearance in Peter Cook's and Dudley Moore's film "Bedazzled." Cf. STARDUST for hotel, restaurant, and casino services; MARVEL for comic books; and the limited run GREMLIN for subcompact cars.

127 SUBCONSCIOUS, SUBLIMINAL ASSOCIATIONS

The feeling a mark conveys may emanate from subliminal associations it evokes, if only among some customers. Thus, in devising a mark one should ask the focus group or others involved what they associate with the mark's sound, appearance, and meaning. The task is to detect subliminal effects and see whether they can help or hurt.

For example, with young people's sportswear, particularly for surfing, skateboarding, and snowboarding, marks designed for appeal to hip youngsters tend to be "cool." Both BILLABONG and REEF, excellent marks for surfing and other outdoor sportswear, meet this call. Each relates to

IV General Considerations

water ("billabong" is an Australian aborigine word for a special kind of water hole), and each has one or more subliminal associations, probably not perceived when the marks were selected nor exploited after the marks were used. For some people could REEF subliminally connect to "reefer," especially because some surf accessories are generically described with the adjective "reefer"? And might BILLABONG be subconsciously associated by some with "bong," particularly by hip consumers not familiar with "billabong's" aboriginal meaning? Other examples are AMWAY and PETERBILT. AMWAY may first give the impression of "American Way," but to some it may subliminally resonate with "I am the way" (John 14:6). Similarly, to some customers PETERBILT may subconsciously resonate with Peter, "the rock upon which my church is built" (Matthew 6:18).

These subliminal associations may only be conjured in relation to some customers or may even be weakly perceived by a few, yet they may contribute to the mark's emotional "look and feel." Before the principal meaning is discerned, when the mind initially processes a *word mark* it may be scanning memory for all associations, meanings, and letter combinations. A word's meaning is derived from its relationship to all other words in the language, so in English, populated with so many idioms, homographs *(¶ 224)*, homonyms *(¶ 220)*, synonyms *(¶ 221)*, and antonyms *(¶ 222)*, a single word can trigger a variety of conscious and subconscious associations.

128 ALPHABETICAL POSITION OF MARK

For service marks particularly, you might choose a mark closer to the top of the alphabet (e.g., AAMCO) because it might appear earlier or be more easily noticed in various listings. This is usually a marginal factor that applies when you have two or more choices each having almost equal merits. It's ever less a factor in the electronic age when search engine placement doesn't typically depend on the starting letter, though in selecting business names listed in yellow pages, the alphabet still matters. Doubling the "A" to get right to the top is often not advisable except to clearly improve the mark, as with AAMCO.

129 TYPING AND KEYBOARD CONSIDERATIONS

Another relatively minor factor is keyboard/typing ease, especially for marks appearing in Worldwide Web domain names entered on keyboards by online users. In relation to the "qwerty" keyboard and the telephone

IV General Considerations

keypad, consider whether entering your mark is a cinch or a finger tangle. For instance, FEDEX is only two buttons on the telephone keypad and four adjacent keys on the typewriter or computer keyboard, whereas VERIZON is more hunt-and-peck. If your mark is a tautonym *(¶ 204)* like PAM PAM, then the dialed or typed numbers will repeat themselves. MIU MIU on the telephone keypad is a repeated triangle 6-4-8 typed counterclockwise and also an easy counterclockwise repeated triangle on the querty keyboard. NEONYM is all on the right column of the telephone keypad.

For those obsessed with word and number games, the quest is for a mark that when dialed on the telephone keypad (1) makes a geometric shape or stays on one column or row; (2) achieves an unusual dialing order such as a palindrome; and (3) expresses some meaning in relation to the product, using the mark's own letters or the other letters on each dialed keypad number. For instance, we developed a mark which when dialed stayed on one column, was a palindrome, and referenced a chapter in the Bible that reflected our client's product.

130 INTERNET CONSIDERATIONS

If the mark will be part of a domain name, the easier to enter on the keyboard, the better. *(See Typing and Keyboard Considerations, ¶ 129.)* That means a shorter mark is better, or if the mark is long, then perhaps it should be capable of abbreviation. Moreover, the more the mark can be easily passed by word of mouth directly to the keyboard, the better; i.e., marks without hyphens or peculiar punctuation or spelling are easier to enter as Web addresses. As of the date of writing this section, Internet domain names can only consist of letters, numbers, and the dash symbol; other typewriter symbols are not yet allowed. Thus, if you pick a mark containing a character or symbol which can't be included in a domain name, you may have difficulty adapting the mark for domain name usage. Marks can even be selected based on their complementary relationship to domain extensions such as .com, .net, .org, and .biz, e.g., com.com, hair.net, cyb.org, and show.biz. Of course, as mentioned throughout this Guide, such cleverness does not often result in strong marks unless the mark has other semantic qualities.

131 DOMAIN NAME AVAILABILITY

So often a much loved word is already part of someone else's domain name. Trademark registries are so densely populated that it is hard to find clearly-

IV General Considerations

available marks; but domain name registries are even more jam packed. Obviously, to the extent the word is used by others in domain names, it may be difficult to find a convenient domain usage. But some domain usage is almost always available: e.g., hypothetically if your mark were PEANUT and peanut.com, .net, etc. were already taken, you could always create a variation or add a hyphen or extra word such as "online" or "usa" to get something like pea-nut.com, peanutonline.com, peanutusa.com, or pnut.com. As a real example, the owner of SHARP for electronics products was forced to take **sharp-usa.com** when a San Diego hospital took **sharp.com**.

The principal question is, if somebody already has a domain registration for the same word, or something close, do you not choose that word in order to avoid public confusion or legal conflict? Again, if you hypothetically selected PEANUT, do you walk away because somebody already has a peanut.com website? When the parties' products are closely related, the answer will often be yes, for practical and legal reasons. Conversely, when the products are unrelated, you might sometimes use and register the mark and assume the risks of conflict and liability. Some factors considered are the similarity between the mark and the domain name, the similarity of the products, how long the website has been operational, and how much public exposure the website has achieved. Only your attorney can judge how serious the risks are.

One solution is to buy the domain name registration. Also, where you have established prior rights in your mark (i.e., used or applied for registration of your mark before the other person's domain name registration), you may be able to take legal action to protect your rights, especially if the other person is deemed a "bad faith cybersquatter." But, as with most legal obstacles, you must act quickly, with an attorneys' help, to remove them.

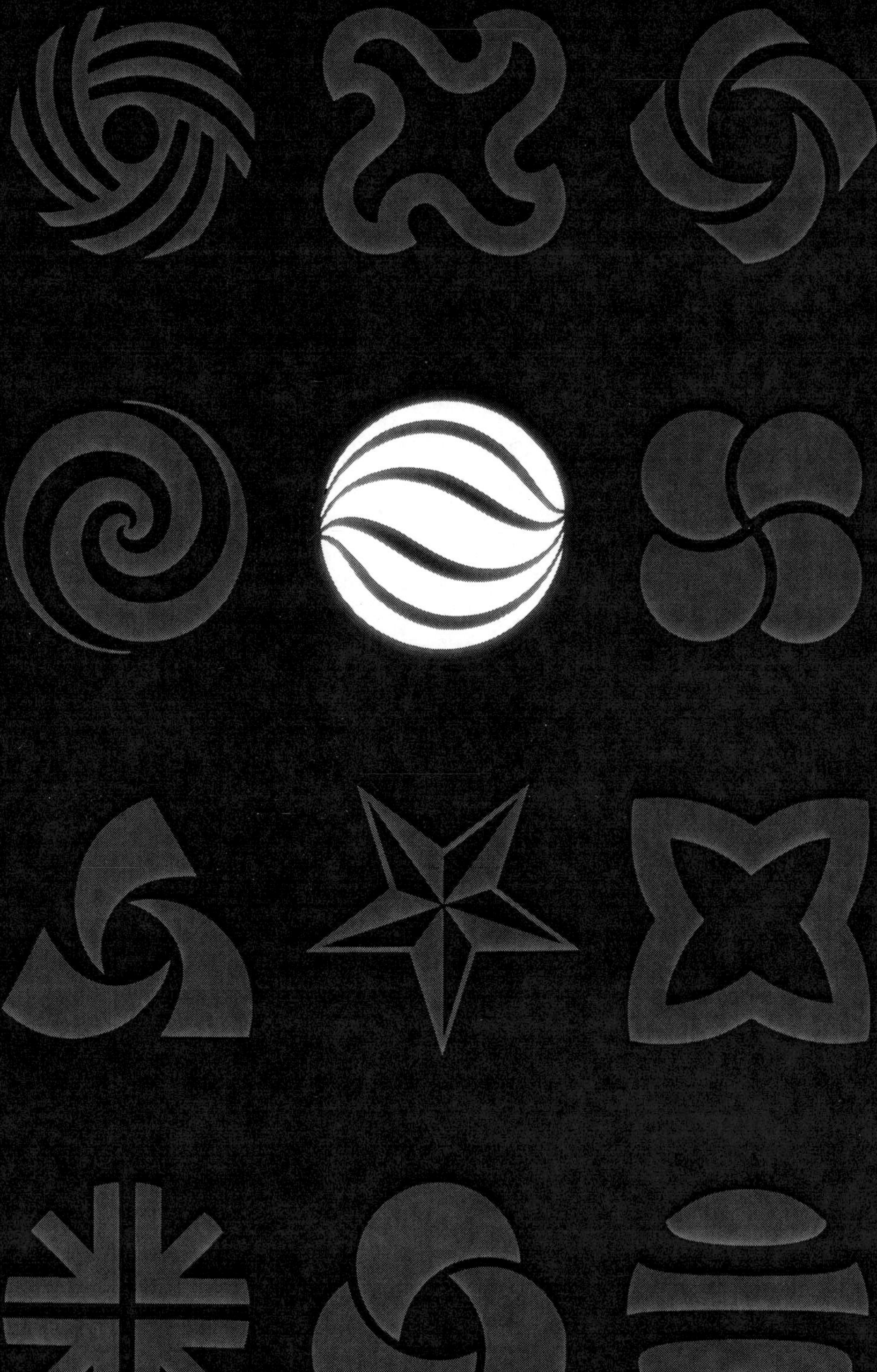

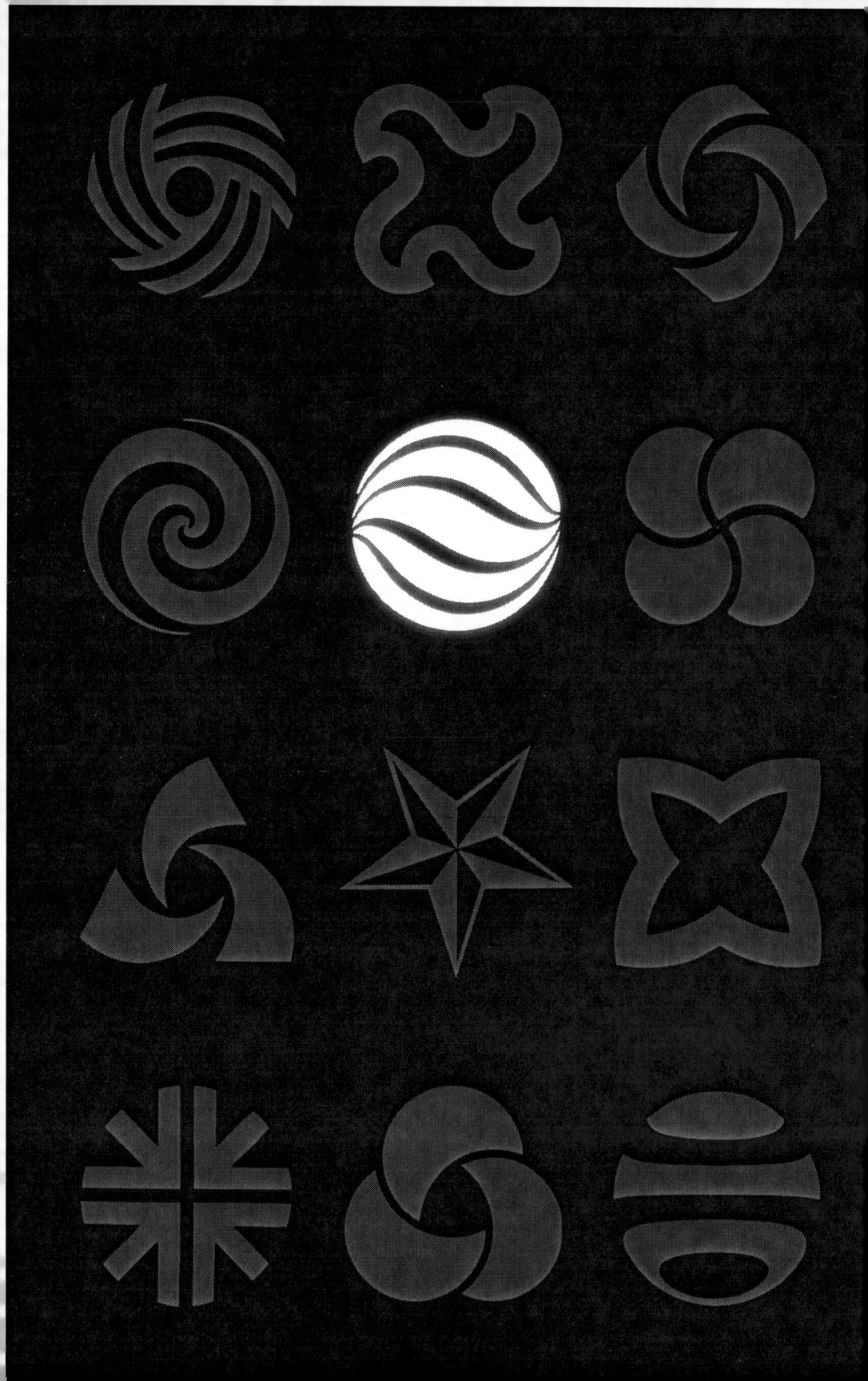

THE KINDS OF SUBJECT MATTER TO CHOOSE FROM

V Subject Matter

"And out of the ground the Lord God formed every beast of the field and every fowl of the air; and bought them unto Adam to see what he would call them: and whatsoever Adam called every living creature, that was the name thereof."

GENESIS 2:19

Trademark protection could extend to marks that appeal to any of the five senses, and valid trademarks now exist in things we not only see but also hear and smell. The following listing describes not only general subject matter categories but also some specific choices for the content of word marks, followed by listings in Sections VI and VII for other kinds of marks.

132 FANCIFUL, CAPRICIOUS MARKS

CONSIDER FANCIFUL AND CAPRICIOUS MARKS, i.e., marks having no real meaning in any language, such as KODAK, VELCRO, PROZAC, BRILLO, TEFLON, EXXON or HÄAGEN-DAZS. These marks often become strong and distinctive, though initially it takes more advertising dollars to tell customers which products are offered with the fanciful mark. By making up unusual new "words" (i.e., "neologisms") you not only create strong, distinctive marks but often avoid problems with conflicting marks, unless, e.g., by some chance your fanciful mark happens to look or sound like some other mark. (Note that because of "soundalike" considerations, simple, shorter, fanciful marks may actually be harder to clear for registration than arbitrary marks having unrelated meaning. E.g., JETTA (fanciful) sounds like GETA, GEDDA, and JEDDA, whereas PLATYPUS (arbitrary) would probably not be mistaken for anything else.)

Even though initially you will probably spend more on advertising a fanciful mark to make it known, the long range results often justify increased initial expenses. Compared to a more *descriptive mark* which tells the consumer

V Subject Matter

something about the products, the more-expensive-to-establish fanciful mark, once established, is usually commercially and legally stronger, more distinctive, more difficult to challenge, and less likely to be confused with competitive descriptive terminology. Another advantage of a coined word like EXXON, KODAK, and CEMEX is that it is neither noun, adjective, or verb and thus capable of all the associations with the products that any part of speech might have. It provides the maximum voltage for the spark of imagination to leap from mark to product and back.

One way to generate ideas for a new word is to use a random word generator. A much better technique is to create a fanciful composite word whose components are derived from product qualities. *(See Composite Marks, ¶ 174.)*

133 ARBITRARY MARKS

Also consider arbitrary marks comprised of words or phrases existing in the language but having no ordinary connection with the products, for instance, KIWI for shoe polish, APPLE for computers, BUMBLE BEE for canned fish, and PENGUIN for books. How about HUSH PUPPIES for shoes since "hush puppy" in the South is a small fried cornmeal cake?

Arbitrary marks may not always be as strong as *fanciful* ones nor as easy to clear for registration, but because they are comprised of real words they can generate pictorial images, as per APPLE for computers and SHELL for fuels; more easily be spelled and remembered by consumers, compared to fanciful marks; and more readily have metaphoric and metonymic relationships with the products. *(See Metaphors, ¶ 71.)* Moreover, as discussed in Patent Considerations *(¶ 116),* the arbitrary mark is often least likely to become *generic* through improper use. Arguably the arbitrary mark is the easiest kind to select and protect because it isn't typically as plagued by soundalikes as the fanciful mark, nor sitting on the fence of *descriptiveness* like the *suggestive mark*.

134 SUGGESTIVE MARKS

Suggestive marks are often excellent choices. These marks don't describe the products but suggest them in some way, metaphorically or otherwise, for instance, STRONGHOLD for nails, ENGLISH LEATHER for toiletries, VALVOLINE for lubricating oil, INTEL for computer chips, V-8 for vegetable juices, and CATERPILLAR for motorized farm vehicles and equipment.

V Subject Matter

REEBOK may even be suggestive because a rhebok is an antelope, an animal which relates metaphorically to shoes a swift runner would use. SPRINT also suggests speed. XEROX may be suggestive because it comes from a Greek word which means "dry," evoking the original dry copying process, xerography.

A premier suggestive mark is WALKMAN for portable, hand-held or headset radios. WHISKAS for cat food is another example. LYCOS, meaning "hunting spider" in Latin, suggests web search services. NEONYM comprising NEO for "new" and NYM for "word" might suggest trademark selection services.

Without describing goods or services, a suggestive mark often indicates what benefits you promise the consumer, e.g., EVEREADY and DIEHARD for batteries, ARCH REST for shoes, and COPPERTONE for sunscreens, though frequently these kinds of marks border on the *descriptive*. A very effective mark is one almost *arbitrary* but also mildly suggestive like CATERPILLAR for farm machinery.

You can often create a stronger suggestive mark by considering the most hyponymous variation of the concept being considered, i.e., the variation most specific in meaning, which is frequently the more uncommon word. E.g., for sport shoes, REEBOK (from "rhebok," a kind of antelope) is more striking and unusual than ANTELOPE, and TERCEL for cars (from "tiercel," a male hawk) is similarly more distinctive than HAWK.

135 DESCRIPTIVE MARKS

Generally avoid descriptive marks, i.e., words or phrases which describe your products or their uses or characteristics. For example, ordinarily you wouldn't want to adopt FAST for delivery services or TASTY for food products (though TASTY is registered for food products based on *secondary meaning*). In specific cases the following marks were once held descriptive: ALWAYS CLOSED for revolving doors, BETTER HOMES for a real estate brokerage (though note numerous registrations for BETTER HOMES AND GARDENS), DUDS for clothes, NO-D-KA for toothpaste, UPC (the initials of "Universal Product Code") for services of developing Universal Product Codes, and TRIM for manicure implements.

Except on the *Supplemental Register* reserved for certain descriptive and otherwise non-distinctive marks, descriptive marks are often not registerable, at

V Subject Matter

least with the USPTO, absent a showing of secondary meaning, a result of extensive advertising and usage. Secondary meaning is often achieved when the public has come to associate the descriptive word or phrase only with one source or origin. Moreover, descriptive marks are usually weak designations of origin. By picking a descriptive or almost-descriptive mark you might initially save advertising dollars because customers may more easily connect the mark with the product. However, such a mark is hard to protect against others using similar descriptive terminology and may ultimately cost more to advertise in order to achieve secondary meaning.

136 INTER-CATEGORY OR HYBRID MARKS

Though it's convenient to categorize marks and names in terms of *fanciful*, *arbitrary*, *suggestive*, and *descriptive*, such categories are only way stations on a continuum. Many marks slip in between these categories, and such "hybrid" marks can be powerful, unusual choices. For instance, CLUB for automobile steering wheel locks is both suggestive of the devices' club-like qualities and arbitrary since CLUB also connotes a close-knit association. Similarly, STAPLES, if connoting key commodities, is almost descriptive of office supplies offered under that mark but if meaning paper fasteners is metonymically suggestive. KASHI for breakfast cereal is virtually fanciful but also suggestive to the extent it reminds one of kasha, the cereal grain mush; the same with JABRA for telephone headsets, which is almost suggestive of talking ("jabber") but also fanciful.

Interestingly, IVORY for soap, inspired by Psalms 45:8 ("out of the ivory palaces"), has been inconsistently labeled by commentators as arbitrary, suggestive, and descriptive. Those labeling it arbitrary apparently imagined elephant tusks, those deeming it suggestive contemplated its relationship to clean skin, and those believing it descriptive perceived the soap's whiteness.

When used with unrelated products obscure dictionary words like ZANTE, TONDO, and CYLIX skirt the borderline between fanciful and arbitrary; the same is true of everyday words for which spelling has been changed and which don't suggest the products, such as COODJU (for a board game), FI'ZI:K (for bicycle parts), and JEZTERZ (for clothing). Finally, we note marks that have different relationships to various products. For instance, WHIRLPOOL is suggestive of washing machines but arbitrary in relation to other household products like refrigerators. One can imagine a single mark being descriptive, suggestive, and arbitrary in relation to a company's products.

V **Subject Matter**

137 GEOGRAPHICALLY DESCRIPTIVE MARKS

Geographically *descriptive marks* should generally be avoided. These are marks which merely tell the consumer where the goods come from, e.g., New York, Kentucky, or Chicago. As with ordinary descriptive marks, these marks are usually hard to protect and register, at least with the USPTO, absent secondary meaning. If registration is available, it may only be on the *Supplemental Register*. Moreover, various Federal and State laws affect use of geographically descriptive marks, such as Federal and State laws which require that wines labeled with names of viticultural areas are substantially produced with grapes from those areas.

An exception is marks indicating regional origin, which are sometimes registerable, e.g., ROQUEFORT for cheese. Typically these regional marks are not registered by individuals but are *collective* or *certification marks*. *(See Collective and Certification Marks, ¶¶ 317 – 319.)* Also sometimes a nickname for a place may be registerable; e.g., O-TOWN was held not geographically descriptive of Orlando even though local residents, but not consumers elsewhere, may perceive the reference.

138 PLACE NAMES; TOPONYMS

On occasion place-name marks may be registrable even if technically "geographically descriptive," especially when the place name refers to a locality owned or controlled by the trademark user. For instance, with marks for bottled water, the trademark user often owns or controls the locality of the springs or at least is the only source of water from that locality. Thus, the following marks have been protected: BETHESDA SPRING, EVIAN, VICHY, and BLUE LICK WATER SPRINGS. Also, place names which have hoped-for metaphorical relations to the product are possibilities; e.g., the romance of the West is reflected in automobile names like TACOMA, DURANGO, LAREDO, SIERRA, YUKON, and TAHOE. You might even consider names evoking a curious mystique, like FUJI and LOCH NESS. TABASCO for hot sauce, named after a southern Mexico river, was chosen primarily because of its sound. One of the most successful toponyms is NOKIA, named after a Finnish city where the company was founded. (Like MARIMEKKO, another famous Finnish mark, NOKIA has the advantage of sounding almost Japanese, appropriate for the mobile phone business as MARIMEKKO is for fabric designs that sometimes mimic a Japanese aesthetic.)

V Subject Matter

Fictional locales can sometimes evoke strong impressions and can be developed as marks. Sometimes the locale can be your own invention, as per LAKE WOBEGON; or the locale can come from legend, like AVALON and CAMELOT, or from literature, like EREWHON and WESSEX. Fictional locale names can hardly be geographically descriptive, but place names from literature can be subject to authors' rights, e.g., for novels and stories still under copyright, so you may need consent.

Remember that many English language toponyms for foreign locations have corresponding endonyms (i.e., foreign language place names used by local inhabitants); for instance, Munich is München in Germany. If such an endonym is better known than the English language toponym and you intend an international mark, you may not want the English variation unless it has a certain cachet. Moreover, occasionally the English variation has social or political overtones. E.g., MUMBAI under British rule was known as BOMBAY, and though for trademark usage BOMBAY is probably better than MUMBAI, people in Asia, particularly in India, might disfavor its colonial overtones.

139 ADDRESSES

Occasionally even street addresses or their derivatives will yield a mark showing the precise location from which the products actually or fictionally emanate. Cf. SAKS FIFTH AVENUE, 4711 (Glockengasse, Cologne, Germany), BAKER STREET, DOWNING STREET, WALL STREET, BROADWAY, and SUNSET BOULEVARD. Such locality markers can contribute to colorful, memorable marks, especially if the address is well-known. Famous streets usually have a slew of associations: i.e., SAKS FIFTH AVENUE is arguably more memorable and effective than would be SAKS NEW YORK or SAKS MANHATTAN. However, though often used, street names common to many localities, like STATE STREET, MAIN STREET, and HIGH STREET, rarely become famous marks.

140 CULTURAL ICONS; LANDMARKS

Related to place names are landmark and cultural icon names that can sometimes be appropriated, like ALCATRAZ, BIG BEN, OLD FAITHFUL, EIFFEL TOWER, and TAJ MAHAL. One advantage of these marks is that they may immediately evoke feelings and images and provide logo material. A

V Subject Matter

disadvantage is that others will use them. Seldom do "landmark" names become famous marks or even succeed as *house marks* perhaps because it may be hard to create unique connections between the user's products and marks which denote notable physical structures and other named physical phenomena. If one's business is located near the landmark or building, that connection may add some spice to using its name. Why select BIG BEN if you're not working within earshot, unless you have some connection to BEN, or the BIG BEN landmark has some interesting metaphoric relationship to your business or products?

141 QUALITY DESIGNATIONS

Generally avoid quality designations, i.e., marks which merely indicate the product's quality or grade, such as GOOD, BEST, BETTER, CHOICE, SELECT, TOP GRADE, HIGHEST, and LOWEST. Note, however, the successful use of BEST, CHOICE, and SELECT for food products. Usually, these kinds of marks are hard to protect, and to achieve *secondary meaning* and protection is often expensive and time-consuming. Sometimes this can be done, e.g., with various BEST marks such as BEST FOODS and BEST gardening products. CHAMPION for spark plugs and STANDARD for bathroom fixtures are borderline quality designations, though each has resulted in well-known marks. When the quality designation is more unusual, like SHARPER IMAGE and BEST WESTERN, it may be stronger and easier to protect. Cf. GOOD & PLENTY, a successful mark for candy.

142 GENERIC DESIGNATIONS

Conceptually close to *descriptive marks* and quality designations are *generic* designations. Unlike the descriptive mark which tells the consumer something about the product's functions, characteristics, or qualities, the generic term identifies the product by its very nature or class. For instance, the following terms have been held generic: AIRBRUSH, MALTED MILK, YO-YO, and SHREDDED WHEAT. Naturally, generic terms are not protectable trademarks.

Note that protectable marks can become generic either from improper usage *(See Adjectival Marks, ¶ 86)* or simply because of such widespread fame that the mark becomes the common name for the product. For instance, ASPIRIN, ZIPPER, ESCALATOR, and CELLOPHANE became generic for products they were sold with. Marks like COKE, SANKA, FORMICA,

V Subject Matter

KLEENEX, POPSICLE, VASELINE, and XEROX have been used improperly by consumers, thus sometimes forcing expensive campaigns by owners to maintain distinctiveness of their marks. For instance, the owners of COKE try to stop restaurants from serving competitive sodas whenever "COKE" is ordered by name.

143 SURNAMES

Generally beware marks consisting only of surnames. Most surnames will be used by other people, generating public confusion and perhaps claims. Also marks that are "primarily merely surnames" are not eligible for USPTO registration on the *Principal Register* without *secondary meaning. (See Surname Prohibition, ¶ 328.)* Of course, there are numerous good surname marks: SMIRNOFF for vodka, KELLOGG'S for breakfast cereals, HONDA for cars, YALE for locks, and HERSHEY'S for chocolate. Surname marks are often company founders' names, e.g., FORD, DELL, and DUPONT. Sometimes the mark refers to more than one person, e.g., WARNER BROTHERS, STEINWAY & SONS, and JOHNSON & JOHNSON. When the surname sounds like a business word, e.g., MAYTAG or BOSCO, so much the better. The mark may be more effective when there's a *design* or product relationship in the surname. Cf. CHEVROLET, which has the benefit of the chevron shape and the OLET suffix for a carriage, like in "cabriolet." The more unusual the name, usually the better the mark, as with BIRDS EYE for frozen foods, named after the founder, Clarence Birdseye.

Because surnames usually have meaning, ensure an appropriate choice. Hypothetically, METZGER, "butcher" in German, might not be best for frozen vegetarian foods; similarly, EPHRON, "like a fawn" in Hebrew, might be unusual for steak houses. Always find the meaning first by consulting a reference book like J.N. Hook's FAMILY NAMES.

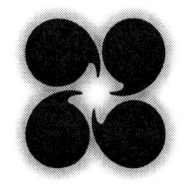

> "The man who could call a spade a spade should be compelled to use one. It is the only thing he is fit for."
>
> OSCAR WILDE

V Subject Matter

144 FIRST NAMES

Generally, first names are not good marks, especially for "high-end" products, including luxury goods and services. But with more "run-of-the-mill" goods, there are numerous successful marks, including DENNY'S for restaurant services, WENDY'S for fast food, and RALPHS for supermarkets. Cf. JIMMY and PETERBILT for trucks. Do not forget the meanings of first names, most of which are derived from Greek, Latin, Hebrew, and Germanic languages. For instance, note the importance of the Biblical names PETER (from Greek, meaning "rock," i.e., the "rock upon which the church is built," Matthew 6:18); PAUL (from Latin, meaning "small," as Saul humbled himself before God on the road to Damascus, Acts 9:4); and MARY (from Hebrew, probably meaning "wished-for child," Luke 1:26-38). This knowledge shows why PETERBILT is such a good mark. (Cf. DENNY'S, from the nickname for Dennis, in turn derived from Dionysus, the Greek god of food, drink, and merriment. Perhaps the originators of DENNY'S were unaware of its Greek origin since all they desired was a replacement for DANNY'S, their previous mark, but the festive meaning didn't hurt.)

When two first names are combined the result is often more distinctive, as in BEN & JERRY'S, HARRY AND DAVID'S, and MAC & JAC, since the sound or meaning of one name will play off the other.

Before selecting a first name, you should learn its meaning to rule out inappropriate names and to ensure the name has some semantic relationship to the business. Numerous "baby naming" websites show meanings of first names.

145 MIDDLE NAMES AND NICKNAMES

Occasionally a middle name like AMADEUS or QUINCY, especially if famous or distinctive, may be chosen. Many full names may not be instantly recognizable without the distinctive middle name, e.g., who are Arthur Doyle, Mary Eddy, and Edna Millay? The same may even apply to middle initials: who is Susan Anthony?

Nicknames are a source, e.g., PEP BOYS for auto parts and CRAZYLEGS, a football player's appellation, later used on a women's shaving gel, thus precipitating a lawsuit by the football player. SPANKY'S is a perky name for portable toilets, with two related associations, "spanking clean" and "spanking one's bottom."

V Subject Matter

For those not already having a product or business nickname they want to protect, nickname software can inspire an original moniker.

146 FULL NAMES

A unique full name can become a valuable trademark or trade name, e.g., in the clothing industry, CALVIN KLEIN, LIZ CLAIBORNE, BILL BLASS, and GEORGIO ARMANI. Cf. MARTHA STEWART and SARA LEE.

The full name or any component should normally be unusual or distinctive. E.g., KLEIN (meaning "small" in German) needed a distinctive first name CALVIN (perhaps meaning "little bald one," derived from the Latin "calvus" for "bald") to succeed, and BILL needed the distinctive BLASS; whereas both LIZ and CLAIBORNE are distinctive. LIZ is an energetic form of ELISABETH, meaning "God's promise" in Hebrew (see Luke 1:5 et seq.) and perhaps the most fertile source of first name variations—dozens. CLAIBORNE, from Old English, probably means clay-banked stream or spring.

To make the full name mark distinctive, should one adopt a mark comprised of incongruent first and last names, e.g., the first name drawn from one culture, the surname from another? Such polarity in names may be striking, e.g., hypothetically, Guillermo Tanaka, Mustafa Stravinsky, or Greywolf Klinghoffer. But the usual choice is more a cultural match, e.g., JACK DANIELS, PIERRE CARDIN, SALVATORE FERRAGAMO, and ENGELBERT HUMPERDINCK. Incongruence between a woman's first and last names may be more accepted because women frequently take on their spouses' surnames.

As with surnames *(¶ 143)*, incongruity between name and business should generally be avoided. Arguably it's better to select an aptronym (a name which matches the business or its owner like Johnny Appleseed for an apple tree planter or Margaret Spellings for a Secretary of Education), even if humorous, rather than an incongruous name which could be ludicrous or misleading. Examples of trademark aptronyms are SCHUMACHER ("shoemaker" in German) for shoes and BETTY CROCKER for cookery products.

Because one aim of adopting a mark is to establish a distinctive, long-term symbol for one's business, anytime the mark is a full name of a real person and the business depends on his/her services, then the mark's usefulness is limited, especially because of the individual's death, disability, or departure. For instance, how many clothing designer "name" marks long survive the

V Subject Matter

designer's death? Of course, this problem doesn't apply to the full name of an imaginary person such as BETTY CROCKER, the homemaker, or JUAN VALDEZ, the Columbian coffee character.

147 OTHERS' NAMES

Using names of other persons is sometimes possible, but under publicity and privacy rights laws and Federal trademark laws, the names of living persons or recently deceased celebrities can't be used without consent. *(See Living Individuals, ¶ 329.)* Though Federal law prevents registration of marks comprising the names of recently deceased U.S. presidents whose spouses are still living, sometimes one may use the names of those long dead. *(See Deceased Presidents, ¶ 327.)* Trade names incorporating WASHINGTON, JEFFERSON, and LINCOLN are common. You should always hire a qualified attorney when using another's name to determine legality and availability and, where applicable, to draft a written consent to be signed by the person or his/her heirs.

Remember, just because you have the same name as a famous person doesn't mean you can use it as a mark or trade name. Ed Sullivan protected his name against a TV and radio sales and repair shop called "Ed Sullivan Radio & TV," mostly owned by someone of the same name.

148 HISTORIC NAMES

Neither King Tut nor Genghis Khan would leap from the grave to challenge trademark use of his name, nor did Socrates object when his name was used on cigars. Also note NAPOLEON, NEWTON, BISMARCK, DA VINCI, CLEOPATRA, LADY GODIVA, and RAMSES. How about PLATO for a dishwashing liquid? The historical figure should generally be widely known and have some trait, sometimes little known, connected to the product, even if only metaphorically.

Strangely, historic names have seldom matured into world famous trademarks, in contrast to fictional names *(¶ 149)* which have fared better. This is true despite legions of meaningful, distinctive historic names available. For instance, in the arts Shakespeare, Beethoven, Mozart, and Van Gogh represent distinctive, meaningful names and famous historical personalities but haven't got standing ovations on the world trademark stage, though Rembrandt, an artist known for a dark palette, is now

V Subject Matter

making teeth whiter, and the GOOGLE website does homage to Picasso via its PICASA photo service (PICASA also connoting "picture house" and rhyming with "mi casa," Spanish for "my house").

149 NAMES FROM FICTION

Trademarked people's names may not only be those of real people but also of fictionalized or fictitious persons or groups from novels, plays, films, and operas, e.g., FALSTAFF for beer, THREE MUSKETEERS for candy bars, YAHOO! for Internet search services, LONG JOHN SILVER for fish restaurants, and RIGOLETTO for cigars. AIDA, CARMEN, and FIGARO have also been used. Starbuck (as in STARBUCKS) was the ship's first mate in MOBY DICK, and more obviously, J. Wellington Wimpy (as in WIMPY restaurants) was the hamburger-loving character in Popeye cartoons. Cf. ALFA ROMEO for sports cars which hints at an "alpha" male lover, though not originally derived from the Shakespeare character.

These character names often make good marks. They reference well-drawn, larger-than-life characters whose fictional existence constantly resonates in consumers' minds so long as the works they inhabit are still read, heard, or seen. Naturally, unless you have formal permission from the work's author or other rights owner, the fictional name should usually come from a public domain work, not one still under copyright or whose character names are otherwise protected.

150 MYTHOLOGICAL NAMES

Mythological names such as ICARUS, ZEUS, THOR, MARS, JUNO, MERCURY, VENUS, SATURN, and ATHENA abound in trademark lore. Also popular are animal-like mythological beings such as UNICORN, GRYPHON, and DRAGON. One trick is to find a god/goddess, hero/heroine, or other mythological figure who characterizes some important quality of your products, e.g., ATLAS for moving services, connoting strength and territory; MERCURY for cars, relating to the god's swiftness; and MIDAS for car parts and services, alluding to the "golden touch."

Without such a direct connection other connections may suffice, e.g., MARS rhymes with bars. Even more remotely the mythological figure may suggest a logo, as with the ARM & HAMMER logo, a symbol of Vulcan, the Roman god of fire and metalworking. To find the right connection, you can review names and descriptions in a mythology encyclopedia.

V Subject Matter

151 ASTRONOMICAL NAMES

Though trademarks are still terrestrial phenomena, "extraterrestrial" subject matter is abundant. The names of moons, planets, stars, galaxies, and constellations permeate trademark registers around the world, such names largely derived from Greek and Roman mythology. Examples are ORION, MARS, VEGA, SATURN, SUN, HYPERION, and IO.

Because of widespread usage these "astronomical" marks are typically solid but not always distinctive. The challenge is to find an unused or barely used astronomical name which connects to the product or business. Unusual names are plentiful, including, e.g., those of Saturn's moons, such as Lapetus, Mimas, Enceladus, Tethys, and Dione. Though SIRIUS and CANOPUS, the two brightest stars, are widely used, you can search for obscure stellar names. Astronomical name sources are plentiful, including specialized dictionaries and encyclopedias.

152 LEGENDARY NAMES

Between the historical and mythological are legendary names like KING ARTHUR, ST. GEORGE, and ROBIN HOOD. Cf. AJAX for cleansers, ODYSSEY and AVALON for cars, and CAMELOT for dolls. As with historical, fictional, and mythological names, legendary names can be good choices, usually so long as the chosen name is not too culturally isolated, obscure, or bound for oblivion. However, because such legends and legendary characters are the frequent subject matter of children's stories, TV shows, and films, their use as trademarks is often best with toys, games, children's products, and the like.

153 GROUP NAMES

Names of cultural, ethnic, and national groups are sometimes used. For instance, many well-known Indian tribe names have been trademarks, e.g., COMANCHE, CHIPPEWA, CHEROKEE, CHEYENNE, IROQUOIS, and LAKOTA. Indian tribe names have so captured the imagination that in some industries it may be difficult to find an available tribe name suitable for the product. South and Central American group names such as MAYA, INCA, and AZTEC have also been used. How about QUAKER, PURITAN, AMISH, SCOTCH, TROJAN, and HEBREW NATIONAL?

However, with extant groups, try to determine whether using the group name will meet public opposition fomented by group members or even

V **Subject Matter**

result in legal actions. *(See Inappropriate Marks, ¶ 81.)* From a moral standpoint, even if you could use a group name without legal obstacles, would you want to use it if your products or business had no real connection to the group, e.g., an ancient Indian tribe name? And even members of the group might hesitate to adopt the group name as a mark without formal group permission. In one case the USPTO refused to register MOHAWK though the applicant was a tribe member.

154 EPONYMS

Sometimes a mark comprising a person's name identifies the products or business. Examples are MARTINIZE for dry cleaning, PILATES for exercise training (now often used *generically*), KELVINATOR for refrigerators, LISTERINE for mouthwashes, WEDGWOOD for china, and STETSON for hats. PILATES, from founder Joseph Pilates, was a good mark for strengthening exercise instruction before being used generically. The pluralized ending connoted a "discipline," and the mark had a Roman flair, "pilatus" meaning "armed with javelin" in Latin, though also strangely reminiscent of Pontius Pilate. Cf. ADIDAS from the founder Adi Dassler, which, to honor the founder, is pronounced Ah-di-Das by company employees but as ah-Di-das by most UK and USA consumers.

Consider P, E, and Z forming PEZ, extracted from the German word "Pfefferminze," meaning peppermint; also TEFLON, derived from polyTEtra-FLuOrethyleNe; and more obviously, ADIDAS from the inventor's name, Adolf "Adi" Dassler.

Preferably the name, which is the root of the mark, will mesh with the company's products. The difference between ordinary name marks described previously *(¶¶ 143 et seq.)* and eponymic usage is that the eponym often becomes almost synonymous with the product, without hopefully becoming generic, like name-derived words such as "silhouette," "poinsettia," "mesmerize," and "pasteurize" (from Etienne de Silhouette, Joel Roberts Poinsett, Friedrich Anton Mesmer, and Louis Pasteur).

121

V **Subject Matter**

155 ACRONYMS, BACRONYMS, AND INITIALS

In general, avoid acronyms and initials unless they have some independent value. Two-, three-, and four-letter combinations are already widely used by others as acronyms, initials or just ordinary letters. In fact, it is often difficult to find a three-letter mark not already in use no matter what three letters you choose! Yet, if you want a short mark, think about unusual letter combinations like QVC, UBS, OXO, DHL, and SBC. (DHL just reflects the founders, Dalsey, Hillblom, and Lynn.) If the abbreviation or initials are meaningful or "jazzy" in themselves, so much the better. For meaningful initials that match the product's nature or purpose, note MADD (Mothers Against Drunk Driving) and NOW (National Organization for Women). Cf. V-8 which symbolized the eight vegetables first used in the beverage, ELF which abbreviates Essence et Lubrifiants de France, REI which stands for Recreational Equipment Inc. and is Latin for "of the business," S.O.S which humorously stands for "save our saucepans," and M & M's which reflects Mars and Murrie, the founders' surnames.

Acronyms usually don't stand out without a catchy meaning, sound or appearance, as exemplified by MADD (Mothers Against Drunk Driving), IHOP (International House of Pancakes), AOL (America Online), KFC (Kentucky Fried Chicken), and DKNY (Donna Karan New York). At least for a limited period, maintaining the long form of the mark along with the acronym often strengthens the business identity. For instance, if KFC and IHOP had been the original marks rather than Kentucky Fried Chicken and International House of Pancakes, they might not have been good on their own, but when perceived as acronyms they are more clever and distinctive. Occasionally, initials will inspire a longer *word mark*. The story goes that JEEP may have come from G.P., standing for "General Purpose" vehicle, and ESSO is just the enunciation of S.O., the initials of Standard Oil.

When the business is already known by a word which seems to be an acronym, sometimes you can create a "bacronym" aka "backronym" to further brand it. A bacronym is virtually the opposite of an acronym, namely a later-developed phrase or combination of words whose initial letters spell the seeming acronym. SAVE OUR SHIP is a bacronym of SOS, and PORT OUTBOUND, STARBOARD HOME a bacronym of POSH, according to encyclopedic listings which indicate that SOS and POSH emerged first and the descriptive bacronyms later. Trademark-related examples of bacronyms are primarily slogans such as AMERICA'S ROAST

V Subject Matter

BEEF, YES SIR from ARBY'S and THE COUNTRY'S BEST YOGURT from TCBY which had originally been an initialism for the unavailable THIS CAN'T BE YOGURT! Bacronyms are generally not great marks but can be effective mnemonic devices.

¶ 156 ABBREVIATIONS

Consider marks which incorporate abbreviations, such as CLUB MED(iterranean), PAC(ific)BELL, MET(ropolitan Opera), PAN-AM(erican Airways), SUDAFED (pseudoephredine), ALKA(line) SELTZER, and FED(eral) EX(press). The slang or abbreviated form of a word may be more catchy and useable than the full word. Is AMWAY derived from AM(ERICAN) WAY or perhaps from (I) AM (THE) WAY (John 14:6)? To be more protectable, the abbreviation usually should not be widely used or recognized on its own, just as ALKA and MED are not generally used to refer to "alkaline" or "Mediterranean." If the abbreviation can stand for the entire company name, so much the better, as with oil company marks like AMOCO (American Oil Company), ARCO (Atlantic Richfield Company), and CONOCO (Continental Oil Company) which are almost acronyms.

¶ 157 EXTRACTIONS

Extraction is akin to abbreviation *(¶ 156)*, except the "extracted" mark may not immediately conjure its origins. The letters P, E, and Z forming PEZ were extracted from the German word "Pfefferminze," meaning peppermint. One story is that OREO was derived from the two O's in "chocolate" surrounding the "RE" extracted from "cream." (It could also have been derived from the Greek word "oreo," meaning hill or mountain, since the original cookie was mound-shaped.) How about TEFLON, derived from polyTEtraFLuOrethyleNe? A more obvious extraction is ADIDAS taken from the inventor's name Adolf "Adi" Dassler. OVALTINE was extracted from OVOMALTINE (from its original main ingredients, "ovum," Latin for egg and malt), and theoretically could have been an extract from OVALENTINE (VALENTINE being derived from the Latin "valens/valentis," meaning strong or healthy). Cf. VODAFONE, from VOice, DAta, and telePHONE. Naturally, the less obscure and more meaningful the extraction, the stronger the mark.

Another variation on the extraction is whole words extracted from well-worn phrases or adages, particularly wording that often would not appear

V Subject Matter

separately outside the phrase or adage. E.g., note PENNYWISE (POUND FOOLISH), (DAVEY) JONES LOCKER, HOPE SPRINGS (ETERNAL), and (ONCE IN A) BLUE MOON; also imagine hypothetically (BETWEEN A ROCK AND A) HARD PLACE and (CAT O') NINE TAILS.

158 NOMINATIVES AND GENITIVES

With certain marks, especially comprising people's names, you might choose between nominative and genitive forms. Consider the following:

NOMINATIVE	GENITIVE
MRS. PAUL	MRS. PAUL'S
CARL JR.	CARL'S JR.
MARTINELLI	MARTINELLI'S

The genitive form is usually more personable since it connotes a direct connection between a person or family and the product; it is also more easily used adjectivally. *(See Adjectival Marks, ¶ 86.)* The nominative is frequently more conservative and "dignified," and thus better for higher-end products.

A compromise is a genitive use without the apostrophe, as with HARVEYS BRISTOL CREAM, ROBINSONS-MAY, and HARRODS.

159 PLURALS AND SINGULARS

Sometimes when the mark is a noun, you may choose between the plural or singular forms. Consider the following:

SINGULAR	PLURAL
HUSH PUPPY	HUSH PUPPIES
Q-TIP	Q-TIPS
BAND-AID	BAND-AIDS

The plural can have the advantage of connoting multiple products sold under the mark but the disadvantage of being used *generically*. The singular sometimes has the advantage of easier adjectival use in relation to the products. *(See Adjectival Marks, ¶ 86.)*

V **Subject Matter**

160 SUFFIXES AND PREFIXES

Remember how important a suffix or prefix is, especially when devising new words. For instance, in the health and pharmaceutical fields the suffixes IN or INE are often used successfully. ASPIRIN was followed by BUFFERIN and ANACIN; see also CLARITIN and TINACTIN. Also compare LISTERINE and OVALTINE. An ON suffix may connote some sort of material, e.g., TEFLON, RAYON, and NYLON. (RAYON and NYLON are *generic*), or ON may reflect "energy" as in EXXON and ENRON.

The suffix ITE might connote a compound, e.g. DOLOMITE (generic for calcium compound). The relatively weak descriptive suffix AID denotes something that is helpful, such as BAND-AID and KITCHENAID. The same is true of the relatively weak ADE which often denotes a beverage, e.g., GATORADE and KOOL-ADE.

Consider the following product-related prefixes and the ending two letters: WIND(ow) in WINDEX; CHROM(ium) in CHROMAX; CLOR(ine) in CLOROX.

A common kind of prefix for contemporary marks is the single letter connoting information technology, e.g., "I" or "E" as in iUNIVERSE and eBAY. A common single letter suffix is "O" as in SPEEDO, and JELL-O, and X-ACTO.

It's remarkable how many famous marks consist of *descriptive* or highly *suggestive* root word plus a one- or two-letter prefix or suffix. But it's surprisingly hard to create such marks—at least good ones—and unusual to find them available.

161 FIRST LETTERS OF MARKS

The first letter of a mark or first letters of words which comprise a multi-word mark are typically the most important. These first letters, which usually dominate their words, can make a big difference. Because of how it looks, sounds, and is physically articulated, each alphabet letter used as a first letter generates distinct impressions, connotations, and feelings.

For instance, in relation to sound, the strong consonant "P" connotes focused energy as in "poke," "point," "projectile," and "pincer." Another strong consonant "T" connotes stored energy as in "tense," "terse," "tight," "tough," and "taut." "B", on the other hand, connotes unfocused, directionless energy as per "bulge," "blunder," "bang," "boisterous," and "brag." "N", a weaker consonant, can connote new age products, as in

V **Subject Matter**

"newton," "neon," "nth," and "number," but also may connote annoyance, as in "nuisance," "noisy," "nosy," and "nitpicker." The vowel "A" has some mystery about it, as in "alpha," "abracadabra," "astrology," and "abacus." "V" by its very shape is both emptiness ("vacuum" and "vessel") and fullness ("voluptuous" and "volume"), focused force ("vanquish" and "vanguard") and a thing to which force is applied ("victim" and "vent"), though in Episode 4, Season 3 of the "Sopranos" Tony cautions against using "V" as a first letter of a business name. Finally, "W" is perhaps the most gossamer of consonants, expressing at a word's beginning the most dispersed energy, as in "wide," "whisper," "wanton," and "wistful."

Considering the impact of sounds, don't forget the connotations of digraphs like SH, TH, and CH, which act as unitary consonants because they express a single sound, not the sounds of the sequence of letters.

To acquaint yourself with the "phonosemantics" of letters, you may peruse articles and books on sound symbolism.

162 LAST LETTERS OF MARKS

Second in importance to the mark's first letter is usually its last. In Latin and certain Romance languages (e.g., Italian and Spanish), the last letter (or sometimes two letters), employed to decline a noun or indicate gender, could make quite a difference. Mario is much different than Maria. An "O" or "US" at the end tends to be masculine, an "A" feminine, and an "UM" neuter as in "barium". However, beware cultural differences, e.g., an ending "O" in Japanese names is often feminine as in Miyoko, and an ending "A" often masculine as in Akira.

Compare the following differences between what is and what could have been:

PINTO	PINTA
PROZAC	PROZAK
EXXON	EXXOM
VELCRO	VELCRA

The same letter at a word's end can have complementary or opposing effects at the beginning. For instance, "P" connoting penetrating energy

V Subject Matter

at the beginning of a word, connotes almost the opposite at the end, that is, a solid container of energy or matter, as in "cup," "scalp," "stop," or "clamp." Compare the unfocused, dispersed energy of "W" at the beginning of a word with its complementary role at the end where it is almost always silent, as in "law," "cow," "new," and "pillow."

163 OMITTED LETTERS AND TELESCOPED MARKS

Many marks are strengthened by omitting letters. For instance, when the last letter of one word and the first letter of the following are the same, the words may be joined using that letter only once, as with TRAVELODGE, EVEREADY, and WORMIX. These are sometimes called "telescoped" marks because they are comprised of two or more joined words which share letters. *(See Combined Words, ¶ 175.)* Or words can be joined by leaving out disparate letters from one or both words, e.g., NAIR ("no hair") for hair removing creams, TWIX ("two sticks") for confections sold in a two-stick package, JAZZERCISE ("jazz exercise") for exercise instruction services, CUISINART ("cuisine art") for kitchen appliances, NOVARTIS ("novae artes" meaning new skills in Latin) for pharmaceuticals, and SILK for soy milk. Letters can also be left out in the middle of the word, as with MAX(W)ELL and TIN(E)ACTI(O)N, creating "syncopes." Moreover, as in QANTAS, letters commonly required for "proper" spelling can be omitted. Cf. FLICKR, NVIDIA, and COMPAQ. (With NVIDIA, the vowel omission has useful purposes, e.g., NAVIDIA would have a nautical connotation, NIVIDIA would sound and look like NIVEA, and NOVIDIA might connote NO VIDEO. With FLICKR the omission makes the mark more distinctive but hardly affects meaning, and the effect is much like an ordinary "contraction" such "you're" for "you are.") Even cutting last letters, i.e., creating apocopes, can make a word more distinctive as per CHARMIN, MOBIL, and ZIPLOC.

Of course, with omissions that create misspellings, the result can be common, trite or "hokey." *(See Trite Use of Letters/Misspelled Words, ¶ 169.)* MOBIL, QANTAS, and ZIPLOC may be distinctive, but GARD instead of GUARD, used in thousands of marks, is mostly not.

164 DECAPITATIONS

A special variation of the missing-letter word *(¶ 163)* is the decapitated word, i.e., the new word formed by striking the first letter of a preexisting

V Subject Matter

Though IKEA supposedly originated from the names of the founder and of his property and village (Ingvar Kamprad Elmtaryd Agunnaryd), the mark has been promoted with awareness that IKEA is one letter away from IDEA, even per the slogan "The IKEA Idea."

word. For example, Intel Corporation's mark ITANIUM has the advantage of starting with IT, symbolizing information technology, while alluding to TITANIUM. ARMONY is HARMONY without the H, ELEPHONE lacks the T, and XPERT is obviously EXPERT without the first E.

A decapitated word can be unusual and even striking yet still exude the original word's essence, as with ITANIUM and ARMONY. Moreover, if the original word were *descriptive* and thus hard to protect, the decapitated version would not likely be so, unless, as with XPERT, the first letter of the decapitation is a rebus *(¶ 172)* for the initial sound of the original word, or unless the first letter of the original word were silent anyway, as in (P)NEUMATIC. Note AMBIEN for sleep medications, connoting "morning wellness" (AM + BIEN), which is both a decapitation of TAMBIEN, meaning "also" in Spanish, and a curtailment of AMBIENT.

165 ADDED LETTERS

Letter omissions *(¶ 163)* are more common than clever letter additions (other than add-ons *(¶ 173)* and typical suffixes and prefixes *(¶ 160)*). However, there are examples of effective added letters, e.g., the second "X" in EXXON, the second "G" in DIGG, the linking "O" in TRAVELOCITY, the ending "E" in FRIGIDAIRE, the beginning Z in ZANTAC (Z + antacid), and the $/S device in WORLD$NET. Sometimes an added letter at the end will partially disguise a real word, as in TRUESTE for fragrance products and COLORA for hair products. Similarly, an added beginning letter can camouflage *descriptiveness*, as with ZANTAC. The added letter often adds an element of ambiguity. With TRAVELOCITY the

V **Subject Matter**

central "O" adds VELOCITY to TRAVEL and CITY, giving the mark extra resonance. TRUESTE connotes TRUEST but at a more subliminal level gives an impression of TRU ESTE, "true East." Where possible the added letter should bring distinctiveness, strength, extra meaning, and more visibility.

166 CHANGED LETTERS

A technique for creating an interesting mark is to change one letter of an ordinary word or a pre-existing name or mark. When the ordinary word is related to the product, that's a plus; if the result is amusing or clever, that, too, may be helpful. Though Kashi is also a Middle Eastern surname, a possible example is KASHI for breakfast cereal, which is one letter away from "kasha," an Eastern European cooked dish made from hulled or crushed grain, e.g., a buckwheat mush. Also note TUSHION for sports and recreational cushions, derived from "cushion" and "tush" which is slang for rear end. LINUX is one letter away from LINUS, the first name of its originator Linus Torvalds, and the more common DANNY'S became the successful DENNY'S. Imaginatively, CINGULAR, one letter away from singular, is related to the Latin words "cingula," meaning belt or girdle, and "cingulum," a zone on the earth, each connoting the terrestrial nature of the CINGULAR telephone network service. ECCO for shoes is one letter away from ECHO and ECCE, "behold" in Latin. Though IKEA supposedly originated from the names of the founder and of his property and village (Ingvar Kamprad Elmtaryd Agunnaryd), the mark has been promoted with awareness that IKEA is one letter away from IDEA, even per the wording "the IKEA idea." Do SNICKERS and SCRABBLE gain energy by respectively being one letter away from SNACKERS and SCRAMBLE? If the changed letter is merely a soundalike of the replaced one, the result may not be as striking or imaginative, as with INFINITI in lieu of INFINITY.

167 REPLACED LETTERS: SYMBOLS INSTEAD OF LETTERS

One way to make a splash is to substitute a symbol for a letter. For example, "$" can substitute for "S" (WORLD$NET, U.S. Reg. No. 1,441,882), "@" for "A" (M@DNOYZ, U.S. Reg. No. 2,558,555), "¢" for "C" (IN¢ENT$, U.S. Reg. No. 2,863,437), "✶" for "O" (PRESENTATI✶N PLATES, U.S. Reg. No. 2,686,671), and "%" for "X" (MA%I-FUND, U.S. Reg. No. 1,369,430 (cancelled)). Other possibilities are "(", "[" or "<" for "C" and "!" for "I" or lowercase "L."

V Subject Matter

Since it is primarily a visual device, this technique can be used not only to create an eyecatching mark but also as a "tweak" to avoid confusion with similar marks. *(See Tweaking Marks, ¶ 12.)* Clearly it's best when the symbol both corresponds to the letter it replaces (e.g., "$" for "S") and relates to the mark's meaning, as per "%" which resembles "X" and also means something in relation to MA%I-FUND, i.e., implying maximum percentage yield.

Despite striking qualities, replacement symbols seldom yield famous marks, consistent with the experience that refined subtlety succeeds more than obvious ingenuity.

168 INFREQUENTLY-USED LETTERS

Consider starting your mark with a less-frequently used letter. A mark which starts with letters such as J, K, Q, X, Z, or Y (high scoring SCRABBLE letters) may stand out more: for example, JEEP, KINKO'S, KLEENEX, Q-TIPS, QANTAS, XEROX, YAMAHA, ZANTAC, and ZENITH. Similarly, unusual beginning letter combinations may be more distinctive, as with TW and DW used in marks like TWIX, TWINKIES, TWININGS, and DWARF. Cf. SCHLAGE for locks and keys.

In relation to *fanciful* marks choosing an uncommonly used letter can be purely an issue of appearance. E.g., JEEP could have been GEEP (which would have matched its purported origin of General Purpose or G.P. vehicle), and KLEENEX could have been CLEENEX. Also, the energic qualities of a mark's first letter are usually more important than its appearance. *(See First Letters of Marks, ¶ 161.)*

169 TRITE USE OF LETTERS; MISSPELLED WORDS

Generally avoid misspelled words and trite use of letters, although sometimes a clever rebus *(¶ 172)* may succeed. For instance, choices like E-Z for EASY or KWIK for QUICK are often weak. Sometimes, such a choice will be "hokey," and misspelling a word usually does not avoid conflict with a mark comprising the properly-spelled word. Moreover, misspelling a *descriptive* term does not usually make it into a protectable mark, e.g., NO-D-KA for toothpaste and EZ FLO for insecticides (though there are numerous USPTO registrations for EZ-FLO and its variations).

V **Subject Matter**

However, a number of good marks use these devices, such as TOYS "Я" US and SUDAFED (for "pseudoephedrine"). When the misspelling is clever and meaningful, it can yield a good mark, e.g., HAIREM for beauty services, L'EGGS for egg-packaged women's hosiery, SKIL for tools, and KIX for breakfast cereal. If consistent with the owner's other marks, a misspelling may be useful even if not particularly clever, as with FROOGLE, a companion to GOOGLE.

170 VOWEL SOUNDS

Consonants represent constriction of the flow of energy and are created by obstructing the flow of outward breath with part of the mouth, be it lips, tongue, or teeth. The sound of "M" is made with the lips, "S" with the teeth, and "L" with the tongue. Vowels, on the other hand, represent the free flow of energy, still shaped by the mouth. Each vowel has its peculiar associations and symbolisms. The short "I" sound in "tick," "pinch," and "kit" connotes constriction and compactness. It's perfect for marks like BIC, SKIL, and INTEL. The long "A" sound in "calm," "father," and "tar" is more expansive and relaxed and thus good for marks like HARMON/KARDON, BALI, and PALMOLIVE. As in Romance languages like Spanish and Italian, the "O" is more robust and masculine compared to the softer, more feminine "A," which is why we have the fashion material LYCRA rather than LYCRO but the more utilitarian VELCRO rather than VELCRA. The short "U" sound in "bum," "cud," and "strum" is the earthy, practical sound of HUMMER, BUD, and VULCAN. These vowel considerations are particularly important when devising a *fanciful mark* in which each letter can make a difference.

171 EUPHONY AND CACOPHONY

As mentioned, the *word mark's* sound *(¶ 48)* and pronunciation *(¶ 53)* are vital considerations. But one should analyze not just overall sound but also component sounds which make the word memorable and attractive. This is where euphony and cacophony are considered.

Euphony is a pleasing, sweet, or harmonious sound or pronunciation; cacophony is its opposite. The euphony or cacophony of a word is determined by its component letters and sounds and by their proximity, repetition, and flow. Specific vowels and consonants are more euphonious or cacophonous than others. For example, the long vowel sounds of AIM,

V Subject Matter

Trademark examples of portmanteaus are MUPPETS (from marionettes and puppets), SPAM (from spiced and ham), and WATSU (from water and shiatsu).

GLEAM, TIME, DOLE, and DUNES are reputedly more euphonious than the short vowel sounds of MAD, HEAD, PIMM'S, BROOKS, and NUNN BUSH. The "liquid" consonants L, M, N, and R are more the subjects of euphony than the "plosive" B, D, G, K, P, and T which can be creatures of cacophony. Generally vowels are more pleasing than consonants because they represent the free flow of energy.

Sound transition is also important. Ease of sound transition, arising from the juxtaposition of letters, is analogous to the flow of cursive handwriting from one letter to another: e.g., the lower case handwriting transition from P to Q is more difficult than that from Q to R. Similarly, the sound transition expressed by the letters A-S-P is slightly harder to accomplish than that of A-P-S.

Besides immediate transition one must consider repetition of sounds. Cacophony rather than euphony results when some consonants are repeated, e.g., the R in "forward," "surprise," and "February," which partially explains why the second R is often not pronounced. Cf. the L's in "slalom" and even the C's in "cacophony." Yet repeated vowels mesh well with euphony, both aesthetically and practically. A repeated vowel (as in "iniquity") is usually easier to enunciate—even if only slightly—than a jumble of vowels (as in "enymatic"), whereas a repeated consonant is often more difficult than a mixture of consonants (compare "Mississippi" vs. "Alabama").

Perhaps surprisingly, euphony does not necessarily yield memorability: the more memorable marks are frequently cacophonous. E.g., letter-for-letter probably more famous marks begin with plosive consonants (B, D, G, K, P, and T) than with liquid ones (L, M, N, and R).

172 REBUSES

Sometimes a rebus is a clever choice. It's a word or phrase comprised of homonymic (soundalike) letters and numerals, occasionally employing

V Subject Matter

pictures. T42, registered for teas, is a rebus for "tea for two"; 4N6 stands for "forensics" as registered for forensic software in the form of 4N6PRT. In U.S. Reg. No. 3,095,201, the mark INNOVIII is to be pronounced as "innovate." Note Q8, K9, B9, and the partial rebus LEO9. Hypothetically, how about QTπ for confections or girls' clothing? B4UP could be one for incontinence pads, CB4UP for bathroom nightlights, and ICUP for specimen containers. Letters and numbers used include, e.g., "A," "B" (be/bee), "C" (see/sea), "G" (gee), "I," "N" (and), "R" (are), "T" (tea/tee), "U" (you), "Y" (why), "1" (one, won), "2" (too, to), "4" (for, fore), and "8" (ate). Beware selecting a mark which may have a meaningful rebus sound in one country but not in another; for instance, the letter Z is pronounced "zee" in the USA but "zed" in many other English-speaking countries, so that EZT might be pronounced "ee zed tea" rather than "easy tea." *(See Homonyms; Soundalikes, ¶ 220.)*

Compare the reverse rebus, wherein the sound is spelled out, as in ESSO, which spells out S.O., Standard Oil's initials; JEEP, the long form of G.P., the initials for General Purpose vehicle; and ARBY'S, which might reflect RB, standing for "roast beef."

173 ADD-ONS

Some successful marks, even distinctive ones, consist of a weak or *descriptive* term coupled with a simple add-on. For instance, note MR. CLEAN, SIR SPEEDY, MRS. PAUL'S, POSTAL PLUS, NEWMAN'S OWN, DR. PEPPER, TOYS, ETC., CHICLETS, and TIMEX. Numbers, including Roman numerals, are frequent add-ons as per MOTEL 6 and MARK IV. When using a date, generally employ one that has a useful life, e.g., CENTURY 21; many marks using 2000 as an add-on have become outdated.

A simple add-on may often enable the user to register marks containing surnames, descriptive words, and other terms that by themselves may not be registerable. Surprisingly these add-ons, when combined only with a surname or descriptive word, comprise so many famous marks. The best add-ons have a synergistic effect with or add new dimensions to the principal word. For instance, DR., when added to PEPPER, not only gives PEPPER a surname connotation in addition to its culinary one but also hints that the beverage may have medicinal qualities.

V Subject Matter

174 COMPOSITE MARKS

Consider composite marks whose elements have separate meanings, individually or in context of the entire mark. For instance, one attorney developed COMPILEX for a computerized information service for personal injury lawyers. The mark had COMP for computers, PI for personal injury, and LEX for law; it also had COMPILE relating to the compilation of data, and the "X" suffix. Each component could be emphasized separately, e.g., in different coloring, though such separate emphasis may sometimes weaken a mark. Another example is NYQUIL, perhaps derived from the "NI" sound in NIGHT and the "QUIL" suffix in TRANQUIL, suggesting a peaceful night after taking this cold and flu remedy. How about DODGE CARAVAN, where CARAVAN not only directly relates to the product but is also comprised of CAR A(ND) VAN? Note also TINACTIN (for an athlete's foot compound) comprised of TIN connoting the tinea fungus, ACT connoting action, and the IN ending implying a pharmaceutical remedy. Graphically the mark has a double TIN separated by AC. A more obscure example is SANKA, presumably derived from the French sans, meaning "without," and KA standing for "caffeine." These marks are often constructed by using "morphemes" which are words or parts of words that have root meanings and can be combined to form unusual marks.

175 COMBINED WORDS

One kind of composite mark is the combination of two words which might otherwise be *descriptive* if not combined, for example, SLIM-FAST for weight reduction products, STRONGHOLD for nails with annular threads, TRAVELODGE for lodging services, and WORMIX for a livestock remedy. How about PALMOLIVE and FRIGIDAIRE? However, like the man who wanted to go to the 13th floor, found no elevator button for it and therefore pressed 6 and 7, hoping to get there, don't count on getting novelty from combining two words. Combining descriptive words doesn't always avoid "descriptiveness." For instance, the following combination marks were once held descriptive: ARTHRITICARE for arthritis preparations, DYANSHINE for shoe polish (though registered with *secondary meaning*), and GOLDCLAD for a chemical composition to electroplate gold. The best combination frequently consists of two ordinary words yielding almost a *fanciful* result, like PALMOLIVE and PEPPERIDGE.

V Subject Matter

176 COMBINATION/BLENDED WORDS; PORTMANTEAUS

New words which are "blended" combinations of others are slightly different than compound words in which the combined words maintain their own identity, like PALMOLIVE and TRAVELODGE. The blended word or "portmanteau" is a new word born out of two or more, like "motel" hatched from "motor" and "hotel"; "brunch," the melding of "breakfast" and "lunch"; and "smog," the blending of "smoke" and "fog." Trademark examples are MUPPETS (from marionettes and puppets), SPAM (from spiced and ham), WATSU (from water and shiatsu), ALDI (from Albrecht, the founders' surname, and discount), VERIZON (perhaps from "veritas," Latin for truth, and horizon), and VASELINE (from the German "Wasser" meaning water, and the Greek "elaion" meaning oil). Cf. JAZZERCISE, MOTOROLA (motor mixed with Victrola), SNAPPLE (from Spice 'N Apple), WIKIPEDIA (from "wiki," a Web site allowing its content to be edited by users, and encyclopedia), PICASA ("picture house," since "casa" is house in Spanish), CRAYOLA (from "craie," French for chalk, and "ola," short for oleaginous, meaning oily), and PETOPIA, which are in between compound words and true portmanteaus (i.e., they preserve one word while substantially truncating the other).

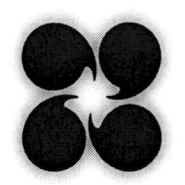

Like putting sprinkles on ice cream, using diacritical symbols, such as Spanish tildes, French accent marks, and German umlauts, can make a mark more distinctive.

If the portmanteau effect is so obscure that nobody will recognize it, then sometimes it's wise to reveal the construction. E.g., with ZILLOW for online real estate services virtually no one would perceive the portmanteau without the founders' explanation, i.e., a combination of ZILLIONS referencing myriads of data points and PILLOW symbolizing the home where one lays one's head to rest. The mark probably succeeds not from the portmanteau device but rather from its mellifluous sound and its emanation of "willow," a tree dense with leaves whose soft shape ornaments the landscape.

V Subject Matter

The portmanteau if clever and well-constructed can frequently yield a good mark. After all, as shown by MUPPETS and SPAM, it exudes the impressions and sounds of the original words while creating a new word (usually a noun) which may perfectly express the product. See PORTMANTEAU DICTIONARY: BLEND WORDS IN THE ENGLISH LANGUAGE, INCLUDING TRADEMARKS AND BRAND NAMES by Dick Turner.

177 DUAL MEANING COMPOSITES

A clever variation of the combined word *(¶ 175)* is the mark having two meanings generated by a middle letter (often an "S") or syllable which ends one word and begins another. Examples are PETSMART for pet supply retail store services, comprised of PETS/MART or PET/SMART; BLUESTONE for music-related services, consisting of either BLUE/STONE, BLUES/TONE or BLUEST/ONE; and HEALTHYSELF for medical services, which is either HEAL/THYSELF or HEALTHY/SELF. Compare TRAVELOCITY, which is either TRAVEL(O)CITY or TRA/VELOCITY. If each of the two or more meanings is almost equally effective and product-related, a delicious ambiguity can be achieved, as with PETSMART and HEALTHYSELF. However, typically this ambiguity is more obvious and "cutesy" than the effects of the more cleverly designed portmanteau *(¶ 176)*.

178 REVERSED LETTERS OR WORDS

Sometimes good marks are merely reversals, for instance, SERUTAN for cough syrup. SERUTAN backwards is NATURES; the natural foods mark EREWHON (the imaginary country of Samuel Butler's utopian novel) is almost NOWHERE backwards. (By coincidence, EVIAN backwards is NAIVE.) Also, sometimes entire words or syllables are reversed such as RUBBERMAID (made of rubber), COMSAT (satellite communications), and MENNON (on men). And even abbreviations can be reversed, as with KOTEX, derived from the abbreviation and reversal of "textured cotton." Every so often, reversing a personal name may work, as with HARPO, a mark and trade name used for Oprah (Winfrey) goods and services. Of course, when the reversal is not apparent, *"look for" advertising* alerting the public to the reversal can be effective, as done with SERUTAN. As with any clever mechanical technique, unless the reversal has a meaningful, metaphoric relationship to the product, however obscure, the mark will probably fail.

V Subject Matter

179 BACKWARDS/FLIPPED LETTERS

Infrequently one sees marks with backwards/flipped letters, an eye-catching device. Perhaps the most famous example is TOYS "Я" US, U.S. Reg. No. 902,125, where the R faces left. Other registered examples are ANOMALY GAMES, U.S. Reg. No. 2,781,800, with a backwards N and L, and REVEL LEVER, U.S. Reg. No. 3,029,125, with all letters in LEVER backwards. Obviously, only letters not vertically symmetric can be flipped to effect, i.e., the effect for capital letters is for B, C, D, E, F, G, J, K, L, N, P, Q, R, S, and Z. (Y may be flipped where the stem is not vertical.) Arguably, those flipped letters which look like letters in other alphabets are more effective. For instance, letters looking like backwards E's, N's, and R's exist in the Russian alphabet.

Because this device is flashy, it seldom yields a famous mark and should only be used when the reversal means something in relation to the word(s) or products. E.g., with ANOMALY GAMES, flipping the N and L elicits the feeling of anomaly. With TOYS "Я" US, an otherwise corny rebus is made interesting by flipping the R; moreover, the flipped R is a clue that the entire mark is a reversal of sorts, i.e., TOYS ARE US is an ungrammatical reversal of WE ARE TOYS.

180 CHIASMUS

A special kind of reversal is a chiasmus, an ancient rhetorical device using reversal to express cleverness and humor. A famous example is Samuel Johnson's critique of a young man's manuscript. "Your manuscript is both good and original, but the part that is good is not original; and the part that is original is not good." (This quip is complemented by Abraham Lincoln's kinder book review: "People who like this sort of thing will find this the sort of thing they like.") Or consider Oscar Wilde's semi-chiasmus, "Work, the curse of the drinking classes." Compare Matthew 16:25. A mark can express a chiasmus in relation to another known word or phrase. Hypothetical examples might be:

V Subject Matter

MARK	KNOWN WORD/ PHRASE	GOODS/ SERVICES
PLAYHORSE	HORSEPLAY	Action Toys
BURNSIDE	SIDEBURN	Men's Hair Products
GOOD ODDS	ODD GOODS	Junk Shop
TALE OF NINE CATS	CAT-O'-NINE-TAILS	Book Title

A successful chiasmus should be meaningful but short, otherwise what should be awfully simple can be simply awful.

181 ANAGRAMS

In addition to reversals, you can play with words in other ways. For instance, playing with anagrams (i.e., shuffling letters of a word to create variations) might yield a mark. Many Internet web sites and computer programs can generate anagrams. Sometimes the mark may be an anagram of the goods, e.g., hypothetically OCEAN for canoe and REGAL for lager. (Is CAMRY derived from MY CAR?) In particular, the mark can be a humorous or zany rearrangement of the product name like CLEMENT SWOOSH (hypothetical) for "women's clothes." Or when you are lucky the anagram says or hints something about the products, e.g., SPANDEX is an anagram of "expands."

Because the mind takes a split second to process the jumble of letters which comprise a word, a mark which is an anagram of other words, particularly those having some metaphoric relationship to the product, can have added "resonance" (¶ 122). Cf. WIRED, for the high energy, high-tech magazine, whose anagrams are WIDER, WEIRD, and IDREW. Anagrammatic resonance may be strongest with words of three to five letters since the anagram is less perceivable, consciously or subconsciously, in words having six or more letters. E.g., in LISTEN it's easy to see ENLIST, but TINSEL and SILENT are more disguised. Very long words yield fewer full anagrams.

V Subject Matter

182 ALPHABETIC/NUMERIC ANALOGS AND TRANSMUTATIONS

One way to construct a mark is to utilize meanings of letters and numbers in foreign and ancient alphabets and in contemporary symbolic and numeric systems. For example, the atomic table is a source for clever marks like CUZN (a soundalike for "cousin") for water filters using a copper/zinc technology. Roman numerals are a possible source, though largely limited to the better-known letters M, D, C, L, X, V, and I. Hypothetically, the palindrome IXXI (9/11) could be used for anti-terrorist security services, with the X's symbolizing eyes.

And alphabetic constructions can be transmuted into other modalities, e.g., Morse code or Braille designs. As mentioned previously *(¶ 172)*, rebuses can be used to transmute letters and numerals into the sounds of words, e.g., 4N6 = forensics and T42 = TEA FOR TWO.

Like facile misspellings (e.g., KWIK for QUICK), most transmutations, even clever ones, don't yield great marks. To succeed, without being obscure the transmutation must not only be clever but also meaningful, often at a deep level.

183 PALINDROMES

Consider a palindrome, a word or phrase which spells the same thing forwards and backwards like DEIFIED and SO MANY DYNAMOS. Trademark examples are ABBA, CIVIC, OXO, XANAX, ROTAVATOR, and ZOONOOZ. XEROX and KODAK are almost palindromes, and TOYOTA would be a palindrome if an "A" were added at the beginning. Though consumers sometimes don't perceive the palindrome nor often appreciate its cleverness, the paired identical letters can yield a striking graphic appearance.

Anagrams, palindromes, reversals, and the like can be used as mnemonic devices to make the public remember your mark, especially by reminding the public that your mark is another word spelled backwards (SERUTAN), the same word spelled backwards (ROTAVATOR), or comprised of the same letters as another word (REGAL, lager, large, and glare).

V Subject Matter

184 NUMBERS, NUMERIC DEVICES, CURRENCY SYMBOLS, AND ALPHANUMERIC MARKS

In creating *word marks*, you are not confined to alphabet letters only; numbers and currency symbols are also usable. For instance, the dollar sign is an excellent symbol, especially in lieu of the letter "S." Take the mark WORLD$NET used in connection with banking software products.

Note 7-UP for soft drinks, 3M for office products, BIG 5 for sporting goods, 409 for cleansers, 7-ELEVEN for mini-markets, MOTEL 6 for motels, CHANEL NO. 5 for perfume, 4711 for cologne, V-8 for vegetable juices, and CENTURY 21 for real estate services. And what about model numbers (not always protected as trademarks) such as 727, 737, 747, 757, 767, 777, and 787 for airplanes? Even mathematical symbols such as "+," "-," "÷," and "∞" are possibilities; see, e.g., U.S. Reg. No. 2,418,223 for 1+1=3. Frequently the number selected is unusual, e.g., an odd number which is "prime" or seemingly so, for instance, PRODUCT 19, 37SIGNALS, 409, 501 (not prime), 4711, or BASKIN 31 ROBBINS. Odd numbers, particularly prime numbers, have more "valence" (in chemistry the combining power of an element) and energy, which is why they are generally more successful for consumer products. Even numbers, particularly appearing in Roman numerals, are more stolid and conservative, e.g., MARK IV and CLASSIC XII.

If the number has secondary significance, so much the better. Consider 76 for oil products, which resonates 1776, the year of the Declaration of Independence. Obviously, 365 for food products connotes "year-round." Cf. 66, registered many times for various products, often connoting the famous Route 66.

185 OTHER ALPHABETS AND NUMERALS

Letters and numbers from ancient or foreign sources can comprise all or part of a mark. E.g., Roman numerals adorn many marks such as Mark IV, CONCEPT XXI, and LOUIS XIV. Since Roman numerals are capital letters in our alphabet, they can also give a mark an (un)intended double meaning: e.g., MCI = 1101 (equals 13 in base 2), CLIX = 159, and LIV = 54. This effect is similar to the Hebrew Gematria, Greek isopsephry, and the Arabic Abjad system whereby alphabet letters are assigned numerical values so that words and even sentences can be read as numbers, sometimes revealing hidden numerical significance. Greek letters like θ, Δ, and π can also be used, and often to good effect because of their mystical and spiritual significance

V **Subject Matter**

(e.g., α (alpha) and ω (omega)) or scientific usage (e.g., α (alpha), β (beta), θ (theta), and Δ (delta)). Of course, if you use a non-Roman letter you may have a problem translating your mark into a useable domain name.

186 PUNCTUATION

Punctuation can add pizzazz, though often its use is trite. An exclamation point at the end of a mark can energize it, e.g., CURE! for laundry detergent and YAHOO! for Internet services. Hyphens are often used, e.g., in ONE-A-DAY (which appropriately turns the three words into an adjective), V-8, and MY-T-FINE. Every so often a slash is used, as with AM/PM; and sometimes quotation marks are used with good effect, e.g., with TOYS "Я" US. Asterisks can make your mark sparkle, e.g., *AETNATEC and CODE*SMART.

Commas and full stops/periods, and even colons and semi-colons, are also used, usually in a functional manner and primarily in *tagline* or *slogan* marks, such as NOW, THAT'S BETTER (a SPRINT communications tagline), THE FUTURE'S BRIGHT, THE FUTURE'S ORANGE (an ORANGE communications slogan), and BETTER MONEY. LIFE TAKES VISA (for VISA credit card services).

Punctuation other than hyphens can create difficulties with Internet usage because many punctuation marks may not be allowed in domain names. And for marks used internationally, punctuated marks may not always transliterate easily into foreign scripts. Moreover, punctuation marks in a name entered in an electronic form are often not recorded properly.

187 MARKS WITH DIACRITICAL SYMBOLS

Using a diacritical symbol in a mark is like putting sprinkles on ice cream: it can make a mark much more distinctive. And the USPTO allows *word mark* registration for marks utilizing symbols like the Spanish tilde, the French accent mark, and the German umlaut. However, successful examples like HÄAGEN-DAZS and ERTÉ are few, and the mark with a diacritical symbol is typically tied to the culture from which the symbol originated. E.g., using a tilde over the letter N may forever tie the mark to Hispanic associations. And the diacritical symbol can't be used when the mark appears in certain formats such as domain names; moreover, it may be inconvenient to use in written communications with customers.

V Subject Matter

Besides enhancing distinctiveness, these symbols can denote correct pronunciation and may avoid confusion with marks having similar spelling but different sounds. Hypothetically, DRANO is closer to BANO than to BAÑO. (Even DRANO has been used with the bar mark over the "A" to indicate a long vowel sound. See U.S. Reg. No. 399,245.)

188 UPPER AND LOWERCASE LETTERING

Generally, legal protection and registration of a *word mark* is best supported by use in all capital letters, often sans serif. Sometimes marks appear with only the initial letter capitalized, perhaps a weaker usage. Entirely lower case usage is not generally recommended though sometimes successfully employed as with **adidas** and **intel inside**. Therefore, if the recommended ALL CAPS form is used, then during the selection process the mark's appearance should be judged in all capital letters. A frequent choice is a mark consisting of two words joined together with the first letter of both words capitalized, e.g., **MasterCard**, **WordPerfect**, and **VirusScan**. However, this is not always the best usage to support a word mark registration or establish trademark rights, especially for a mark consisting of two *descriptive* words. By using the middle capital letter to divide the mark into two descriptive or quasi-descriptive words, the mark in its entirety becomes more descriptive.

189 INTERNET DOMAIN NAMES

Internet domain names, when used in a trademark sense, can be good marks, for instance, **amazon.com** and **monster.com**. However, if the domain name is merely an extension of a well-known trademark (e.g., **mcdonalds.com**, **microsoft.com**, or **porsche.com**), it may add little to a trademark program. The trademark status, including trademark registration, of a domain name is particularly important when the business is known primarily by its domain name, as with **amazon.com**. The USPTO has provided special rules and information on trademark registration of domain names which can be found at **uspto.gov**. The key factor in getting trademark status for a domain name is its use as a genuine trademark and not merely as an Internet address, which means the domain name must be used as a true designation of origin with appropriate trademark symbols. To get trademark rights in a domain name you should consult an attorney.

V Subject Matter

190 TITLES

Creators of many successful works of authorship, including books and movies, turn their product titles into trademarks. But a title by itself, especially as applied only to the work for which it is the name, is usually not a fully protectable mark. For instance, JURASSIC PARK solely as a book or movie title is only a title, not a trademark, but once the title is applied as a "mark" to a host of goods—as with JURASSIC PARK and other movie titles yielding numerous licensed products—then the title can be a trademark. As another example, MEN ARE FROM MARS, WOMEN ARE FROM VENUS as a book title alone would not be registerable at the USPTO, but when also applied to audiocassettes, computer disks, calendars, and greeting cards it could be a protectable mark. Thus, if you want registerable and protectable trademark rights in a title, you must use the mark either on different products (e.g., books, computer disks, and calendars) or on a series of related products (e.g., a series of books or magazines).

191 CLASSICAL ROOTS

Many marks have classical roots even in dying languages like Latin or once universal languages like Greek. Latin is the origin of LYCOS, from "lykos," meaning hunting spider, an apt mark for online search services; MAGNAVOX, originally for radios, meaning "great voice"; SONY, emanating from "sonus," signifying "sound"; VOLVO, aptly meaning "I roll"; and AUDI, meaning "hark," a translation of the founder's German name Horsch. Greek has contributed XEROX derived from "xeros," meaning "dry" as in the original dry copying process; NIKE, the goddess of victory; MARATHON, a place name; and THERMOS, from "therme" meaning "heat." PENTIUM perhaps comes from the Greek "penta" meaning "five" (as per "pentagon" meaning five-sided shape). Or maybe PENTIUM also emerged from "pent," meaning "shut in," as per the slogan "INTEL INSIDE." These marks can enjoy high "cultural resonance" whenever the root words are embedded in today's living languages.

Because of the universality of classical Greek culture, Greek-derived marks like NIKE, ORACLE, and HYPERION, embodying Greek names, words, and concepts, can be simultaneously atavistic and futuristic. In contrast, Latin-derived marks, like MIRAMAX, TAURUS, and MAGNAVOX, may lack the same universality and spirituality of their more ethereal Greek cousins but may emanate solidity, strength, and majesty.

V Subject Matter

192 FOREIGN LANGUAGE TERMS

Often foreign language terminology will provide a good mark, especially when the products are associated with the country or language involved. For instance, take the marks ALTAVISTA ("high view"), LA ROSA ("the rose"), BON AMI ("good friend"), and DOS EQUIS ("two X's"). Latin and Greek terms are often effective, e.g., MAGNAVOX (Latin, meaning "great voice") or XEROX (Greek, derived from "xerography," the dry copying process). Cf. AUDI (meaning "listen!" or "hark" in Latin), a translation of the founder's German name Horsch. And Japanese marks often connect with nature, e.g., YAMAHA (mountain leaves), HITACHI (sunrise), MINOLTA (ripening fields of rice), and TOYOTA (rich field).

If you have an unusual product for which no suitable English word is apt, oftentimes the answer is a foreign language rich in related terminology. E.g., if you had a cold weather product you might adopt one of the dozens of Eskimo words for different types of snow; or if you had a hot weather product, you might consider one of the dozens of Arabic words for different types of camels.

Problems with *descriptiveness (See Descriptive Marks, ¶ 135)* are not usually avoided by adopting foreign language equivalents of descriptive English terms, e.g., GAZA (a soundalike of GASA, Spanish for "gauze") was held descriptive of toilet paper, as was BAGEL NOSH (Yiddish for "bagel snack") in relation to bagel sandwiches (though registered for restaurant-related services). However, sometimes when the otherwise descriptive foreign word is very obscure, protection may be available. For instance, a court held that the applicant had no duty to tell the USPTO that COHIBA for cigars means "tobacco" to the Taino Indians of the Dominican Republic since USA cigar smokers would not know such meaning. Who would suspect that CWM and TY mean respectively "valley" and "house" in Welsh? (The USPTO online database entries for such marks do not show that registrants have generally disclosed the Welsh meanings to the USPTO, probably because they were not aware of such meanings.) VOLKSWAGEN, meaning "people's car," a concept sponsored by Adolf Hitler—who even made his way into trademark lore—might be considered somewhat descriptive, but its widespread use abroad would have made it distinctive.

If the foreign word is not phonetic in English, when registering the mark in an English-speaking country you may want to specify pronunciation in the registration, as done with U.S. Reg. No. 305,349 for PINAUD (French) pronounced PEE-NO and U.S. Reg. No. 2,484,068 for ASE (Norwegian) pronounced OH-SUH.

Whenever an irresistible cachet may attach to a foreign sounding name, then sometimes one can devise foreign sounding words having no meaning in any language, e.g., HÄAGEN-DAZS.

193 TRANSLATIONS

Rather than import foreign terminology, sometimes a straight translation of English words will do. That is, start with a concept expressed in English, then translate. Microsoft Corporation filed at the USPTO for the marks ISKOOLA POTA (Sinhalese for "school book") for font-related software and MEIRYO (Japanese for "clear," "lucid" or "plain"), also for font-related software Cf. FACILPAGO used by the Home Shopping Network en Español ("ease of payment"); QD QUAQUE DIE ONLINE ("quaque die" in Latin is "everyday"); and ORO FINO NUGGET ("oro fino" in Español is "fine gold"). Infrequently, where an English word might be unprotectably *descriptive*, a foreign equivalent will not, particularly a word from an obscure language. Putting equivalent foreign words alongside English words, as per ORO FINO NUGGET, makes the mark stand out.

Beware the "metaphrase," i.e., a word-for-word translation, because literal translations can result in marks having different idiomatic meanings in other languages. For example, the owner of PURE LIFE for bottled water realized that in Spanish speaking countries the metaphrase VIDA PURA was less appropriate than PUREZA VITAL. Conversely, one Chinese writer lamented that a gentle feminine Chinese mark for a beauty product could be literally translated as FANGFANG in English.

194 ANGLICIZED WORDS AND NAMES

Foreign terminology can be anglicized, a process that has generated many surnames, e.g., CAMPBELL's for soups is derived from the French "champs belle," meaning "beautiful field." Similarly, BEACHAMS comes from the French "beau champs," also meaning "beautiful field." REDFIELD is an anglicized version of ROSENFELD (German) or ROOSEVELT (Dutch) and a more modern version of RALEIGH. The trick is to find expressive foreign terminology and then, often without translating it, merely change the sound and spelling to comport with English usage. Cf. BOO-KU ("beaucoup"), LEGO (from the Danish "leg godt," meaning play well),

V **Subject Matter**

Truly onomatopoeic marks are rare. Successful examples are SCHWEPPES, which matches the carbonated hiss, and FERRARI, which mimics the car's powerful engine.

NUVO ("nouveau"), and CAMAY (from the French "camee," meaning cameo). Anglicization is just a form of transliteration, with English as the target language.

The anglicized mark, though frequently lacking the panache or cachet of its foreign source, can often be made shorter, more phonetic, and more distinctive. Sometimes an unprotectably *descriptive* foreign word might be salvaged by creating a English-looking soundalike. E.g., hypothetically, if ROJO ("red" in Spanish) were descriptive of the products, one could argue that ROWHOE, connoting a farm implement, was not.

195 INCONGRUOUS MARKS; MULTI-LANGUAGE MARKS

To avoid obstacles facing *descriptive* terminology, some companies develop marks having a descriptive English word coupled with a foreign word. Occasionally registration has been allowed even where the foreign word, when translated, does not remove overall descriptiveness. For instance, LA YOGURT for yogurt and LE CASE for jewelry and gift boxes were held registerable with disclaimers for the descriptive words YOGURT and CASE. However, typically less registerable is the mark having the opposite construction, with the English word as the article or other add-on and the foreign word as the descriptive term: e.g., hypothetically imagine THE CHAPEAU for hats or THE BOLSA for handbags. Trademark miscegenation is usually a gamble, as shown in Word Origins (¶ 89). The risk is magnified when the two or more words from different languages are comparable in importance. Hypothetically, imagine that instead of RED BULL or TORO ROJO one used RED TORO or ROJO BULL.

196 COLLOQUIALISMS, SLANG, AND IDIOMS

Slang is a fertile source of marks. Sometimes you can construct a mark using a colloquialism or other informal speech device which contains a

V Subject Matter

word relating to your product or business. For instance, if your product has anything to do with "cleaning," whether a floor or hard drive, colloquial words containing WASH might be considered, e.g., WHITEWASH, HOGWASH, BRAINWASH, EYEWASH, or WISHYWASHY. Or where the product relates to "heat," how about HOTROD, HOTHEAD, HOTSEAT, HOTHOUSE, HOTSPOT, or HOTSHOT? At the border between nonsense and meaning, slang offers something colorful and fresh. Registered examples are WISHY WASHY, WACKO, NITTY GRITTY, KLUTZ, GOO-GOO, and YOO-HOO.

Obviously a colloquial mark will usually not be a dignified one, but less obvious is that it may lose meaning over time. As Oscar Wilde said, "No age borrows the slang of its predecessor." Colloquialisms of one generation may be unknown to or unused by the next because words at the periphery of language often emerge, then disappear.

Less ephemeral than slang are idioms, many of which have crawled out of the sea of slang. An idiom, like "bought the farm," which usually means "died" rather than "purchased agricultural property," is typically an expression whose common meaning is not its literal one. Trademark examples are LET IT RIP and CUT TO THE CHASE. Though often catchy, idioms like slang are frequently not dignified nor successful choices. Also, though an idiom may predominately signify its common meaning, for purposes of conflicts it may also be judged in relation to its literal meaning.

197 OBSCURE WORDS

You can derive an almost-*fanciful mark* that has linguistic and semantic roots by finding an obscure word, e.g., by perusing the complete edition of the Oxford English Dictionary. If the word suggests the product, that's a plus; even if not, you may have an unusual *arbitrary* mark. Examples of registered marks are VIRAGO (an heroic or manlike woman)(U.S. Reg. No. 2,199,841 for books); ZANTE (European smoke-tree wood) (U.S. Reg. No. 2,399,171 for footwear); TONDO (a circular painting or carving)(U.S. Reg. No. 2,348,526 for books); CYLIX (a shallow-stemmed two-handled drinking cup)(U.S. Reg. No. 1,212,734 for data transmission and computer programming services); and OBELUS (a sign used in ancient manuscripts to mark suspect, corrupt, or spurious words or passages) (U.S. Reg. No. 2,259,241 for stainless steel flatware). Such unusual marks tend to be distinctive and less likely to conflict with other marks, especially in relation to meaning.

V Subject Matter

Less arcane, but sometime apt, are "fossil" words, i.e., obsolete words which, like a crab in a shell, only survive within idiomatic expressions, such as "fettle" which only occurs within the expression "in fine fettle." KITH, as in "kith and kin," is a trademark example, as is SPIC AND SPAN. Though fossil words can be distinctive, their advantage may be lost unless used arbitrarily or otherwise imaginatively.

Still somewhat obscure, but less so than "fossil" words, are "jargon" words and expressions. Jargon is vocabulary peculiar to a particular trade, industry, occupation, profession or similar group, for example, legal jargon like "sua sponte" (meaning "of his/her own volition") or military jargon like "alpha strike." If jargon words spark imagination, like the mark EVENT HORIZON, so much the better. Otherwise, to be effective, a less imaginative mark like FORCE MULTIPLIER must be used arbitrarily or very imaginatively. After all, jargon terms by their very nature can be dull and lifeless.

198 PUNS ON WORDS

Puns on words are sometimes good marks or trade names. Paul Newman cleverly chose FIG NEWMANS to slipstream FIG NEWTONS. What about SCRIPTEASERS ("stripteasers") for an organization that offers a forum for people to read literature aloud, or GHOSTHUSTLERS ("ghostbusters") for a business that places the services of ghost writers? How about TUMBLESTEEDS ("tumbleweeds") for rodeo horses? Even foreign languages may be exploited, e.g., imagine COUP DE GRASS ("coup de gras") for grass cutting equipment.

To create a pun you find a word already amusing or interesting and change one of its components (sometimes a morpheme, syllable, or letter or two) to yield an expression having a different, more humorous meaning in relation to the products. For example, from the interesting word TUMBLEWEED you get not only TUMBLESTEED but also TUMBLESEED, TUMBLEBEAD, and TUMBLEFEED, which might cleverly apply to certain products. Though puns and spoonerisms may be clever and funny, surprisingly few have become famous marks.

199 DOUBLE ENTENDRE

Much like a homograph *(¶ 224),* when a phrase or word combination has two or more meanings, a clever result may be achieved. Typically, when

V Subject Matter

one uses a double-entendre device, all or most of the words in the mark will have a double meaning, and each word may be a homograph: e.g., JUST DESSERTS for food products and PART COMPANY for a talent agency. More humorous would be SHRINKRAP for an online psychiatry forum, the humor achieved because both components together connote packaging, while each component is also a slang word.

These marks are constructed using lists of phrases and homographs. Often each double-meaning word has roots in different parts of speech, such as noun vs. verb, e.g., PART verb vs. PART noun, JUST adjective vs. JUST adverb, and POST verb vs. POST prefix. When combined, the two or more double-meaning words also must have two or more meanings. This concoction usually takes the talent of someone who has "a way with words." However, these intellectually clever marks are generally not great successes.

200 PARODIES

Parodies can be memorable, humorous marks. However, beware parodies on someone else's name, trade name or trademark because you could attract legal claims. For instance, note the lawsuit involving Johnny Carson's objections to HERE'S JOHNNY portable toilets. The owner of THE GREATEST SHOW ON EARTH was concerned about THE GREATEST SNOW ON EARTH, and the owner of WHERE THERE'S LIFE...THERE'S BUD was not pleased by WHERE THERE'S LIFE...THERE'S BUGS. Also, BAGZILLA for "monstrously strong" garbage bags drew fire from GODZILLA, and LOUIS VUITTON for luxury goods growled at CHEWY VUITON for dog toys and beds. But the owners of FIG NEWTONS allowed Paul Newman to use FIG NEWMANS under license.

Successful parody takes substantial skill. As Yogi Berra said, "If you can't imitate him, don't copy him." For the subject of the parody, the trick is to find and cleverly change a well-known word or phrase somehow related to the product. Preferably the part(s) of the original subject matter changed will be distinctive. One technique is to make as much change as possible without losing the impression of the original word or phrase. This technique is applied when someone owns the original subject matter and you are trying to avoid a claim. When developing a parody mark, always consult an attorney.

V Subject Matter

201 RHYMES AND SEMI-RHYMES

A rhyming mark is often easy to remember and sometimes memorable, e.g., 7-ELEVEN, "TUSH-CUSH," YOO-HOO, FAMOUS AMOS, PIGGLY-WIGGLY, MAC & JAC, and LEXIS NEXIS. You may also benefit when the mark rhymes with the product or a principal component, as with MARS bars, GO-GURT yogurt, RONZONI macaroni, and SPAM ham. Sometimes the rhyme is subtle when relating to a product quality, e.g., VELUX for skylights rhymes with DELUXE. (It also has LUX, Latin for "light," the beginning "VE" connoting an opening as in "vent" and the Spanish "ventana," and a similarity to "velum," meaning "covering" in Latin.)

Taglines and *slogans* occasionally feature rhymes. E.g., note "DON'T SAY GLUE, SAY YOOHOO!," "NATIONWIDE IS ON YOUR SIDE," and the TCBY "GOOD TASTE. NO WAIST." Though rhyming taglines/slogans may be memorable, unless cleverly devised they may lack the positioning capacity of less gaudy phrases.

To generate rhymes, print, software, and online rhyming dictionaries are useful.

Occasionally assonance or semi-rhyme is effective. Assonance is achieved when the vowels in the stressed syllables of two or more contiguous words are the same, even if the vowel is sounded differently in each word. LOCK AND LOAD (also alliterative) is an example; so is HARMON/KARDON. Yet marks that almost rhyme, like HARMAN/KARDON, may be harder to remember. Semi-rhymes can also be tongue-twisters, and if so should be avoided. (Tongue twisters like "she sells sea shells by the seashore" and "Betty Botter had some butter" are constructed using semi-rhymes and alliteration.)

202 ALLITERATION

Alliterative marks containing words starting with the same initial sound can catch the ear, e.g., BURT'S BEES, BROOKS BROTHERS, ROTO-ROOTER, BOB'S BIG BOY, REYNOLDS WRAP, VOLKSWAGEN, PAYPAL, and CISCO SYSTEMS. When the first or last letters of the two or more alliterative words are the same (e.g., BOB'S BIG BOY or BROOKS BROTHERS) rather than just sounding the same (e.g., REYNOLDS WRAP), then the sound effect is also reflected in appearance, which has some advantages, as in signage. The alliterative effect is also more faintly achieved when the product has the same initial sound, e.g., PLANTERS peanuts, BECK'S beer, SCHICK shavers, VOLVO vehicles, CANON cameras, and BANTAM books. And alliteration

V **Subject Matter**

can be carried over to themes, *taglines*, and *slogans*, such as "M & M's Melt in Your Mouth," "Welcome to the World Wide Wow," "It's NERF or Nothing," or "Better Buy BIRDS EYE."

203 RHYTHMIC MARKS

Rhythm is sometimes lively and memorable as exemplified by RIN TIN TIN, ABRACADABRA, RUB-A-DUB, COCA-COLA, and HOWDY DOODY. This device is probably more effective when rhyming is also present, e.g., TRADITIONAL MEDICINALS. Rhythmic harmony can also exist between the mark and the product, e.g., CHIQUITA bananas, RONZONI macaroni, and LA ROSA spaghetti, though this kind of rhythm will probably be less noticeable than rhythm in a mark. On rare occasions a *tagline* or *slogan* will show signs of rhythm, like the Radio Times' "If it's on, it's in." Rhythmic marks are relatively rare, which suggests that rhythm, though memorable, may be hard to achieve while preserving more important semantics.

204 TAUTONYMS; REDUPLICATED WORDS

Reduplicated words, aka tautonyms, are possibilities, though not often successful. In English examples are beri beri, bye bye, couscous, tom tom, mahi mahi, and yo-yo. These words often originate from "native" languages. The relative ease of repeating a sound already formed by the mouth explains infantile tautonyms like mama, dada, wee wee, goo goo, etc.

Many first names, typically nicknames, are tautonyms, such as Mimi, Bebe, Kiki, Zsa Zsa, Coco, and Gigi. Most of these women's first names are registered trademarks at the USPTO, typically for women's products. Other examples of repetition are MIU MIU, PAM PAM, TOMTOM, DUM DUMS, M & M'S, EMINEM, and repeating surnames such as JOHNSON & JOHNSON. COCA-COLA is almost a tautonym and obviously more effective than if it were, as are the ricochet words *(¶ 205)*. Adding an "AND," "&," or middle syllable often makes the mark more useable or palatable, as in JOHNSON & JOHNSON and M & M'S. Sometimes the reduplication is disguised or submerged, as in TINACTIN, CANOSCAN, and KINDLEKIN.

Because of the "diminutive" and sometimes primitive effect of pure tautonyms, they are not often suitable for large businesses or major product lines, except perhaps in the fashion industry.

V **Subject Matter**

205 RICOCHET WORDS

Close to alliteration, rhyme, rhythm, and reduplication are "ricochet" words like chit-chat, dilly-dally, flim-flam, mish-mash, razzle-dazzle, tip-top, tiki-wiki, hodgepodge, pell-mell, riff-raff, boogie-woogie, bric-a-brac, and namby-pamby. Though some are rhymes (e.g., namby-pamby), some alliterative (e.g., chit-chat), and some rhythmic (e.g., higgledy-piggledy), they share common characteristics. The first such characteristic is that each of the two components—they are typically two-word constructions—has the same number of syllables. Second, each ends with the same vowel sound (namby-pamby) or consonant sound (tip-top). Third, in each word the matching vowel sounds are either both short (flim-flam or spitter spatter) or both long (okey-dokey or rosy posy). Typically the short "i" sound is followed by a short "a" or "o" sound, though a short "e" sound could follow the "i" sound, as in pig pen. (A short "u" sound is rare.) In words in which the vowel sounds are different, the shorter vowel sound usually comes first, e.g., the short "i" as in tip top, flim-flam, and pig pen; therefore, with terms that could be reversed, the reversal in not as catchy, as in chat-chit, flam-flim, and dally-dilly. Also, if no rhyme is present, the initial consonant or vowel sounds of the two components are usually the same, as in chit-chat and dilly-dally.

Examples of well-known ricochet trademarks are TIC TAC, KIT KAT, PALL MALL, TUSH-CUSH, SPIC AND SPAN, and SHAKE 'N BAKE. HARMON/KARDON is almost a ricochet. Cf. CRACKER JACK. As with rhymes *(¶ 201)* and alliteration *(¶ 202)*, the ricochet effect can be achieved when the mark is juxtaposed with the product name, as per SPAM ham or MARS bars.

The virtue of the ricochet word is its memorability. The staccato effect of the two-syllable version (TIC TAC or KIT KAT) is particularly catchy because words play off each other almost as echoes.

206 COLORS IN WORD MARKS

Colors in a *design mark* can be attractive but can also be useful in a *word mark*, for instance, VISA GOLD, RED BULL, BLUE CROSS, BLAUPUNKT ("blue dot"), BROWN COW, SILVER SHADOW, GREEN GIANT, and GREEN & BLACK'S. Naturally, when the word mark denotes a color, logos and packaging color schemes often follow suit. The most frequently used "color words" are black, white, gold, silver, red, blue, and green. Perhaps other color words are not as pleasant sounding, like yellow and purple, or

V Subject Matter

represent colors which might not stand out in logos, like pink and lavender. One should consider the cultural, political, and social associations of colors *(Colors in Designs, ¶ 275)*; e.g., AKAI, meaning "red" in Japanese, positively connotes the color of the rising sun; RED CROSS has no controversial color associations, but hypothetically, what about RED DISPATCH for a political newspaper, perhaps connoting leftwing leanings?

207 SOUNDING LIKE THE PRODUCT; ONOMATOPOEIA

Sometimes the mark may sound like the product itself or a major component, with an extra twist or connotation. For instance, consider marks that sound like the product name, like SNAPPLE sometimes used with apple-based drinks, LECTRONIC for electric shavers, UHU for glue, and PIXAR for computer pictures, i.e., pixilated animation. RINGLING, a surname (from the German "Rüngeling"), reminds one of circus rings. Cf. JELL-O, WINDEX, and CLOROX. Although the cleverer marks like SNAPPLE and RINGLING have indirect, metaphoric, or metonymic associations with the product, perhaps the most successful were created by adding a single letter or syllable to the sound of the product name, e.g., JELL-O, Q-TIPS, and TIMEX.

Uncommon are marks that sound like the product's essence, i.e., truly onomatopoeic words such as "hiss" and "hiccup." Trademark examples are KABOOM, KERPLUNK (GERPLUNK), SCHWEPPES which matches the carbonated hiss of the beverage, and, to some extent, FERRARI, which mimics the car's powerful engine.

208 PRODUCT COMPONENT MARKS

Some marks relate, in whole or part, to a product component and thus have a metonymic *(¶ 219)* relationship to the product. Examples are PEPTO-BISMOL (derived from the active ingredient bismuth), ZINMAX (for supplements containing zinc), KAOPECTATE (includes kaolin-pectate), and YAMMIT for a product containing powdered yam. Perhaps the most famous of these marks is COCA-COLA, from the original ingredients that included coca leaves and kola nuts. Did PEPSI come from "pepsin," the digestive enzyme? Occasionally the mark alludes to something not even in the product, as with VALIUM for a tranquilizer not containing the sedative herb valerian. Compare the VICODIN product which contains hydrocodone bitartrate, not codeine.

V Subject Matter

209 LOOKING LIKE THE PRODUCT

Sometimes the mark suggests the product's appearance. Automotive marks often subtly suggest the shape, like RABBIT, GREMLIN, JAGUAR, BUG, and BEETLE. HUSH PUPPIES for soft suede shoes, FAT BOY for motorcycles, and ROCKET POPS for desserts on a stick also come to mind. Cf. LIFE SAVERS for round candies and CHEERIOS for breakfast cereals. However, with "appearance" marks one must avoid *descriptiveness* in relation to the product, its functions or characteristics; the car marks above only suggest what the car looks like. A very imaginative example is DOMINO'S which suggests the dots on dominoes as evoked by sliced pepperoni on pizza. LIFEBUOY remotely suggests soap bars that can float in water. Even more arcane is the shape metaphor of ADOBE, as originally used for fonts, i.e., the various shapes of adobe structures remotely suggesting typographic shapes (though named for Adobe Creek, located near the home of one of the founders).

210 DIMINUTIVES

When the mark will almost totally reflect the product, particularly a small product, a diminutive may occasionally flourish. Examples of "small-size" marks are WHEATIES, WHEATETTES, CHICLETS, and NACHITOS. Naturally this kind of *descriptive* choice often results in an unimaginative noun mark in contrast to the more imaginative *fanciful* or *arbitrary* noun marks (¶ 213) like CROAKIES, TWINKIES, and HUSH PUPPIES. I.e., merely adding a suffix like "ies" or "ettes" to the product name does not promise a strong mark, though some such marks, like WHEATIES, have become strong.

211 EXPERIENTIAL, EVOCATIVE MARKS

Sometimes a great mark conjures an experience associated with the product. A wonderful example is BALLPARK for frankfurters. Anyone who has eaten a stadium hotdog knows that unforgettable experience evoked by BALLPARK. And anyone who has spent time in the mountains can relate to MOUNTAIN DEW which evokes that experience and perhaps the feeling of an Appalachian brew. Less directly, another brilliant mark, BAZOOKA, brings "gun" and "gum" together in relation to the popping sound of bubble gum.

One concern is, can a mark that rouses a pleasant experience, and successfully introduces the product to the customer, live up to that experience? If not,

V Subject Matter

one faces customer let-down and no second sale. If BALLPARK franks tasted nothing like stadium hotdogs, the brand might fail.

212 REIFICATION OF VERBS; AGENTIVE WORDS AND GERUNDS

Where the product performs a function which can be described with a verb, one can embody that function in a noun derived from the verb. This device is often used because relatively few successful marks are pure verbs. *(See Verb Marks, ¶ 214.)* Most marks consisting of ordinary words are comprised of nouns or adjectives combined with nouns, and should be used adjectivally in connection with the products with which they are associated. *(See Adjectival Marks, ¶ 86.)* Verb-to-noun conversion can be achieved, e.g., by adding an "ER" suffix to the verb or using the verb's gerund form, that is, adding an "ING" at the end. "ER" examples abound with cars, e.g., LAND ROVER, EXPLORER, and VOYAGER. Cf. ENERGIZER and ENFORCER. Gerunds, less successful, also serve to reify a verb, as in CLIMBING, MOVING and CARING. These "nouned" verbs are useful if the verb expresses an action you want associated with the product but the mark must be expressed with the solidity of a noun.

Occasionally, the reverse technique of back-formation is employed, e.g., creating a shorter new word from an extant longer one, just as the verb "burgle" was created from the noun "burglar" and the noun "diplomat" from the adjective "diplomatic." Trademarks incorporating back-formed words are INTUIT from "intuition" and BURGER KING from "hamburger," in turn derived from "Hamburg."

213 NOUN MARKS

Though marks are generally better when suited for "adjectival" use *(¶ 86)*, sometimes a good mark is a *fanciful* one which can become a noun. This is often true for personal use products, especially novel products or those having no one-word *generic* name. For example, CROAKIES prospers for eyeglass cords, HUSH PUPPIES succeeds for soft comfortable shoes, and TWINKIES thrives for cream-filled confections. VELCRO was a triumph for "hook and loop" fastening material: VEL connotes a material like velvet, velour, or vellum; CR gives the feeling of gripping or hooking; while the masculine "O" ending is better for such a utilitarian material than an "A" like the "A" in the fabric LYCRA. (VELCRA would not have been as

V Subject Matter

good.) SLINKY is another masterpiece, consisting of a snake-like "S," the word LINK having a metallic sound and connoting linkage, the "cutesy" diminutive-sounding "Y" at the end, and, of course, the word SLINK connoting the toy's movement.

However, noun usage is risky since it also weakens a mark and may cause it to become unprotectibly generic. Thus, if considering such a "noun" mark, plan on advertising materials that stress that the word is a trademark, e.g., "CROAKIES brand eyeglass retainers."

214 VERB MARKS

Pure verbs are infrequent choices, relatively speaking. By "pure verbs" we mean those not homographs *(¶ 224)* for nouns, i.e., also nouns like SPRINT, WISK (pseudospelling for WHISK), and MARVEL. Examples of pure verb marks are QUICKEN, ENSURE, DISCOVER, OUST, and EXCITE. Intransitive verbs (verbs having no object) are even more unusual, e.g., GO, LOOK, and DEPEND. Verbs are seldom good choices because it is often linguistically awkward to use them adjectivally *(¶ 86)* with products, for instance, in the format of "VERB brand product," as in "DEPEND brand napkins."

Though pure verbs are seldom used very successfully, they can be very active and striking, e.g., when used with punctuation marks, adverbs, prepositions or short nouns, as in HANG TEN and GOT MILK? Cf. SHAKE 'N BAKE and PICTURE IT! (not quite pure verbs).

215 PURE ADJECTIVES

Though marks are almost always used as adjectives in relation to the products they accompany *(¶ 86)*, relatively seldom do pure adjectives (adjectives having no homographic noun counterparts) make famous marks. E.g., though color-connoting ORANGE for wireless phone services is a famous mark in the UK, the word also has a homographic noun counterpart, i.e., the same letters denoting the fruit. One reason for the relative dearth of famous "pure adjective" marks is that if the adjective already describes the products, it may be difficult to protect *(¶ 135)*. A misdescriptive adjective may also face problems *(¶ 322)*.

Though a *suggestive* or *arbitrary* noun may make a good mark because of its tangential or metaphorical relationship to the product (e.g., WALKMAN for portable radio headsets and APPLE for computers), suggestive or arbitrary

V **Subject Matter**

adjectives might seem unsuitable for the products. For example, though the nouns BROTHER and LIFE may be strong marks, the comparable adjectives (FRATERNAL/BROTHERLY and LIVING) are probably weaker.

A concept's noun form typically has more metaphorical relationships to the product it's used with than the pure adjective. Compare URBAN vs. CITY, RITZY vs. RITZ or BLUE vs. SKY. E.g., in its connotations RITZY is more obvious and less imaginative than RITZ. With the noun more is left to the imagination: more trademark "capacitance" and "voltage" than with the more direct adjective.

216 ADVERBS

A rare choice is an adverb, i.e., a word like "quickly" or "honorably" which modifies a verb or less frequently an adjective or other adverb. Examples of USPTO adverb registrations are those for QUICKLY (tea), GENTLY (bathroom tissue), and HOW (graphic design magazines). Verbs themselves are infrequent choices *(See Verb Marks, ¶ 214)*, so words which modify them would seem even less desirable. Perhaps one reason for few adverb marks is that adverbs, as well as verbs, lack the "solidity" *(¶ 78)* which makes for a strong mark; perhaps that is also why nouns probably comprise a plurality of registered non-*fanciful word marks*. Compared to a noun (particularly a concrete noun in contrast to an abstract one), a verb usually has less ability to conjure a visual or metaphoric/metonymic association; therefore, adverbs, which generally modify verbs, are even more abstract. Another reason for adverb scarcity may be that adverbs are linguistically awkward to use adjectivally, as marks must be used. *(See Adjectival Marks, ¶ 86.)* Nonetheless, adverb use is sometimes present, particularly when the letters spell both an adverb and an adjective or noun. For instance, FAST is not only an adverb but also an adjective and a noun.

217 OTHER PARTS OF SPEECH; CONJUNCTIONS, PREPOSITIONS, AND ARTICLES

The principle of "parsimony" *(¶ 98)* teaches that unnecessary words be omitted. This principle particularly applies to "function" words from parts of speech such as articles ("A" and "THE"), conjunctions ("AND," BUT," etc.), and prepositions ("OF," "IN," "ON," "FROM," etc.). The prime reason for omission is that if such a word is not necessary, it may make the mark less distinctive and memorable, and less suitable for adjectival

V **Subject Matter**

Animals with unusual or striking characteristics, even insects and snakes (like BEETLE, CATERPILLAR, PYTHON, and COBRA), can be more distinctive than duller, cuddlier creatures.

use. For example, adding an article like THE or A at the beginning of a mark typically detracts from adjectival use because it is easier to say "HOME DEPOT building supplies" than "THE HOME DEPOT building supplies." Leaving out a conjunction like AND typically adds more rhythm, bounce, and interest to a mark. For instance, with a double surname mark like JOHNSON & JOHNSON one would not abandon the conjunction and be left with JOHNSON JOHNSON. Yet compare how much stronger and sharper SMITH BROTHERS is compared to SMITH & SMITH; the same is true of SMITH BARNEY versus SMITH & BARNEY.

Unnecessary prepositions usually add little interest to a mark. Thus, hypothetically a mark like GO ON UP containing two prepositions and one intransitive verb would probably be less distinctive and memorable than one incorporating at least one "tangible" word or concept, e.g., hypothetically GO BY KITE. Compare COME ON IN to COME ON STRONG, marks actually registered at the USPTO.

These kinds of connecting or limiting words generally evoke no mental images or graphic designs and can clutter a mark, particularly when the *word mark* is a phrase. Thus, whenever such words appear in a mark, try tweaking the mark to eliminate them without losing essential meaning.

218 MIXED METAPHORS; OXYMORONS

Some successful marks contain two or more incongruous words; the trendier the industry, the greater the incongruity. For instance, with older rock band names, recall LED ZEPPELIN, IRON BUTTERFLY, GRATEFUL DEAD, and PINK FLOYD. Also, note in the computer field NETSCAPE and DATASTORM. Many of these marks embody contradictions or are true oxymorons like BLACK SUN, TRUE LIES, and LIQUID DIAMOND. On the whole, "oxymoron" marks are more suitable for unusual products or

V Subject Matter

everyday products marketed unusually. The better oxymorons are probably those where the relationship between the words stirs the imagination.

Occasionally, a strong mark is deliberately metaphorically inconsistent, partly or entirely, with the product's main attributes. Success may come if the seemingly incongruent mark subtly suggests the product's essence. For instance, THE SOPRANOS was wildly successful for television programs dominated by characters who hardly match boys, girls, and women with high voices. Yet, the mark's "choir boy" motif complements the more sensitive familial and interpersonal aspects of the show.

219 METONYMS

A metonym is often an effective mark. Metonyms are words used in a transferred sense, e.g., the name of one thing put for that of another related to it, as the effect for the cause. For instance, "the bottle" is a metonym for "drink" as was "Kremlin" for the Soviet government. RED LOBSTER could be considered a metonym for a fish restaurant; and VINEYARD, used in the Bible (e.g., Matthew 20:1-16, 21:33-44) in relation to the Kingdom of God and the arena of travail where salvation is sought, is a metonymic mark for religious teaching and training services. STAPLES, meaning "leading commodities," is not metonymic in relation to office supplies but is metonymic when signifying paper fasteners as per TV ads. Metonyms can be good choices when suggesting products in a clever or aesthetic fashion, sometimes without *descriptiveness*.

220 HOMONYMS; SOUNDALIKES

Words having the same sound but different meanings or spellings can be useful devices. E.g., MAID often replaces MADE as in MAID IN THE SHADE for plants, SUN-MAID for dried fruits, and MINUTE MAID for frozen orange juice. WRIGHT, WRITE, RIGHT, and RITE are frequently interchanged, e.g., in the marks PLAYWRIGHT, PLAYRIGHT, PLAYRITE, and PLAYWRITE. Even more unusual are switches when the sounds are close but not identical as EYEFUL for EIFFEL.

Unless the replacement homonym is meaningfully related to the product or the word it replaces, it is often trite and dull. In a related fashion, always check whether your *fanciful* selection is a homonym for an unrelated word. Clearly, the creators of JOOST knew it matched JUICED which

V **Subject Matter**

semantically relates to the computerized entertainment services offered. But did the owners of CIALIS for erectile dysfunction medications consider that it could be heard or pronounced as SEE ALICE?

Sometimes you might consider heterophones, including words that mimic a target word, typically a product name or function but not someone else's mark or *trade name*. This mimicking effect may be achieved by techniques such as rhyming (e.g., MARS bars) and assonance (e.g., SPACKLE for cracks, though SPACKLE is also a back-formation of "spackling").

221 SYNONYMS

Synonyms, different words with the same meaning, frequently play a key role in selection. Whenever you choose a word that is unavailable or not quite right, sometimes a synonym will be better. As Samuel Butler observed, "'The Ancient Mariner' would not have taken so well if it had been called 'The Old Sailor.'" Thesaureses and synonym finders, both print and software versions, are sources of words having similar or related meanings, e.g., MAUDLIN/SENTIMENTAL or TRIP/EXCURSION. Choices often emerge from two origins, Anglo-Saxon/Old English and French/Latin. Anglo-Saxon/Old English words tend to be earthier, the French/Latin words more analytical but sometimes more "poetic." Ponder the following lists of what is and what could have been.

ANGLO-SAXON	FRENCH/LATIN
SWEAR	PLEDGE
TUCKS	INSERTS
GLAD	PLEASED
WHOLE FOODS	COMPLETE NUTRIENTS

Even phrases and *slogans* have semantic analogs. E.g., A TO Z is matched by ALPHA TO OMEGA (Rev. 1:11), and in other contexts by SOUP TO NUTS, WOMB TO TOMB, and FROM HERE TO ETERNITY.

As with A TO Z being matched by SOUP TO NUTS, sometimes the synonym comes from a different realm of experience or represents a poetic expression of the original word. Compare two health company marks, the Biblical EDEN and its semantic counterpart GARDEN OF LIFE. If the synonym is a

V **Subject Matter**

poetic translation or emanates from a different frame of reference, public confusion is often avoided.

Always carefully weigh semantic differences between synonyms. For example, consider the differences between TRAVEL and JOURNEY. To "journey" to another place connotes a venture more arduous and tortuous but perhaps more interesting since it also connotes more stops and sightseeing, whereas "travel" often connotes what we do on short holidays, i.e., quickly go someplace, perhaps with short stops elsewhere. We might metaphorically allude to "life as a journey" but would not do the same with "travel." (As with many other semantic choices, the words' connotations slightly betray their origins since "journey" is derived from the French "jour" meaning "day" and originally connoted a day's travel or work, whereas "travel" is related to the French "travail" connoting excessive labor or effort.)

When you can't use a word because of a conflict or otherwise, and you don't want a synonym, you might consider another form of the word. That is, you might try the various members of a lexeme to preserve some of the intended meaning. Hypothetically, with the lexeme GROW you might try GROWER, GROWN, or GROWING, or a company wanting to mimic CRAIG'S LIST without creating confusion might test second words like LISTING, LISTINGS, LISTER, etc. Seldom does this kind of tweak succeed, but it's worth considering.

222 ANTONYMS

Occasionally an antonym, a word opposite in meaning to another, can work. The antonym can be the opposite of another's mark or of the product itself. For instance, in contrast to MR. CLEAN one might risk MR. DIRT. Or for clothing the counter-descriptive mark GRUBB, suggesting "grubby," was once upheld. When using an antonym of someone else's mark, particularly one which satirizes it, you risk a claim. Also, when the counter-*descriptive mark* is deceptively misdescriptive, you may forfeit protection. *(See Misdescriptive Marks, ¶ 322.)*

Antonymic marks can sometimes be generated by adding/subtracting a prefix or suffix. Something larger can be made smaller with an "ette" suffix (see, e.g., U.S. Reg. No. 2,266,752 for NEONETTE); a word can be negated by adding an "A" or an "UN" at the beginning (as in UNCOLA, U.S. Reg. No. 1,201,356) or perhaps even an "ANTI" (cf. U.S. Reg. No. 2,517,775 for

V **Subject Matter**

ANTISENILIN); and a masculine word can be made feminine with an "A" at the end, or a feminine word made masculine by changing to an "O" at the end, e.g., as on "Seinfeld" where the imaginary man's bra is called "BRO." The antonymic mark may suggest a function of the product, perhaps in an imaginative way. E.g., note LOJACK for vehicle anti-theft devices designed to prevent a "hijack," and which reflects the original placement of the devices, usually toward the vehicle's bottom.

223 CONTRONYMS

Words, phrases or expressions having opposite meanings can sometimes be memorable. A famous contronym was "sacer" in Latin which meant both "sacred" and "taboo." Trademark examples of contronyms are the following registered marks:

MARK	MEANING/CONNOTATION 1	MEANING/CONNOTATION 2
TRIM	Addition	Excision
BOLT	Tie Down	Escape
TRIP	Stumble	Move With Agility
SCREEN	Show	Hide

Words or expressions containing directional indicators like up, down, around, in, and out can be contronyms, such as WINDUP, connoting both preparation and dissolution.

The contronym is essentially a homograph (¶ 224) with the added requirement that the different meanings are opposite, i.e., a "homographic antonym." *(See Antonyms, ¶ 222.)* When the opposite meanings both connect to the business and its products, you've possibly hit a jackpot.

224 MULTIPLE MEANINGS; HOMOGRAPHS, HETERONYMS, AND CAPITONYMS

Certain words have multiple meanings or shades of meaning. Homographs (words having the same spelling but different origins and meaning) can give a mark delicious ambiguity. Good examples are RUN, PART, and

V Subject Matter

PLANT. POST supposedly has twelve separate meanings, and the champion SET may have as many as two hundred meanings. Sometimes the meanings can be quite disparate: consider JAM as it relates to "door," "traffic," "session," and "fruit" and FLY referring to "travel," "insect," and "zipper." For instance, hypothetically (UN)KNOWN PARTS could be a trade name or perhaps a mark for a travel agency, barbershop, auto supply warehouse, or talent agency. Cf. U.S. Reg. No. 2,198,822 for PARTS UNKNOWN for clothing. HOME RUNS might be useful for a sports agency, delivery service, real estate agency, home maintenance service, clothing repair kit, or toilet paper. Cf. U.S. Reg. No. 2,058,372 for HANAFORD'S HOME RUNS for home delivery services. VAULT is a homograph whose two meanings, leap and valuables' storage place, eminently suit a magazine covering offshore business and investment.

When words spelled the same way not only have different meanings but also different sounds (like "lead" the metal and "lead" the verb), they are known as "heteronyms." A heteronymous mark has even more room for anomaly and strangeness than a homographic, though English heteronymous marks like BASS, CONVERSE, and DOVE are less common, probably because there are relatively few true heteronyms in the language.

A "capitonym" is a heteronym where the dual meaning and dual pronunciation are created by capitalizing it. E.g., consider "reading" and the mark READING (pronounced "redding" like Reading, the English city), "job" and the mark JOB (when inspired by the Biblical character), and "rainier" and the mark RAINIER (when related to the surname). Capitonymic marks are uncommon and typically used when the customer will readily perceive that the capitalized meaning and pronunciation are intended.

> **Non-descriptive vegetable marks are comparatively rare, perhaps because vegetables typically lack the warmth, sweetness, juiciness, and distinctive shapes associated with fruits and have rarely captured the poetic imagination, as have fruits.**

V **Subject Matter**

225 BODY PARTS

Body parts are fertile subject matter since a high percentage of products accompany, serve or mimic the human body's parts or functions,. E.g., note PALM, HANDSPRING, L'EGGS, ANUSOL, HEAD & SHOULDERS, ARM & HAMMER, and WALKMAN. And the creators of the following marks also must have noted a bodily connection: LEGO, TUCKS (buttocks), and IMAX (eye). (Note that LEGO is derived from the Danish "LEG GODT" meaning "play well" and also means in Latin "I read" or "I put together.")

Body parts also appear in designs that accompany word marks, e.g., the ARM & HAMMER, ALLSTATE (hands), and HANG TEN (feet) logos. These designs usually enhance *word mark* recognition.

226 ANIMAL MARKS; THERONYMS

So many marks come from animal names that no one should ignore this possibility, either in relation to *product marks* or symbolic character-based marks. Automobile marks are a good example of animal characteristics applied to mechanical vehicles: JAGUAR, IMPALA, RAM, BEETLE, MUSTANG, and SABLE. Animal character marks include CHARLIE THE TUNA, SMOKEY BEAR, and TONY THE TIGER. Though barnyard animals like cows, pigs, and chickens may relate to food products (BROWN COW, COW AND GATE, and CHICKEN OF THE SEA), they are not usually suitable for classy goods. Conversely, obscure animals like mongooses and platypuses may suit specialty products but not necessarily canned tuna or breakfast cereals. Some animal name marks have the advantage of generating animal-related logos, shapes, themes, and even sounds. Remember, obscure, rarely-used animal names still survive: cf. Toyota's TERCEL, a variant of "tiercel," a male hawk. And animals with unusual or striking characteristics, including insects and snakes (like BEETLE, CATERPILLAR, PYTHON, and COBRA), can be more distinctive than duller, cuddlier creatures. Even animal words from other languages may be viable, as per AVIS (Latin for bird) or REEBOK (from the Afrikaans/Dutch spelling of rhebok, a kind of African antelope).

As with other subject matter, always note cultural differences. In many lands a dog is a man's best friend while in others only tablefare; in China a dragon may be auspicious while in Western countries often monstrous.

By the way, note the unsuccessful Anheuser-Busch, Inc. application, U.S. Serial No. 78/944,873, to register a live Clydesdale horse as a trademark and

V Subject Matter

the successful registration of a point of sale display comprising eight live Clydesdale horses hitched to a beer wagon with uniformed human drivers and a dog, U.S. Reg. No. 3,238,974.

227 LITERARY OR COMMONLY-USED EXPRESSIONS

Consider literary or commonly-used expressions, for example, SPIC AND SPAN for detergents and cleansers, IT'S A JUNGLE OUT THERE for outerwear, GET A GRIP for bowling ball accessories, UNDERNEATH IT ALL for women's underwear, PLAY IT AGAIN SAM for used sports equipment, and SEEDS OF CHANGE for food products. Biblical phrases and terminology are possibilities such as GOOD SAMARITAN, BREAD OF LIFE, SALT OF THE EARTH, and TENDER MERCIES. "Phrase generators" are available on disk or on the Web. Typically, you enter a word or concept and the software generates phrases which incorporate that word or concept. However, even if you get trademark protection for such a phrase doesn't mean you can always stop others from non-commercially using it to express ordinary thoughts, e.g., "He failed to get a grip on reality," "The seeds of change were sown years ago when...." or "She acted like a good Samaritan."

228 NEWLY-DEVISED SLOGANS AND PHRASES

If no well-worn phrase suits your fancy, then make up your own, e.g., YOU'RE IN GOOD HANDS associated with the ALLSTATE insurance mark, DRIVERS WANTED for VW cars, IT PAYS TO DISCOVER for the DISCOVER credit card, THE WORLD'S FAVOURITE AIRLINE for British Airways services, THE WORLD ON TIME for FEDEX delivery services, WE TRY HARDER for AVIS car rentals, and SOLUTIONS FOR A SMALL PLANET marketed with IBM office products. When the phrase is catchy or conveys a visceral image, it may be as successful as the *house mark*. For instance, the ALLSTATE phrase and imagery is distinctive and well known.

Typically, these newly coined phrases are used in *slogans* and not often as house or *product marks*, whereas well-worn expressions, with established meaning and recognition, have more use as product and even house marks. The best such slogans and phrases are short and distinctive. Exceeding four or five words usually makes the slogan less powerful and memorable. Imagery and metaphor are the goals, not necessarily literary devices like rhymes and alliteration, which are surprisingly infrequent in famous slogans.

V Subject Matter

229 TAGLINES

Though the terms "slogans" and "taglines" are often used interchangeably, there is a subtle difference. A slogan is a short phrase or statement that helps promote interest in a company or its products, whereas a tagline is typically a shorter phrase or combination of words that reflects the tone, essence or premise of a company or its products. The slogan is usually more *descriptive* and direct and often touts a specific quality or benefit, whereas the tagline is often more metaphoric and imaginative. Slogans are more likely to change or disappear and may accompany only a single advertising campaign, whereas taglines are typically designed to last longer. Tagline examples are the NIKE tagline "JUST DO IT," the MCDONALD'S "I'M LOVIN' IT," and "IMPOSSIBLE IS NOTHING" associated with ADIDAS. Arguably, because of their durability and distinctiveness, taglines may merit more investment in selection and protection than more descriptive slogans. The tagline is often an important device in positioning the *brand*, and creating terse and powerful taglines is an art in itself. Often more than the word mark, the tagline expresses an attitude or feeling which defines the brand, so the tagline does not necessarily contain words which linguistically relate to the *word mark* but rather words that conceptually or emotionally position the company or product.

Like the examples mentioned in the last paragraph, the best taglines are very short, three or four words at most. This brevity gives them more lasting trademark significance, in contrast to more descriptive slogans. One technique for achieving brevity is to craft a short phrase that captures the brand's aim, cachet, or essence and then compress the expression to its minimum. Writing haiku is good training for writing taglines.

230 "MISSION" MARKS

For companies having non-monetary political or social goals, a mark suggesting the company mission may be viable. RAINFOREST is used as a component of many *product marks* by companies which support rainforest preservation. Cf. ECOPOWER, U.S. Reg. No. 2,582,743 for renewable energy; PAX WORLD FUND, U.S. Reg. No. 2,275,410 for securities investment services by a company sponsoring socially responsible investing; and MOTHERS AGAINST DRUNK DRIVING, U.S. Reg. No. 1,603,041.

A common concern with mission marks is making the mark distinctive. E.g., so many RAINFOREST, ECO____, and NATUR__ marks exist that it is hard to

V Subject Matter

stand out using such components. The trick is to find an uncommon *suggestive* component.

Because using such a mark generally connotes support for a cause, the trademark owner is typically expected to direct its activities, or donate a portion of profits, to the cause or else risk loss of credibility.

231 ACTION MARKS

Many marks are derived from verbs or adjectival phrases which indicate something about behavior of or surrounding the product, for instance, IN-N-OUT BURGER for drive-through fast food, ONE-A-DAY for vitamins, REACH for dental floss, ENSURE for weight control products, and BOOST for nutritional supplements. Whenever *descriptive*, these kinds of marks may be difficult to protect. An action mark making a visceral connection may succeed.

232 SERENDIPITY; SELF-CONNECTED MARKS

Sometimes a great mark is as close as the nose on your face. For instance, the Weinstein brothers derived MIRAMAX from their parents' names Miriam and Max, a brilliant mark connoting "great wonder" in Latin, and also rhythmic and alliterative. BETTY CROCKER came from a director of the Gold Medal Flour Company, William C. Crocker. Semantically BETTY CROCKER is an effective mark for foods and recipe books since CROCKER connotes the kitchen ("crockery"), and BETTY is not only a friendly, wholesome name but also evokes BETTER. WENDY'S was named after Dave Thomas' daughter (her nickname), not Peter Pan's friend; the same with SARA LEE, the daughter of a bakery entrepreneur, and BARBIE, named after Barbara, a company founder's daughter. Supposedly, KINKOS came from the founder's kinky

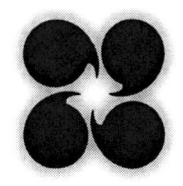

> "APPLE for computers succeeds probably because the apple is a symbol of knowledge, health or wholeness; a prize given to a goddess; a gift to a teacher; or the perfect fruit: nutritious, nicely packaged, and not easily damaged."
>
> PETER KARLEN

V Subject Matter

hair. And LINUX obviously came from Linus Torvalds, its originator. Cf. VICTORINOX, from the founder's mother Victoria, plus INOX, the international symbol for stainless steel.

These self-connected marks can give a business and its workforce a sense of comfort, closeness, and purpose. Sources can be names of relatives, participants, and even pets. The trick is not only to use personal material and establish an inner connection but to adapt that material so it connects to the product in the public's eye, as with MIRAMAX.

So many famous marks emanate from company location names (like NOKIA), names or nicknames of company founders or their relatives, and other personally-connected subject matter, that serendipity ranks with resonance (¶ 122) and parsimony (¶ 98) as a top selection source and consideration.

233 MISCELLANEOUS SUBJECT MATTER

When stumped, try miscellaneous subject matter, particularly for *arbitrary* marks. For instance, fruits, herbs, and Biblical names are fertile subject areas. Marks with geographic connotations are common, e.g., LANDS' END, BLUE SKY, OCEAN SPRAY, SANYO ("three oceans" in Japanese), LAND O'LAKES, AVON (Celtic for "river"), TIMBERLAND, and TROPICANA.

Yet, not every miscellaneous area is fertile. For instance, though famous or strong non-*descriptive* fruit marks like APPLE, KIWI, and ORANGE thrive, non-descriptive vegetable marks are comparatively rare, perhaps because vegetables typically lack the warmth, sweetness, juiciness, and distinctive shapes associated with fruits and have rarely captured the poetic imagination, as have fruits. Non-descriptive "grain" marks have done slightly better than their vegetable counterparts because of metaphors associated with grains, e.g., wheat as the "staff of life" and oats as "energy" as in "WILD OATS." Yet, corn, once generic for grain and mentioned in the Bible 102 times, perhaps more than any other staple, is hardly used non-descriptively. I.e., when you see CORN, you are probably getting (pop)corn.

234 PRESCRIBED FORMAT MARKS; CALL LETTERS

Some marks fall into predetermined formats, dictated by law or practical limitations. For example, radio and TV station call letters, which can sometimes act as marks, are so prescribed. In the USA they are usually four letters long, occasionally three; in the West they start with K, in the East with W, thus leaving the owner with only three (or two) letters to add.

V Subject Matter

When the format is so limited, essential selection considerations like memorability *(¶ 69)* and audibility *(¶ 49)* apply most strongly. This is best illustrated with station call letter marks. The most easily remembered may be those derived from already-established relationships, as per station marks like KABC and WCBS. The ABC and CBS components are so well known that the station marks are instantly recognized. Next best in terms of memorability may be call letters containing a *suggestive* word like KJOY (soft music station) and WHLO ("Hello" radio). Another ploy is the use of pun, rebus, or double entendre as in KRAP and WRIP. Also possible is a mark which uses a group of letters that doesn't have obvious meaning but whose meaning, if advertised or deciphered, might add something to the mark, as in KQED (quod erat demonstrandum). Finally if the letter combination appears entirely random to most listeners, it should at least obey the laws of euphony. *(See Euphony and Cacophony, ¶ 171.)* I.e., the sounds of the letters in the rebus format *(See Rebuses, ¶ 172)* should easily flow from one to the next and avoid tongue twisting. For instance, if KPBS were not derived from PBS and thus not easily recognizable, it would not be a good choice because the P is confusingly similar to the B. The same is true of WGBH, a jumble of letters which if not locally associated with Great Blue Hill might twist the tongue and be hard to remember.

A number of lists and publications on call letter origins can be found on the Web, which seem to indicate five major sources of call letters, namely: (1) euphony: the sounds of call letters, including call letters which spell a word; (2) radio frequency: the dial position reflected in the call letters; (3) ownership: the initials or name of the original or successor licensee; (4) location: the geographic feature, region, town, or city reflected in the call letters; and (5) slogan: a promotional phrase, often reflecting the licensee.

235 MISCELLANEOUS STATE MARKS

Various State jurisdictions have registration systems for a variety of special marks, including laundry marks; quality marks; estate, villa, farm, and ranch names; and trade names. Whenever you have such registerable subject matter, you may want to register under the State schemes in a manner consistent with federally protecting your mark.

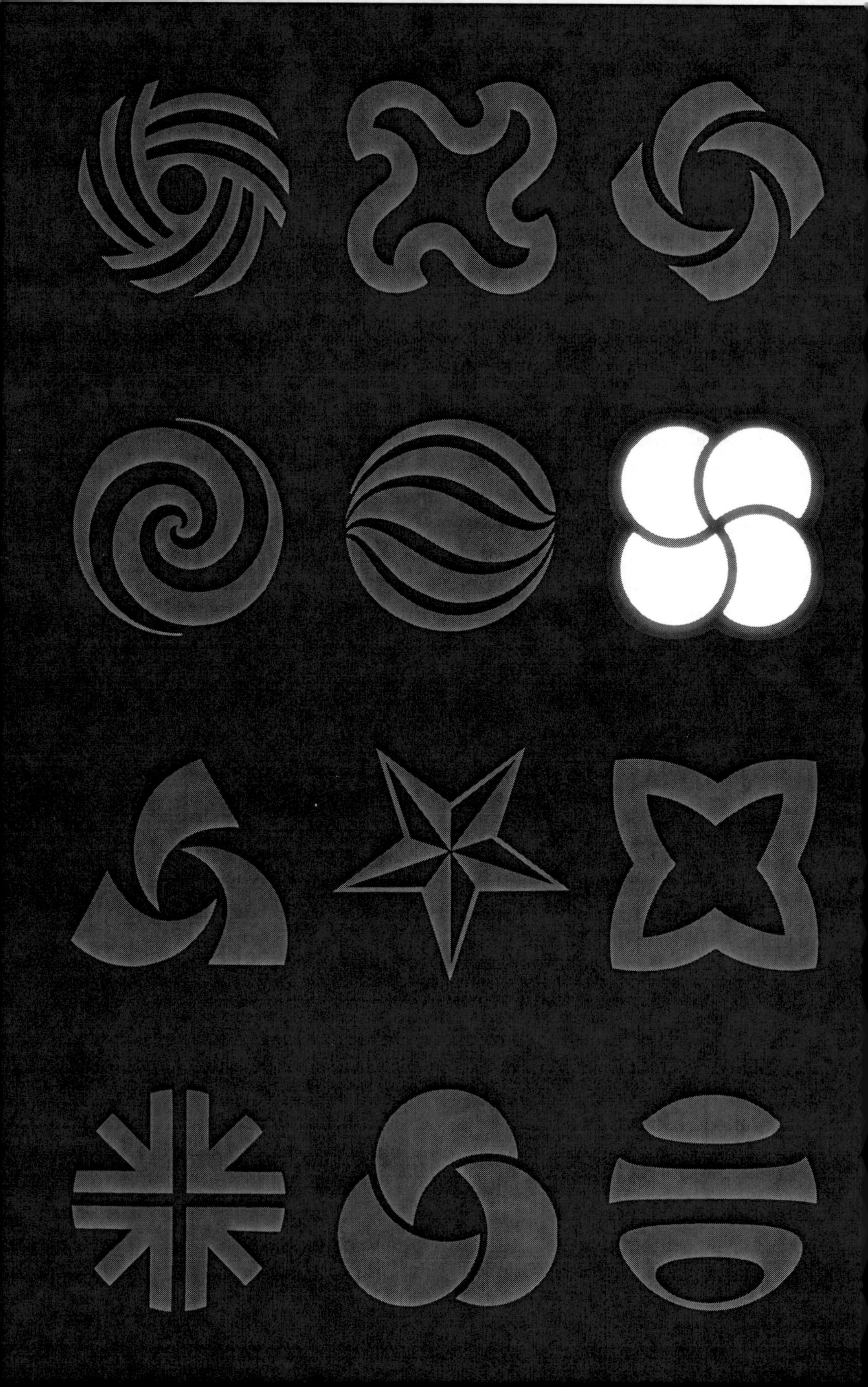

CONSIDERATIONS FOR CREATING 2-D DESIGN MARKS

VI Design Marks

"Graphic design is the paradise of individuality, eccentricity, heresy, abnormality, hobbies, and humors."

GEORGE SANTAYANA

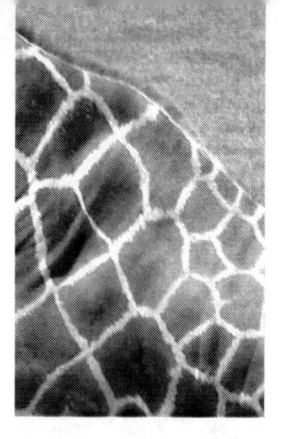

Selecting a design

rather than a word mark is sometimes more difficult since pictorial and graphic designs are harder to categorize and analyze than words. Still, many concepts applying to word marks also apply to designs. The following are some considerations for selecting two-dimensional design marks.

236 DESIGN GOALS

AS WITH THE WORD MARK, creating the *design mark* starts with inventorying the product's qualities. A good design captures the product's essence, or for a *house mark* captures the essence of the company and its product lines. What might be expressed in a word or phrase must be translated visually into a design. The design's visual movement, density, complexity, color(s), and other characteristics must metaphorically convey the message. A good design is like a commercial fingerprint, conveying a unique brand identity. Though you can describe what you want and even create images on paper or on a computer screen, only a professional designer should prepare the final image.

Occasionally a product is sold only with a design mark, but most products sold with a design also bear an identifying *word mark*. In such cases one goal is to ensure that the design reflects or complements the word(s). Though they say "a picture is worth a thousand words," this adage seldom applies to trademarks. Rather the word mark, existing in realms of sight, sound, and semantics, typically trumps the design, and the design is typically created around the word, not vice versa.

VI Design Marks

237 DESIGN FACTORS

There are many theories of and factors in two-dimensional design. A useful list of design factors is in Wucius Wong's PRINCIPLES OF TWO-DIMENSIONAL DESIGN. Among the factors he lists and illustrates are form, repetition, structure, similarity, gradation, radiation, anomaly, contrast, concentration, texture, and space. Once you see these factors illustrated with numerous examples, you will be able to meaningfully interact with your graphic designer. Acquainting yourself with graphic design essentials is particularly important when the *design mark* will be mostly or entirely abstract.

238 DESIGN SELECTION PROCESS

The selection process for designs is much the same as for words. An early step is often to view existing *design marks* for closely related products, which for store stocked goods means viewing products on store shelves. Then the usual course is to create and examine numerous candidates, select a few, apply them to packaging and other usage materials, and begin to tweak them until a short list emerges. The final candidates might then run the gauntlet of focus groups, trademark searches, trial use on sales and advertising materials, and test marketing. Though wordless designs are typically more expensive to search than words because of complexities in categorizing designs, compared to *word marks* such designs usually encounter fewer conflicts with other marks. And unlike the word mark which is often difficult to change once heavily advertised, designs are usually more susceptible to gradual change and evolution, frequently becoming simpler and more abstract.

239 ENERGY FLOW AND FENG SHUI

Selecting the right *design* is almost like practicing "energy work" or Feng Shui —on paper. After all, considerations like orientation *(¶ 244)*, directional movement *(¶ 245)*, density *(¶ 248)*, location *(¶ 250)*, size *(¶ 251)*, and gravity *(¶ 246)* are Feng Shui subject matter. This is also true when the mark is a three-dimensional construction like a kiosk, building element, car ornament, or even clothing attachment. Like individual alphabet letters which constrict and channel the flow of breath **(Solidity, ¶ 78 and Vowel Sounds, ¶ 170)**, two- and three-dimensional designs, at least metaphorically, express the flow or constriction of energy.

VI Design Marks

Even if one does not trust the accuracy or application of "energy work" or Feng Shui principles, applying them to selection may nurture sensitivity to the issues addressed by these disciplines.

240 VISUAL ACTIVITY

Consider a *design* having some visual ambiguity, perhaps suggesting two or more different images at the same time, even though one image may predominate. (A Necker cube is such a device.) Cf. U.S. Reg. No. 2,385,359 for a dark square standing on one of its corners with two musical notes carved out, U.S. Reg. No. 2,571,610 for a stylized infinity symbol, and U.S. Reg. No. 2,560,030 showing a highly abstract building design. Compare three renderings of the letter "T": the TOYOTA "T" at U.S. Reg. No. 1,797,716, also looking like a hat on a man's head; the Deutsche-Telekom/T-MOBILE "T" at U.S. Reg. No. 3,221,551, concurrently resembling a man's face; and the TRAVELERS "T" at U.S. Reg. No. 1,161,313, masquerading as an umbrella. This ambiguity keeps the mind and eye active and gives the mark visual "movement." Such activity is enhanced by the subtle interplay of foreground and background.

241 SYMMETRY

They say a symmetrical face may be more handsome or beautiful yet perhaps less interesting. The same is partially true of *designs*. Examples of symmetric designs are the CBS eye, U.S. Reg. No. 645,893; the Wool Bureau's wool content symbol, U.S. Reg. No. 790,140; the Purina checkerboard, U.S. Reg. No. 930,599; the BASS beer triangle, U.S. Reg. No. 1,926,947; and marks using the infinity symbol, the number 8, or the letter H. Although these marks may be more visually static, they can be more "timeless" and durable. *(See Timeless Designs, ¶ 273.)* I.e., they can be more iconic and symbolic. By flowing curves or bold contrasts the symmetrical mark may still retain visual activity, as per the wool content, checkerboard, number 8, and infinity symbol marks.

The most timeless and iconic are designs that are both horizontally and vertically symmetric, like those described previously. A mark symmetric in only one dimension is generally less powerful though sometimes more expressive. Compare the fully symmetric "H" design used by Hannah Creations, Inc. for jewelry (U.S. Reg. No. 2,782,146) to the vertically

VI Design Marks

symmetric HONDA "H" (U.S. Reg. No. 2,651,962), or the fully symmetric "8" in V-8 to the horizontally symmetric "3" in 3M. Or compare the Roman numerals II and V.

Symmetric designs, particularly fully symmetric, are better suited for *house marks* since they radiate an aura of stability via their balance and inertia. Also the fully symmetric design is generally more compatible with a conservative business image.

242 ANOMALY

With abstract *designs* in particular, anomaly often creates interest or excitement. Cf. the irregular-shaped box in U.S. Reg. No. 2,266,269 and the irregular circular design in U.S. Reg. No. 1,688,288. Pure symmetry or regularity can sometimes be static and dull. Even a slight anomaly may create feelings of movement, energy, ambiguity, or mystery. This is also true for stylized words and lettering; often the best typefaces have interesting but subtle irregularities. Anomaly frequently arises from a contrast between the "majority" portion of the design which gives stability and the "minority" which lends interest.

243 BALANCE

For any *design*, especially an abstract one, balance will usually be an important consideration. A balanced design may be more pleasing and harmonious and lend a sense of stability to the brand. Balance is achieved by setting off against each other the various "masses," forces, motions, colors, and other features of the design. And balance can manifest in different ways, e.g., static, asymmetric, and radial balance. The most basic balance is achieved through symmetry, i.e., "static" balance. As mentioned in the discussion of symmetry *(¶ 241)*, the symmetric design, particularly one symmetric both horizontally and vertically, may achieve balance with little or no movement. These symmetric designs, like the CBS eye (U.S. Reg. No. 887,916), the Purina checkerboard square (U.S. Reg. No. 787,875), and the Wool Bureau's wool content logo (U.S. Reg. No. 790,140), can become timeless, symbolic, and iconic emblems.

If static balance is like two equal size adults on opposite ends of a seesaw, "asymmetric" balance is like an adult at one end balanced by two children at the other; in other words, balance is achieved via unequal elements at

VI Design Marks

different positions in the design. Examples are the designs depicted in U.S. Reg. Nos. 2,381,564 and 2,526,447. Value, color, shape, texture, and line can be used to balance different sized elements. For instance, a large empty square can be balanced by a black or intensely colored small circle on the other side. Asymmetric balance within a simple design has the advantage of life and movement.

"Radial" balance arises from forces moving into or away from a central point and can be achieved centripetally, centrifugally, or concentrically, and even with spiraling. With centripetal radial balance, the forces or movement are propelled toward the central point. Examples are the old Metropolitan Life logo consisting of the inward facing shape constructed with four "M" letters (U.S. Reg. No. 1,855,918, cancelled, also statically balanced) and the diamond shaped logo in U.S. Reg. No. 2,738,105. With centrifugal radial balance, the forces or movement are directed away from the central point, as in U.S. Reg. Nos. 2,914,546 and 945,743 (expired). Concentric radial balance is achieved when the force or energy radiates in rings or spirals from the central point, as per the TARGET design (U.S. Reg. No. 2,778,472, also statically balanced) and the AMSTEL LIGHT beer logo (U.S. Reg. No. 1,461,239).

And the spiral balancing device is illustrated in U.S. Reg. Nos. 2,767,075 and 1,691,166.

244 ORIENTATION

The direction a mark faces may have a subtle or even profound effect. *(Cf. Gravity, ¶ 246.)* Right vs. left orientation should be considered whenever a choice arises. Clearly this phenomenon applies to *word marks* because they read left to right in most languages, but it also applies to designs since most designs used on labels, packaging, advertising, letterhead, and business cards appear on the left or center, encouraging the mark's rightward orientation or movement. Rightward and upward orientations are metaphorically positive, alive, and forward-looking; leftward and downward can be otherwise. ("Left" in Latin is "sinister"; in French it's "gauche.")

Notice with coinage designs that busts of dead figures (presidents or monarchs) tend to face left while those alive tend right. To be "positive" and forward looking, designs showing wheelchairs almost invariably face right, e.g., U.S. Reg. Nos. 2,322,919 and 1,714,499. Some designs are registered both ways, with the right-facing isotope usually being the more "friendly."

VI Design Marks

Cf. U.S. Reg. Nos. 2,352,951 and 2,352,943 for left- and right-facing moon crescents used for bakery goods and U.S. Reg. Nos. 2,617,369 and 2,630,709 for left- and right-facing equine designs for horse registry services.

245 MOVEMENT AND ROTATION

A mark's movement should be considered, including circular movement. For circular movement, clockwise is sometimes better because it metaphorically mimics the forward-looking sweep of clock hands, as per U.S. Reg. Nos. 2,524,075 and 941,316. However, with designs having a 3-D appearance, counterclockwise movement may align metaphorically with the earth's rotation, as per U.S. Reg. Nos. 2,564,873 and 2,027,054. Rotational movement may sometimes be used to draw the eye into the design's center. Even frontal movement may be achieved, e.g., approaching or receding. That effect can sometimes be created through color usage since some "warm" colors "approach" the viewer while "cooler" ones may "recede."

246 GRAVITY

A special aspect of directional movement is up-or-down "gravitational" appearance. A *design* heavily "weighted" at the bottom often appears drawn down by gravity, while those more weighted at the top may appear buoyant and upward-moving. An airline would probably not want an earthbound mark, nor a banking business embrace a very buoyant one. Compare the United Airlines logo (U.S. Reg. No. 1,598,941) with the Washington Mutual logo (U.S. Reg. No. 2,368,337). Also note the famous TRAVELERS insurance umbrella, U.S. Reg. No. 1,161,313, a top-weighted, buoyant design yet suited for insurance because the umbrella is a symbol of protection.

247 PERCEPTIBILITY

Select a *design* which stands out and immediately grabs the customer's attention, especially when your product sits next to others on a shelf. Also consider designs easily perceived even when materials on which they appear are not oriented right side up. (Symmetrical designs like those in U.S. Reg. Nos. 2,144,136 and 2,248,739 are logical choices if recognizability from various angles is important.) This factor is more important in markets where customer choices are often based on split-second decisions, perceptions, and recognitions. Where the new mark will join other marks

VI Design Marks

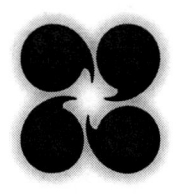

> "There. I guess King George will be able to read that!"
>
> JOHN HANCOCK ON BOLDLY SIGNING HIS NAME TO THE DECLARATION OF INDEPENDENCE IN 1776

on a product or packaging, consider how visible the new mark should be in relation to the others, e.g., in relation to size and location.

248 DENSITY; CONCENTRATION

A factor analogous to "gravity" *(¶ 246)* is density or concentration of graphic elements. Dense or concentrated *designs* have substantial areas of concentrated dark colors or black. A design may enjoy concentration towards a line or towards a point. Cf. the dense B of A design, U.S. Reg. No. 983,025, and the less concentrated banking logo in U.S. Reg. No. 2,600,861. For most applications, marks with substantial concentration are best, while wispy marks have fewer uses. For example, there are probably many more solid block-letter word designs than ones in outline typeface. With designs incorporating text, "kerning" (the spacing between characters) is important, especially between letters that might slope into each other, like W and A, W and M, and V and A. A dense font can have a different effect than one less concentrated. Cf. the denser GLAD (U.S. Reg. No. 1,987,137) and PRUDENTIAL (U.S. Reg. No. 978,340) versus their lighter, more expanded counterparts, GLAD (U.S. Reg. No. 1,981,233) and PRUDENTIAL (U.S. Reg. No. 1,580,456). Font condensation or expansion is often employed to match a design's other graphic elements.

249 ANGULAR VS. CURVED

Another *design* dichotomy is angular vs. curved. A very angular design is one for EXTREME ADRENALINE SPORTS (U.S. Reg. No. 3,017,593), whereas a curved, rounded design is exemplified in U.S. Reg. No. 3,216,067 depicting three curved lines mimicking a smiling face. A design with both energies is the VW logo (U.S. Reg. No. 804,869) comprised of the angular VW letters enclosed within a circle. Roundness may be associated with unfocused energy, relaxation, openness, and grace, while straight, angular lines and shapes may express focused energy, vigor, tension, directness, modernity, and structure. This dichotomy is reflected not only in figurative and abstract design but also typeface. For remarkable insights into angular and curved shapes, you might read Edwin Abbott's FLATLAND, a fantasy novelette about two-dimensional life.

250 LOCATION

Occasionally a mark's preferred or required placement on goods will dictate the *design's* content. For instance, on certain goods there may be only one logical place to put the mark, e.g., because of space or visibility constraints; therefore, some kinds of designs may be unsuitable for such placement. An example might be design marks to appear on book spines. Vertical designs may be more suitable than horizontal ones because thin spines may not effectively house a horizontal design. See, e.g., the Penguin Books penguin logo (U.S. Reg. No. 557,412), and the Simon & Schuster tree logo (U.S. Reg. No. 1,200,407), compact vertical designs suitable for book spines. Because most service marks appear to the left or center in business cards, letterhead, and printed advertisements, this factor affects the mark's content, e.g., its orientation *(¶ 244)*.

251 SIZE; SCALABILITY

Size not only relates to reproduction quality *(¶ 255)* but other factors as well. For example, if your mark will most frequently appear in large size (e.g., on business signs or sides of trucks), certain colors or shapes may be overwhelming or conversely less distinctive compared to their effects when the same mark is used on letterhead. Similarly, one must consider the mark's proportionate size in relation to the background materials on which it appears. The mark's optimal size may not mesh well with the size of the background materials. When the mark is so large that it appears more like an illustration than a symbol, it may be perceived as an "ornament" rather than a trademark. For instance, the complicated design with the words I WAS ABDUCTED BY ALIENS AND ALL I GOT WAS THIS LOUSY T-SHIRT—a fantastic idea—in U.S. Serial No. 75/205,749 (abandoned) could be perceived as an illustration or ornament unless carefully used.

252 3-D EFFECTS

Many two-dimensional *designs* have subtle or dramatic 3-D effects which make them stand out. Examples are the DELL logo (U.S. Reg. No. 1,860,272)

VI Design Marks

in which the "E" overlaps the two contiguous letters, creating a slight 3-D effect of letters in more than one plane; the DD design mark (U.S. Reg. No. 1,665,695) for computer equipment, showing the letters "DD" one over the other, generating a 3-D effect; and the EquiFirst banking services logo (U.S. Reg. No. 3,022,077) which creates the impression of a 3-D box. 3-D effects can be achieved not only by overlapping but also by intimations of perspective, addition of shadow, use of texture, and variations in color and grayscale values. Even holograms *(¶ 300)* are possibilities.

253 4-D EFFECTS

Beyond 3-D effects *(¶ 252)* are those from the fourth dimension, time. When it hints at movement or change occurring over time, a *design mark* reflects time, or rather a space-time effect. Examples are the marks subject to U.S. Reg. Nos. 2,573,116 (depicting background and foreground human figures the relationship between which creates a sense of motion); 2,681,747 (depicting a triangular measuring square in motion); and 1,738,756 (showing the letters W and I and their reflections, suggesting movement). Though this kind of active design is not yet common and contrasts starkly with most frozen images, it may be a wave of the future. Even when the design itself does not immediately reflect change, "morphing" marks programmed to change, like changing electronic signs, may become popular. (*Cf. "Moving" Marks, ¶ 301.*)

254 TEXTURE

Even with two-dimensional *designs*, or designs appearing on almost flat services, visual and tactile texture may be significant. Visual texture may appear in the form of glossy versus matte or fuzzy versus straight-edged. Tactile factors such as smooth versus rough are discussed later in this Guide *(Tactile Marks, ¶ 304)*. Somewhere in between the visual and the tactile are marks that feature embossing through which numerous effects can be achieved by adjusting the height and edge of the elevated surface. Examples of textured designs are U.S. Reg. No. 1,413,427 for a repeating raised pattern on a fabric surface and U.S. Reg. No. 947,706 for an edge design consisting of serrations and indentations.

To gain trademark rights, avoid selecting textural elements which are merely functional since functional design elements are often unprotectable. For

VI Design Marks

instance, if a raised textured surface is merely the button on a device, it may not be perceived nor protected as a trademark.

255 REPRODUCTION QUALITY

Select a *design* which reproduces well in all sizes. A mark with numerous words, very thin lines or a number of detailed or complex features may not reproduce well in small size. How well would the numerous words and design features of U.S. Reg. Nos. 2,098,781 and 2,417,211 reproduce in small size, e.g., on business cards or letterhead? Remember, your mark may have to suit various-sized packaging and labeling materials, including stickers and tags, and maybe stationery and business cards. Perhaps your mark may even appear on billboards or on cars and trucks. A graphic artist's rule is that a mark should be clearly distinguishable when reduced into a half-inch square and not so overpowering that it is not readily distinguishable when enlarged into a six-foot square.

256 BLACK-AND-WHITE USAGE

Sometimes one chooses between color and black-and-white, or uses two versions of the mark, one color, the other black-and-white. See, e.g., U.S. Reg. Nos. 1,297,161 and 1,835,705 for the black-and-white and colored versions of THE HOME DEPOT logo; U.S. Reg. Nos. 1,023,923 and 1,094,740 for the black-and-white and colored versions of the U-HAUL logo. Even if color is chosen, often the mark should also be suitable for black-and-white use in case color reproduction on certain materials is not feasible. This often means avoiding certain colors. *(See Black-And-White Reproduction, ¶ 257.)*

257 BLACK-AND-WHITE REPRODUCTION

In selecting a colored mark, particularly one designed on computer, don't forget that once the mark is printed on paper, paper copies may be photocopied in black and white, e.g., by fax or copy machine. Unless there are significant differences in grayscale values between various colored elements, the black-and-white photocopy may not properly show the mark. For instance, if your design has red lettering on a black background, or vice versa, the black-and-white copy may show all black since some reds appear as black on black-and-white photocopies. E.g., how will the red-

VI Design Marks

and-black designs in U.S. Reg. Nos. 2,616,736 and 2,614,008 appear when photocopied in black and white? Moreover, some colors (e.g., certain yellows and light blues) will not even copy in black and white. If black-and-white reproduction is a concern, then you should try photocopying a color design before selecting it.

258 GRAYSCALE VALUES, STIPPLING, AND SHADING

Because visual perception of *designs* ultimately depends on grayscale values, even for colored marks one must consider the effects of shading, stippling, and other techniques employed to show contrast less than black against white. For marks used in large size, these techniques may be valuable and achieve special effects, e.g., on label designs and packaging. But such techniques are often unsuited for small size logo designs. When the logo appears in small size, e.g., on business cards, the lesser contrast often weakens the logo's recognizability, form and content. Especially when creating figurative images, inexperienced logo designers may try too hard to intricately depict the subject matter, e.g., by using special shading or stippling. In doing so they may forget to create an eye-catching, more abstract logo. The goal, after all, is usually a symbol, not an illustration.

Another faux pas is logos featuring adjacent colors with little difference in grayscale values, so the design may not reproduce well in black and white and even create visual anomalies when perceived in color. Adjacent colors with the same grayscale values may look virtually the same when reproduced in black and white. And because the underlying basis of vision is black and white via the eyes' rods, two adjacent colors with the same grayscale values may create visual discomfort.

A related consideration is the degree to which grayscale values of various elements must be different in order to achieve adequate contrast. For instance, even a 25% difference in grayscale values between adjacent elements may produce insufficient contrast, especially if the design appears in small size or the elements have little surface area.

259 MEDIA OF USE

Consider the physical materials on which the *design* will appear. A mark suitable for labels or business cards may not be good for embossing on

VI Design Marks

goods; a clothing mark suitable for hang tags might not reproduce well on clothing nor on sewn-in labels. Moreover, a design mark effective on computer screen may be dismal on paper, and vice versa. For Internet services and computer software, one consideration might be adapting the mark into a screen icon. As with *word marks* which should be tried in different fonts and on various materials, prospective designs also need trial spins, especially in electronic formats.

260 ELECTRONIC DESIGNS

If your *design* will be mostly or only used electronically (e.g., online), then you might consider the contrasts with non-electronic designs. Online designs can be more complex and colorful, and even boast more colors, especially since the practical and cost constraints of color printing do not apply. Is this why the eBAY letters (U.S. Reg. No. 2,410,023) and MSN butterfly (U.S. Reg. No. 2,795,999) online designs were created, each with seven colors? Cf. the MSNBC online and TV logo incorporating the NBC peacock image and flaunting six colors (U.S. Reg. No. 2,193,387). Even colors or color combinations unsuitable for print media might succeed online. Moreover, black-and-white reproduction considerations *(¶257)* may be less important.

Electronic designs need not be as scalable as other designs because online size differences are typically smaller than those between business cards and business signs, though you must consider sizing in relation to handheld devices. Also online designs can utilize special effects like texturing, gradients, and shadowing which, aesthetically and financially, may be impractical on paper. However, you must exercise care in

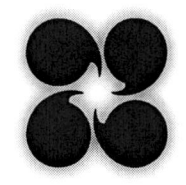

Colors can have profound emotional, visual, aesthetic and even biological effects; and one must consider the various spectra of color responses, e.g., masculine/ feminine, stimulating/ calming, conservative/ radical, and spiritual/ worldly.

183

the technical aspects of electronic graphics. For instance, colors selected should be "Web-safe" so they will appear consistent regardless of browser, hardware, or operating system employed.

261 CHANGEABLE DESIGNS

Adaptability may be important. Sometimes logo *designs* must be modified to conform to changing fashions, trends, and markets. Though some logos like the General Electric "monogram" (U.S. Reg. No. 2,752,236) and the CBS "eye" (U.S. Reg. No. 887,916) may be relatively "timeless" and subject to minimal change, most designs should be mutable. Figurative designs depicting humans and animals are easily adapted. Witness the various versions of the U.S. Postal Service's eagle designs (U.S. Reg. Nos. 1,917,921 and 2,494,399), the KFC image of Col. Sanders (U.S. Reg. No. 806,104 and Ser. No. 78/909,943), the MICHELIN man (U.S. Reg. Nos. 888,288 and 3,183,905), and the DUTCH BOY character (U.S. Reg. Nos. 383,644 and 1,161,535). Other realistic images are similarly changeable to reflect new styles and markets. Also, designs incorporating well-known symbols, lettering and other notation can generally be changed without dramatic effects on public recognition. E.g., the HONDA "H" (U.S. Reg. Nos. 800,926 and 2,272,458) and the KELLOGG'S "K" (U.S. Reg. Nos. 1,259,406 and 1,278,007) could be considerably altered without great loss of recognition. Note the evolution of the OAKLEY "O" (U.S. Reg. Nos. 1,904,181, 2,301,660, and 3,151,994).

But highly abstract designs are often more difficult to adapt without lost recognition. After all, unlike the figurative design which has a relatively unchanged meaning when modified—an eagle is still an eagle even if redrawn—the highly abstract design's meaning is purely metaphoric or metonymic and may be lost once the design is substantially changed. Even the timeless abstract logo, if greatly changed, must be relearned and reassociated.

262 PRODUCT/DESIGN CONGRUENCE

A *design* should generally mesh with the product, e.g., a staid design mark is usually not best for a cutting-edge product, and vice versa. For instance, Ford Motor Co. uses on cars a conservative blue elliptical design which represents the solidity and history of the company but is not necessarily the best mark for more jazzy car models. See U.S. Reg. No. 1,399,080. On the other hand, the newer Chrysler "wings" design is both futuristic and atavistic and thus adaptable to both conservative minivans and sporty sedans. See U.S. Reg. No. 2,357,408. This congruence is analogous to metaphoric consistency between *word mark* and product.

263 FORM OF EXPRESSION

The *design's* form of expression should reflect or complement the company's image and products. Expression can range from abstract and symbolic to romantic and expressive. "Symbolic" expression is characterized by qualities such as dense, heavy, monotone, architectural, abstract, iconic, and simple. Opposite from symbolic is the "romantic" form represented by expressive, musical, poetic, emotive, subjective, personal, complex, and colorful designs. Midway in the spectrum is "classical" expression epitomized by qualities such as figurative, sculptural, objective, integrated, and balanced.

The symbolic design is manifested in typefaces such as Helvetica, Bauhaus, and various sans serif boldface fonts such as Arial Black. This kind of design may be appropriate for house marks and marks for technical products such as electronic and computer equipment. Witness U.S. Reg. Nos. 1,860,272 (DELL logo) and 1,252,912 (cancelled) (the old MICROSOFT logo), U.S. Reg. No. 1,542,937 (AT&T logo).

The classical design is reflected in balanced serif fonts like Times Roman, Palatino, and Bookman Old Style and may be suited for reputable products requiring substantial client contacts, e.g., insurance and financial services. See, e.g., U.S. Reg. Nos. 1,580,456 (PRUDENTIAL logo) and 1,635,681 (TRANSAMERICA logo).

The romantic design is characterized by typefaces such as Script, Vivaldi, and Amaze Italic and may be recommended for personal care products such as beauty supplies, jewelry, and clothing. E.g., note U.S. Reg. Nos. 410,701 (CARTIER logo) and 393,492 (expired) (old MAYBELLINE logo).

264 SIMPLER DESIGNS

Simpler *designs* are generally better than complicated ones because of easier reproduction and recognition in all sizes. For instance, complicated designs, especially when irregular and asymmetric, may not be easily recognizable in small size. Compare the simpler design in U.S. Reg. No. 982,182 (SAMSONITE logo) to the slightly more complicated one in U.S. Reg. No. 1,654,205. To be easily recognizable, complicated abstract designs

VI Design Marks

often should have some symmetric qualities. Triumphs of simplicity are the NIKE "swoosh" logo (U.S. Reg. No. 1,145,473) and the TARGET "target" design (U.S. Reg. No. 972,082). Simpler designs have a better chance of becoming strong iconic symbols.

265 GEOMETRIC DESIGNS

Ordinary circles, ellipses, rectangles, diamonds, squares, triangles, and other simple geometric shapes are not usually protectable without *secondary meaning* because they are often not distinctive. However, such geometric shapes coupled with other elements (e.g., pictorial, graphic or alphabetic) can usually be made distinctive. For example, a word, letter, or figure (human or animal) within a triangle or ellipse might be protectable. See, e.g., U.S. Reg. No. 2,413,735 for the letter "E" within a triangle, and U.S. Reg. No. 2,144,407 for a chevron-type design within an ellipse. Note the famous red triangle associated with BASS beer, shown in U.S. Reg. No. 1,926,947. Of course, the added material, not the geometric shape, is typically the more distinctive component.

266 PICTORIAL DESIGNS

At the other extreme from geometric *designs* are pictorial ones which depict real objects or beings, such as the ARM & HAMMER design showing an arm and hammer (U.S. Reg. No. 1,970,953), the TACO BELL design depicting a bell (U.S. Reg. No. 2,105,501), and the U.S. Postal Service's eagle (U.S. Reg. No. 2,494,399). These kinds of designs, especially if highly stylized, will usually be protectable. The more "pictorial" the mark, the more it can be analogized to a *descriptive, suggestive,* or *arbitrary word mark*, in contrast to an abstract or geometric design analogous to a *fanciful* word mark. For instance, a pictorial mark may have the advantage of being readily recognizable and more easily related to the product, but it can face legal problems relating to descriptiveness and confusion in relation to other marks, even word marks. Thus, the design of an orange could be confused with the word ORANGE, and for selling oranges such design would probably be weak or unprotectable. *(See Descriptive Designs, ¶ 267.)*

267 DESCRIPTIVE DESIGNS

If your *design* is *descriptive*, it may be weak or even unprotectable. For instance, when selling bicycles, the design of an ordinary looking bicycle

VI Design Marks

might not be easily protectable; a cow's picture usually indicates dairy products. Sometimes, however, even where the mark depicts products, it might enjoy protection if the depiction is unusual or highly stylized. See, e.g., the stylized bicycle in U.S. Reg. No. 2,145,378 for bicycle sales and service. But compare U.S. Reg. No. 2,524,859 depicting a relatively less stylized lamp for retail and online lamp services. As with *word marks*, never forget that your mark is supposed to be a symbol, not a sign. Analogously, the mark is not an ordinary road sign with an arrow pointing to the destination; rather, it's more like an emblem symbolizing the destination.

A stalwart of trademark folklore is the signature. Well known are those of JOHN HANCOCK for insurance, THOMAS A. EDISON for electrical equipment, and MARY BAKER EDDY for religious materials.

268 QUASI-FUNCTIONAL DESIGNS

Because of the breadth of trademark subject matter, even the goods can be shaped in a protectible fashion, usually so long as the shaping is non-functional. For instance, U.S. Reg. No. 2,339,374 was granted for a "paisley-like shape for the sound hole of a guitar." Cf. U.S. Reg. No. 2,237,052 for a boomerang-like shaped cut-out on the body of a saw blade and U.S. Reg. No. 2,080,375 for an oval-shaped cut-out on a bicycle saddle's underside.

The task is to determine what holes, appendages, and other topological aspects of your product can be distinctively and non-functionally shaped in order to achieve trademark status. Then the challenge is to make the public aware that the distinctive shaping is a designation of origin, not just an ornamental feature.

269 COPYRIGHTABILITY

Sometimes one should consider the *design's* copyrightability. Though individual words and short phrases are not generally copyrightable (at least in the U.S.A.), copyright protection exists for pictorial and graphic images

VI Design Marks

which embody a certain minimum creativity. Thus, the more artistic and elaborate the design, the more likely it may enjoy copyright protection, whereas simple geometric shapes may not be copyrightable.

Copyrightability may be a factor when the mark is also used collaterally as an ornament or illustration for promotional items like T-shirts, mugs, magnets, and other products on which the design appears but not in a trademark sense. Having copyright protection when trademark rights are weak may offer an advantage in protecting the design. Examples of designs which may be copyrightable are the BUDWEISER bottle label in U.S. Reg. No. 2,163,450, the QUAKER oats logo in U.S. Reg. No. 1,803,603, and numerous pictorial logos appearing on alcoholic beverage packaging and containers.

270 DESIGN SUBJECT MATTER

If stumped for subject matter, the USPTO website at **www.uspto.gov** shows a listing of design subjects under the link to Design Search Code. The Table of Categories, each of which includes numerous sub-categories, reads:

- 01 Celestial bodies, natural phenomena, geographical maps
- 02 Human beings
- 03 Animals
- 04 Supernatural beings, mythological and legendary beings, fantastical beings, and unidentifiable beings
- 05 Plants
- 06 Scenery
- 07 Dwellings, buildings, monuments, stadiums, fountains, structural works, and building materials
- 08 Foodstuffs
- 09 Textiles, clothing, headwear, footwear, and sewing accessories
- 10 Tobacco, smokers' materials; fans; toilet articles; medical devices and apparatus including tablets, capsules or powders
- 11 Household utensils
- 12 Furniture and sanitary fixtures
- 13 Lighting, cooking, heating, cooling, and refrigeration equipment
- 14 Hardware, tools and ladders; nonmotorized agricultural implements; keys and locks
- 15 Machines and parts thereof, including industrial agricultural, home and office machines; electrical equipment

VI Design Marks

16 Telecommunications, sound recording and reproduction equipment; photography, cinematography, and optics
17 Horological instruments and parts, jewelry, weights and measures
18 Transport, equipment for animals, traffic signs
19 Baggage, containers, and bottles
20 Writing, drawing or painting materials, office materials, stationery, and books
21 Games, toys, and sporting articles
22 Musical instruments and their accessories, bells, sculptures
23 Arms, ammunition, and armor
24 Heraldry, flags, crowns, crosses, arrows, and symbols
25 Ornamental framework, surfaces or backgrounds with ornaments
26 Geometric figures and solids
27 Forms of writing
28 Inscriptions in various characters
29 Miscellaneous

271 CHARACTER IMAGES

Pictorial *design marks* may also consist of character images, e.g., the images of Colonel Sanders for KFC products (U.S. Reg. No. 806,104), Green Giant for canned vegetables (U.S. Reg. No. 1,445,475), Elsie the Cow for dairy products (U.S. Reg. No. 647,962), and Charlie the Tuna for canned tuna (U.S. Reg. No. 1,260,124). Character images are particularly effective when associated with slogans and well-known characters, including animated characters. However, preparing a successful character design also usually entails developing the character's personality and even voice for use in various media.

If the character is a real person, like Colonel Sanders, then you probably need an attorney-drafted consent to use the image, even for recently deceased persons.

272 CLASSIC SYMBOLS

Classic symbols like the Yin/Yang circle (U.S. Reg. No. 2,130,983), the Sanskrit lettering for OM (U.S. Reg. No. 2,621,742), and the mathematical symbol for infinity (U.S. Reg. No. 1,954,583) can occasionally become protectable marks if *secondary meaning* is achieved or the symbol is

VI Design Marks

enhanced by stylization or added material. Nonetheless, it is difficult to imagine how secondary meaning can be achieved in the USA (or exclusive protection secured in any Western or Christian country) for Christian symbols like the Cross; after all, they might not be perceived as indications of source but rather as tokens of the producer's religious beliefs. Though designs which include stylized depictions of the Cross have been registered (e.g., U.S. Reg. No. 2,200,332), often the registrant specifically disclaims exclusive rights in that symbol.

The classic symbol is most effective when *arbitrary* or at least only *suggestive* of the products. A good source of these symbols is the DICTIONARY OF SYMBOLS by Carl Liungman which presents 54 categories of symbols. Analogously, heraldry is a fertile source of ideas since coats of arms were family insignias designed to last for generations. For example, with automobile marks note the ALFA ROMEO logo (U.S. Reg. No. 228,220) inspired by the coat of arms of the powerful Milanese Visconti family; the PORSCHE logo (U.S. Reg. No. 618,932) in part taken from a Stuttgart dynasty's coat of arms; and the FERRARI logo (U.S. Reg. No. 862,632) utilizing the family crest.

273 TIMELESS DESIGNS

Rather than create a *design* which can be changed with changing times *(See Changeable Designs, ¶ 261)*, one might seek a timeless icon which can weather social and aesthetic change. Surprisingly, design books for decades past, displaying well-known corporate logos, show that relatively few companies have achieved timeless designs. Examples might be the GE "monogram" (U.S. Reg. No. 2,752,236), the CBS "eye" logo (U.S. Reg. No. 887,916), the PURINA "checkerboard" logo (U.S. Reg. No. 787,875), and the Wool Bureau's "wool content" symbol (U.S. Reg. No. 790,140).

Timelessness is achieved in a few ways. Timeless logos tend be to fairly integrated and simple, without extraneous features that might become outdated. The CBS "eye" design and the Wool Bureau symbol are such marks. Or they may incorporate "classic" images locked into historical consciousness, again the CBS eye. (Even the PURINA logo is reminiscent of heraldry.) They may have an element of universality insofar as they reflect a common cultural history or incorporate themes, styles, or images familiar to people around the world. Or they encapsulate an "old-time" or atavistic image that the company wishes to convey to the world. Cf.

VI Design Marks

the PABST "Blue Ribbon" design (U.S. Reg. No. 542,096) and the classic COCA-COLA design (U.S. Reg. No. 1,432,152).

274 EVERYDAY SYMBOLS

Publicly viewed everyday symbols, if not trademarked or copyrighted by others, or not specifically excluded from protection *(See Flags And Insignias, ¶ 326)*, are possible subject matter, especially when adapted. Sources of inspiration are road, parking, safety, and prohibitory signage; rail, air, and other transportation symbols and signage; and clothing care and automobile dashboard symbols. See, e.g., U.S. Reg. No. 1,678,597 depicting a "Slippery When Wet" road sign and U.S. Reg. No. 1,748,360 for a mark consisting in part of marine signal flags.

Be careful to avoid *descriptive* use; *suggestive* or *arbitrary* use is best. For instance, a mark incorporating an image of the Route 66 road sign may not be strong if used for a business with outlets only on that highway; after all, how can the owner persuasively argue that other businesses on Route 66 can't use that sign in their advertising?

Nature is a vast reservoir of shapes adaptable for design marks. Examples are sea shells, clovers, maple leaves, palm trees, lotus petals, and animal footprints.

275 COLORS IN DESIGNS

Now that color, even by itself, can sometimes be protected as a trademark *(See Color Marks, ¶ 307)*, it is often an important element of a protectable *design*. Usually colors in an abstract design should be few and easily recognizable. For instance, a mark with ten colors is not likely to be very useful, reproducible, or recognizable. U.S. Reg. No. 2,465,306 shows a six-color mark which stretches the outer limits of color variety. Cf. U.S. Reg. No. 2,629,751. Unusual colors are not ordinarily recommended. Generally the choices are primary colors and basic combinations thereof, such as red, blue, yellow, green, and orange. If the customer can't immediately perceive and name the color in your mark, then you probably haven't chosen well.

VI Design Marks

On occasion the exact color is specified using Pantone standards, as per the BEST WESTERN logo in U.S. Reg. No. 2,105,546 and the toothpaste container in U.S. Reg. No. 2,503,242.

In selecting a color mark, remember that it may have to be adaptable for embossing and black-and-white reproduction. Consult reference materials on color usage and effects of various colors on consumer perceptions and choices. Colors can have profound emotional, visual, aesthetic, and even biological effects; and one must consider the various spectra of color responses, e.g., masculine/feminine, stimulating/calming, conservative/radical, and spiritual/worldly. Also, don't neglect the social, political, and cultural associations of colors or color combinations. For instance, certain color combinations may mimic flags of countries either associated with or antagonistic to the products.

Color combining in multicolor marks is tricky since a color's appearance and effects may be different when seen alone or in combination with other colors. Even though adjacent colors may appear to contrast with each other, because perception of colored elements depends on the colors' underlying grayscale values, when these values are roughly equivalent, that equivalency can set up a vibration that makes the two or more colored elements harder to perceive. For example, even red letters on a green background may be hard to read where the particular red and green have the same grayscale value. Thus, it is important to differentiate the colors in relation to both hue and grayscale value so the mark converts well to grayscale and is clearly visible to people having color vision disabilities.

276 APPROPRIATE DESIGNS

As with words, not every *design* is appropriate in every country or culture. For example, accidental use of religious symbols from other cultures must be avoided. A symbol with positive connotations in one culture may be negative in another, a consideration for marks used internationally; e.g., a swastika might be favorably regarded in parts of India where it is an ancient symbol but unfavorably almost everywhere else. Compare the somewhat more benign left-facing Buddhist swastika in U.S. Reg. No. 2,538,512 with the right-facing Nazi swastika. A pentagram might have satanic connotations to some, but there is nothing evil about the Texaco star-in-a-circle design, U.S. Reg. No. 150,620 nor the CONVERSE five-pointed star design, U.S. Reg. No. 741,662. To see whether your design has

VI Design Marks

symbolic meaning, including negative connotations, consult works like the DICTIONARY OF SYMBOLS *(¶ 272).*

277 STYLIZED WORDS

Whenever a word or phrase appears in stylized letters, the stylized form may become distinctive and independently protectable. Most famous *word marks* also exist in stylized versions, and often the ordinary word mark and the stylized version are both registered. Usually, the word mark registration will be more valuable than that for the stylized version. Naturally, the typeface or particular stylization should be consistent with or amplify the themes associated with the word(s) alone. *(See Font/Typeface, ¶ 61.)*

A good example of stylization is the SUPERMAN mark originally registered by D.C. Comics both as a word mark and in large stylized block letters. See U.S. Reg. Nos. 1,216,976 and 371,803. Another famous example is the dual registration for the IBM *design marks.* See U.S. Reg. Nos. 640,606 and 1,205,090. Often registration is not available for the word either because it is *descriptive* or registered by others, so only the stylized version can be claimed, e.g., the original U.S. registration depicting the stylized PEOPLE for magazines (U.S. Reg. No. 1,137,391).

In stylizing words, remember all the ordinary and special effects available, e.g., italics, reverse italics, different styles of block and outline lettering, shadows, and halos. Many stylizing special effects can be analogized to kinds of word play, e.g., anagrams and palindromes. For instance, comparable to palindromes a few designs are actually ambigraphs, i.e., stylized words which spell the same thing when turned upside down. Cf. U.S. Reg. No. 2,334,391 for ASTROPOWER (shown right side up over upside-down reflection); U.S. Reg. No. 2,205,939 for PP (one "P" on its foot next to the other on its head); and U.S. Reg. No. 1,255,898 for EXTEK (right side up over upside-down reflection).

278 SIGNATURES

A stalwart of trademark folklore is the signature, perhaps one of the original trademarks. Well known are those of JOHN HANCOCK for insurance (U.S. Reg. No 557,033), THOMAS A. EDISON for electrical equipment (U.S. Reg. No. 2,443,841), MARY BAKER EDDY for religious materials (U.S. Reg. No. 403,487), and D. GHIRARDELLI for chocolate (U.S. Reg. No. 426,706).

VI Design Marks

Sometimes the signature will be that of an historical figure or other person not associated with the company (like John Hancock), but if using the signature of a living or recently deceased person, beware publicity and privacy rights laws which prohibit non-consensual use.

Signature marks are usually best when the signer or signature is already famous or when the signer is the products' originator. A real rather than contrived signature may be preferable since it reflects the signer's personality and creates a direct personal connection between the consumer and the signer. If the real signature is illegible or unstylishly irregular, frequently it can be redesigned by a top notch artist and still reflect the signer's unique personality. Even a very legible signature can be refined and tweaked. Cf. the Edison signature mentioned at the beginning of this section and the KELLOGG'S surname signature, U.S. Reg. No. 147,454.

279 HAND-DRAWN MARKS

Almost all *designs* are professionally created using graphics software or at least drawing tools designed to provide "clean-edged" results. But some are actually hand drawn or appear to be so. The hand drawn signature *(¶ 278)* is the classic example, but so are logos like that for Lucent Technologies (U.S. Reg. No. 2,388,016); the one depicted in U.S. Reg. No. 2,431,472, a hand sketch of a tree with a "pencil" trunk; and the crayon lines in U.S. Reg. No. 2,460,550. Unlike many designs which can be replicated on a computer, computer replication of the hand-drawn design is only achieved by having a graphics file for the design or scanning the design to create such a file. The better hand-drawn mark will usually be bold and structured in contrast to wispy and disjointed. However, even some good hand-drawn designs may not be suitable for electronic use.

280 MONOGRAMS

Some of the most famous *designs* are monogram marks comprising companies' stylized initials, often incorporated in a circle or other geometric shape, e.g., the USS design for U.S. Steel (U.S. Reg. No. 1,234,035), the GE design for General Electric (U.S. Reg. No. 1,181,959), and the 3M monogram for Minnesota Mining and Manufacturing Company (U.S. Reg. No. 561,629). Sometimes you can protect a design incorporating company initials if highly stylized and unusual even when others have used or registered the initials as *word marks*. But only your attorney can opine on that issue.

VI Design Marks

281 DESIGNS WITH WORDS

Many image *designs* incorporate words, either stylized or in ordinary typeface. In fact, a design may incorporate multiple devices in a single mark, e.g., an overall geometric or figurative shape, a descriptive tag line, and perhaps even an acronym or other short *word mark*. See, e.g., the MASSENGILL design mark, (U.S. Registration No. 2,461,532) where the mark is described as:

> "...the word "MASSENGILL" depicted in a stylized manner, specifically, the letter 'M' is shown with a flower design appearing between the two peaks of the letter, within a ribbon design; under the ribbon design appears a panel showing a bathroom scene, featuring a bathtub with towel draped thereover and folded towels and washcloths and soaps in the background; to the right of the panel appear the words "EVERYDAY FRESH" and a Seal Design with the same stylized "M" featured in the ribbon design described above."

Cf. DUNKIN' DONUTS and design (U.S. Reg. No. 907,303) and PRUDENTIAL and design (U.S. Reg. No. 1,580,456).

When all elements are contained within the geometric or other shape, then the combination of elements may be protectable as one design mark. However, sometimes words, phrases, or alphanumeric characters appear outside the shape, so the issue arises whether a single composite mark appears or whether two or more marks are being used in relative proximity. One test is the commercial impression given to the ordinary consumer. Does the consumer perceive a single distinguishing device or two or more devices which happen to appear together? When devising such a composite mark, consult your attorney to ensure that its use will yield legal protection for the entire mark.

282 SINGLE LETTERS

A widely used device is the single letter *design*, usually representing the first letter of the company name or house mark, e.g., the stylized "N" on NEW BALANCE shoes (U.S. Reg. No. 1,344,589) and the "P" for PRINCE tennis racquets (U.S. Reg. No. 1,175,337). Cf. "E!" for entertainment industry television services (U.S. Reg. No. 2,545,008) and for clothing (U.S.

VI Design Marks

Reg. No. 2,387,961), "K" in a circle for convenience retail stores (U.S. Reg. No. 2,150,616), "H" in a rounded square for HONDA cars (U.S. Reg. No. 2,272,458), and "L" in a circle for LEXUS cars (U.S. Reg. No. 1,619,755).

Like a nickname, the letter can be an easy reminder of the full mark or trade name. Often the letter appears at an angle or always in the same color(s). Some letters are more distinctive and suitable for this use, e.g., E, K, N, S, and K compared to L and O. The single-letter design may not be viable when a competitor already uses such a mark, though exceptions persist, e.g., the "H" designs used on HONDA (U.S. Reg. No. 2,272,458) and HYUNDAI (U.S. Reg. No. 1,569,538) cars.

283 PACKAGE SURFACE DESIGNS

A *design* or pattern uniformly covering packaging surfaces can sometimes be a protectable mark, e.g., a design comprised of polka dots or stripes. For instance, designs on canned goods, such as soup can designs, are often protectable if uniformly applied. See U.S. Reg. No. 1,544,679 for a CAMPBELL's design. Cf. U.S. Reg. No. 1,531,069 for the design of TOOTSIE ROLL packaging.

For packaged goods standing alongside competitors' products on supermarket shelves or department store aisles, the packaging design should not only be distinctive in itself but also in relation to competitors' packaging. Color is an important factor in packaging. E.g., with food packaging one might select red which stimulates the appetite but avoid blue which suppresses it; though blue may be good for detergent packaging, brown usually isn't.

284 PATTERNS

If distinctive and non-functional, sometimes patterns may be protected marks, e.g., not only packaging *designs (Package Surface Designs, ¶ 283)* but also patterns one might see on a strung tennis racket or travel luggage. See, e.g., the checkered pattern for LOUIS VUITTON luggage, U.S. Reg. No. 2,421,618. Cf. the colored pattern on a fabric wrapped around cord and cable in U.S. Reg. No. 543,697. What about sneaker sole designs which, though largely functional, are often highly artistic and distinctive? See U.S. Reg. No. 1,588,960 for the CONVERSE sole design. The challenge is to devise a pattern so distinctive that potential customers will immediately perceive its trademark function. If consumers don't see the pattern as a designation of origin, then *"look for" advertising* may be used to educate them as to the pattern's trademark function.

285 WORD ART

Occasionally individual letters or words, or even myriads of words, can be arranged to form pictorial images. Hypothetically an example might be the shape of a rabbit comprised of scores of the word RABBIT. For other instances of shapes and patterns arising from repeated words, see, e.g., U.S. Reg. No. 1,482,342 covering a mark described as a "sinusoidal curve having a repeating pattern of the word 'permclip' in various shapes"; U.S. Reg. No. 1,340,720 for the word DIOR in a repeating pattern; and U.S. Reg. No. 2,386,386 for the letter "B" and the word FRITES appearing together repeatedly at various irregular angles to each other. Sometimes a *word mark,* repeated scores or hundreds of times, occupies the entire cover of an advertising leaflet or the whole surface of packaging material.

In the hands of a good calligrapher, letters, particularly Arabic, can be shaped to form pictorial images. A challenge is to create an abstract or figurative design which contains all the letters of a word mark. Examples of "letter art" are U.S. Reg. Nos. 2,737,383 (the letters GG shaped to form a butterfly); 3,081,473 (the letters IB shaped into a butterfly); 3,153,559 (the letters CD shaped into a heart), and 2,494,019 (the FEDEX logo showing an arrow between the second E and the X). Sometimes, instead of horizontal arrangement, letters of a stylized word may appear vertically, diagonally, or in other directions.

286 NATURAL SHAPES

Nature is a vast reservoir of shapes adaptable for *design marks.* Examples are sea shells, clovers, maple leaves, palm trees, lotus petals, and animal footprints. See, e.g., U.S. Reg. No. 2,312,067 depicting inter alia an acorn, oak leaf, and tree branches; U.S. Reg. No. 2,043,809 depicting a cat's paw print. However, the better known and easily identifiable shapes are already used, so it is often hard to find unused natural shapes or adapt used ones.

If you choose a less known shape like that of a camel's foot or sassafras leaf, then the shape should usually have a meaningful connection to the business or product; also you might offer explanatory *"look for" advertising* which identifies the shape and in some cases its connection.

VI Design Marks

287 MEDALLIONS AND SEALS

Medallions and seals (like gold seals pasted on packaging) can be protected if distinctive, unusually shaped, and properly placed, but generally only with *secondary meaning*. Secondary meaning is often required because the consumer might not ordinarily think that a seal or medallion is being used as a trademark. Advertising which prompts the consumer to "look for" the gold seal or other device *("look for" advertising)* can help establish public recognition and secondary meaning. Cf. U.S. Reg. No. 430,729 for the LEE clothing seal, U.S. Reg. No. 1,439,275 for the NCAA medallion, and U.S. Reg. No. 739,469 for the MOTHER'S food medallion.

288 STITCHING DESIGNS

Stitching *designs* for garments, if distinctive, can often be protected with *secondary meaning*. An example is the orange stitching design on the back pockets of LEVI'S jeans as per U.S. Reg. No. 404,248. See also the GUESS? pocket stitching design, U.S. Reg. No. 3,075,822, and the BIKINI JEANS stitching mark, U.S. Reg. No. 2,186,472. Secondary meaning is generally required because even distinctive stitching might not be perceived as trademark usage, but *"look for" advertising* can help establish secondary meaning. To get a stronger mark, one should choose a design less likely perceived as an ornament or decoration. E.g., it is easy to see how certain blue jeans stitching designs may only be perceived as decorations.

289 ORNAMENTAL DESIGNS

Many designs perceived as merely "ornamental" cannot be protected without *secondary meaning*. For instance, floral designs on dishware or cookware, even those adorning all the manufacturer's products, might only be perceived as decorative. Therefore, the new user who wants protection should try to exclusively use such designs and make the public aware through *"look for" advertising* that these designs are indications of origin, not mere decorations. Cf. U.S. Reg. No. 3,012,841 for corn ear designs applied to a package lid; U.S. Reg. No. 2,567,941 for a six-petal floral design for paper napkins; and U.S. Reg. No. 1,740,915 for floral ornamentation applied to fork and spoon handles, all registered with secondary meaning.

VI Design Marks

290 CUTOUTS AND BRANDS

As with *word marks, designs* can also be cut into the goods or other materials on which they appear. Nothing even excludes protection for cutouts having somewhat ordinary shapes, if non-functional and distinctive, such as punch holes and clipped corners. See, e.g., U.S. Reg. No. 2,032,160 featuring heart-shaped holes in baby pacifiers. Cf. U.S. Reg. No. 2,316,631 featuring holes and indentations in breakfast cereal. And marks can be etched, burnt, and "branded." See, e.g., U.S. Reg. No. 1,915,975 for a design for "TT" which is burned, stamped, or welded onto ornamental objects, furniture, etc. Perhaps the very first mark was a brand, which is why trademarks are frequently called "brands."

291 OTHER NON-INKED MARKS

Depending on your product you might select a mark suitable for "non-ink" usage, for instance, as a watermark, embossing, engraving or neon light *(¶ 306)*. See, e.g., U.S. Reg. No. 2,533,131 for a watermark applied to security papers; U.S. Reg. No. 1,986,364 for an embossed butterfly design for tote bags and clothing; and U.S. Reg. No. 3,114,470 for an engraved YVES SAINT LAURENT bottle for perfumes and other toiletries. Holograms *(¶ 300)*, too, fall into this category. Of course, whenever these kinds of marks are not clearly visible without careful examination, they are more suitable for sophisticated, careful consumers looking for quality markers, e.g., on premium papers and other luxury items.

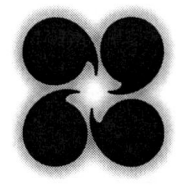

Signature marks are usually best when the signer or signature is already famous or when the signer is the products' originator.

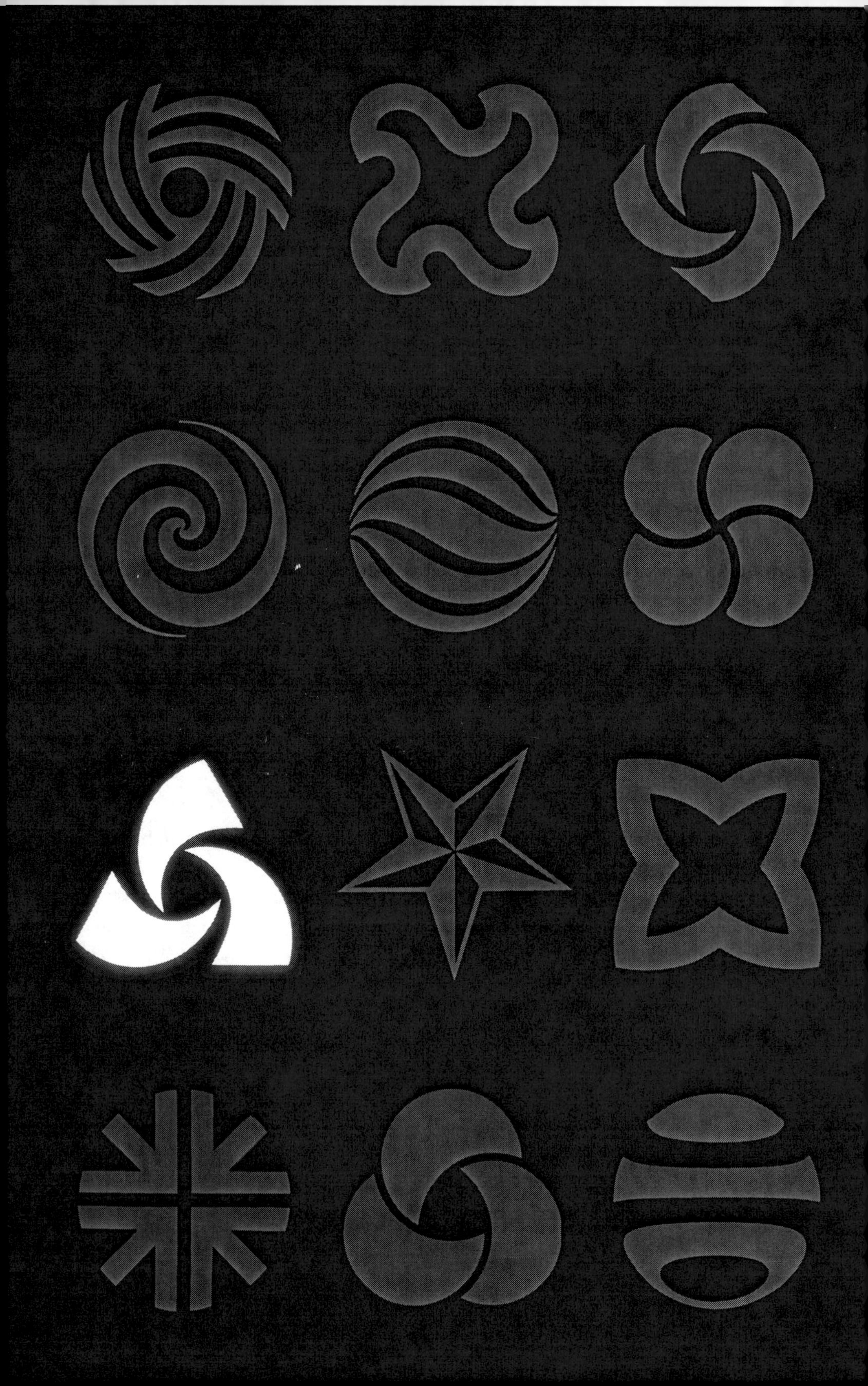

MISCELLANEOUS TRADEMARK SUBJECT MATTER

VII Other Kinds Of Marks And Devices

"A strange but provocative notion is that businesses seldom star on a national or international stage without strong trademarks. The mark often makes the business, not the other way around."

PETER KARLEN

The following is a potpourri

of special kinds of marks other than word marks and two-dimensional designs.

292 THREE-DIMENSIONAL CONFIGURATIONS

TRADEMARKS NOT ONLY EXIST in two dimensions but also three *(See Vehicles, Buildings, Clothing, Container Shapes, ¶¶ 293 et seq.)*. Examples of three-dimensional marks are MCDONALD'S arches (Expired U.S. Reg. No. 772,552), FOTOMAT kiosks (Expired U.S. Reg. No. 911,388), and even buildings such as the Transamerica building or models thereof. See U.S. Reg. No. 1,872,759 for a replica of the Transamerica building. As with other devices, the configuration must be used distinctively to indicate a single source of products. I.e., the consumer should see the 3-D configuration as a business symbol, not merely a structure.

293 VEHICLES

One kind of three-dimensional mark is a vehicle's distinctive appearance. For instance, yellow cabs enjoy some protection in jurisdictions where distinctive of one company; the brown color of UPS vehicles is another example, as per U.S. Reg. No. 2,131,693. The checkered band design owned by the Checker Cab Company also was protected. See U.S. Reg. No. 589,868. Cf. U.S. Reg. No. 2,058,985 for a "mark consisting of the markings on the aircraft and the wording 'DELTA.'" Distinctive non-functional shapes or dramatic three-dimensional ornaments on a vehicle might also be protectable. See, e.g., U.S. Reg. No. 2,580,468 for the configuration of a light truck body and U.S. Reg. No. 1,539,614 for sculptural mouse body parts mounted on a motor vehicle in connection with pest and termite control services.

VII Other Kinds of Marks & Devices

294 BUILDINGS AND STRUCTURES

Distinctive buildings have yielded trademark registrations, including those for the DISCOUNT AUTO PARTS building (U.S. Reg. No. 2,539,168), the MCDONALD'S quick service restaurant design (U.S. Reg. No. 1,753,026), and the distinctive sign structure for HOLIDAY INN (U.S. Reg. No. 592,541). Cf. U.S. Reg. No. 2,212,098 for QUAKER STATE in white lettering on a colored roof line design, placed on a certain part of a building, and U.S. Reg. No. 3,076,949 for the green, yellow, and white canopy of a BP service station. A key to success is maintaining uniformity in the buildings used by the trademark owner and its franchisees.

295 CLOTHING

Distinctive outfits and uniforms, like cheerleaders' uniforms and mascot costumes, can enjoy protection. See, e.g., U.S. Reg. No. 2,110,368 for a basketball costume used by the Cleveland Cavaliers. Again, the keys are distinctiveness and uniformity of usage. Note that white uniforms for selling ice cream have been found insufficiently distinctive. How about the brown uniforms of UPS personnel? See U.S. Reg. No. 2,159,865 for UPS clothing. Cf. the U.S. Postal Service registration for design elements and color combinations appearing on letter carrier uniforms, U.S. Reg. No. 3,061,548.

296 LABELS, TAGS, AND TABS

Labels and tags frequently bear trademarks but sometimes by themselves may be valid marks, particularly for clothing. Typically a label or tag is made distinctive by its unusual shape, size, or location; color and pictorial image may also be factors. The small tabs sewn on the back pockets of LEVI's jeans are examples. See U.S. Reg. No. 1,157,769. Cf. U.S. Reg. No. 1,959,592 for hangtags attached to back pockets in the form of packets containing seeds. *Secondary meaning*, generally required for protection, can sometimes be achieved with *"look for" advertising*.

297 CONTAINER SHAPES

Distinctive container shapes can be protected upon achieving *secondary meaning*. For instance, the classic thick-glass Coca-Cola bottle earned a U.S. trademark registration, No. 1,057,884. Grooves cut in a container are sometimes protectible, as per U.S. Reg. No. 1,830,915 for a mark consisting

VII Other Kinds of Marks & Devices

of "a plurality of angularly extending grooves formed in a container...." Practical constraints which limit creativity apply to container shapes, e.g., in relation to storage, shipping, display, and product dispensing. Yet, even with such constraints one can often create a shape which metaphorically expresses the product or one of its functions, or which parallels another branding element such as the brand logo. Note U.S. Reg. No. 2,737,196 for a perfume bottle in the shape of a female torso. The container shape shouldn't be designed without considering how and where the consumer will experience the shape. E.g., the simple yet elegant VOSS water bottle shown in U.S. Ser. No. 78/507,373 excels in a festive restaurant atmosphere, but does it in a supermarket?

298 CONTAINER FEATURES

Specific or combined container features, especially color features, can sometimes be protected, if distinctive. See, e.g., U.S. Reg. No. 1,277,688 for a CHANEL perfume bottle and its features. A container feature, like a brightly colored bottle top, can be more powerful than any *word mark*, e.g., with certain lines of vitamin products. Note the bright orange bottle tops for NATROL brand ESTER–C supplements. Cf. U.S. Reg. No. 2,568,837 for features of an ARROWHEAD water bottle including "the configuration of a cylindrical bottle with a red cap and a decorative wave pattern."

Container features are most important for goods sold on store shelves, where the container should immediately identify the product and grab the consumer's attention. Container features are typically selected after viewing containers for competing products, especially in a store setting.

299 PILL AND TABLET SHAPES

Pill and tablet shapes are potentially protectable, but *secondary meaning* must usually be shown to secure USPTO registration on the *Principal Register*. See U.S. Reg. Nos. 2,934,291 (heart design), 2,684,917 (almond shape), and 2,594,558 (modified pentagon shape). Obviously, practical considerations may predominate in designing such shapes. E.g., with pharmaceutical products, large or sharp-edged tablets may be perceived as hard to swallow, small ones hard to handle, and flat ones hard to pick up. When devising a shape, one must also consider the color. As an example, for many purposes a red or pink heart will arguably succeed better than a

VII Other Kinds of Marks & Devices

purple one. Pill and tablet design provides ample opportunity for creative non-functional features, mostly visual but some tactile. *(See Pill And Tablet Colors, ¶ 311.)*

300 HOLOGRAMS

Some jurisdictions may provide protection and registration for holograms which often give the illusion of three-dimensional shapes and movement. Naturally, searching and registering holograms is not always easy. Registration is possible at the USPTO, for instance, U.S. Reg. No. 2,288,159 for SEBASTIAN in a hologram and various AQUAFRESH hologram marks, e.g., U.S. Reg. No. 2,324,607. However, purely functional holograms may not be registerable. For instance, a hologram used as an anti-counterfeiting device may not be registerable unless consumers would perceive it as a trademark, i.e., as a distinctive designation of origin. Also, if the hologram has two or more views, the USPTO examiner may refuse registration based on the rule that an application cannot seek registration of multiple marks.

301 MOVING MARKS

Moving images are sometimes protectable. Where registration is available, often the mark is depicted to the registry as a series of still pictures combined with a detailed description of the mark's sequence of movements. Such a mark may exist in two or three dimensions, e.g., in a video format or as a moving solid. See, e.g., U.S. Reg. No. 1,928,424 for 20TH CENTURY FOX, a mark consisting of "a computer generated sequence showing the central element from several angles as though a camera is moving around the structure. The drawing represents four 'stills' from the sequence." Cf. U.S. Reg. No. 2,315,036 for a computer-generated sequence showing images of the brain, covering information services in the field of neurological surgery.

302 OLFACTORY MARKS

Marks consisting of scents should generally be readily recognizable, created with non-toxic and non-allergenic components, placed on or in association with the products, and maintain a consistent smell with little deterioration over a significant time period, e.g., long enough to stay with the products until the customer buys them. One must consider the strength of the fragrance, especially if scented products are offered in enclosed

VII Other Kinds of Marks & Devices

spaces. The scent should not be ordinarily associated with the product (e.g., using lemon scent to sell lemons) nor metaphorically inappropriate (e.g., using lemon scent to sell cars). Some of the best fragrance marks will be *arbitrary* and metaphorically interesting in relation to the product and obviously pleasant and memorable.

Scent selection, creation, and application is highly technical, requiring scientific expertise, and the results should not be thrust into the market without substantial testing. Even regulatory restrictions may apply.

The first olfactory mark registered at the USPTO, Reg. No. 1,639,128 issued in 1991, was a "high impact, fresh, floral fragrance reminiscent of plumeria blossoms" for sewing thread and embroidery yarn. See also, e.g., U.S. Reg. No. 3,143,735 for a "vanilla scent or fragrance" of certain office supplies and U.S. Reg. No. 2,568,512 for a grape scent applied to lubricants and motor fuels. Though one might only think of scented goods, possibilities may also exist for services.

Under current USPTO regulations, a scent may be registered on the *Principal Register* if it has attained *secondary meaning*; otherwise registration is on the *Supplemental Register*.

303 FLAVORS

Arguments are being made for and against trademark protection for distinctive flavors. Naturally, protection would rarely extend to food flavors since the essential characteristic of a food is its flavor, which would only be *descriptive* of the food. Hypothetically, one could imagine a distinctive flavor not ordinarily associated with the food product, especially when used as a short-lived "teaser," e.g., a special flavor which floats to the top of a soda can so only the first sips give that flavor. Flavors can be distinctively used with pharmaceuticals, whether liquids or chewables. However, because relatively few distinctive flavors are actually used with pharmaceutical products (e.g., orange, cherry, peppermint, and spearmint), monopolies on flavors might limit legitimate competition and consumer choice. Compare U.S. Reg. No. 1,623,869 for an "arcuate configuration of five flavors of ice cream... arranged from bottom to top, as it is sold on a cone."

304 TACTILE MARKS

Tactile devices might be marks if not functional. Rough versus smooth, round versus flat, ridged versus rounded or flat, and dimpled versus smooth can indicate function. For instance, on old stereo speaker cords, flat versus ridged wire coverings may indicate polarity of the two wires, a functional indication. Such devices can also indicate origin especially on goods sold to the visually-impaired. *"Look for" advertising* can make tactile devices useful with consumers; however, we are not aware of very many registrations for tactile marks. One of few examples is U.S. Reg. No. 2,273,173 for the "configuration and visual and tactile configuration of a [plant] pot made from fibrous material...." See also U.S. Reg. No. 2,495,311 for a trash can design with "sides having a pebbly texture...."; U.S. Reg. No. 2,320,497 for a champagne glass having a "crackled texture"; and U.S. Reg. No. 2,093,825 for the configuration of a padlock body with roughened and smooth surfaces. *Secondary meaning* may be required for USPTO registration on the *Principal Register* since a number of these marks appear on the *Supplemental Register*.

305 SOUND MARKS

Distinctive sound marks usually consist of a short series of individual notes, alone or with chords, often mid-range notes played on a single instrument. Cf. the NBC chimes (U.S. Reg. No. 916,522) and the "INTEL INSIDE" sound bite (U.S. Reg. No. 2,315,261). Sometimes words accompany the sounds as with U.S. Reg. No. 2,369,787 owned by Glaxo Wellcome, Inc. for a mark consisting of "the melody notes E flat, F, B flat in octave below, B flat, followed by the spoken words of 'BREAKTHROUGH MEDICINES FOR EVERYDAY LIVING' and a musical chord consisting of the melody notes E flat and E flat in two octaves."

Animal noises are also possible subject matter, e.g., the roar of the old MGM lion (U.S. Reg. No. 1,395,550). More unusual marks are being developed, even sounds from exhaust pipes used to advertise motorcycles. Nonetheless, such unusual marks, unless cleverly employed, will be hard to protect and less distinctive, especially if somewhat *descriptive*.

Even where sound is not necessarily registerable, it can be part of a branding strategy. E.g., supposedly JAGUAR car engine sounds are designed to complement the JAGUAR name and design.

306 LIGHT MARKS

All marks other than those perceived through smell, touch, or hearing depend on light but usually light reflected off a surface to give the

VII Other Kinds of Marks & Devices

impression of the mark. Some visual marks, however, may consist of light emanations, including flashing or blinking light bulbs, flashing screens, and other patterns of illumination, still or moving. Examples are U.S. Reg. No. 2,535,181 for a mark consisting of "a formation of light beams resembling the conical framework of a tipi [teepee] emanating from a circular source of light," and U.S. Reg. No. 2,323,892 for a "pre-programmed rotating sequence of a plurality of high-intensity columns of light projected into the sky to locate a source at the base thereof." Often these light emanations are *service marks* designed to attract attention to a location, but they can also be *trademarks* when distinctive non-functional light beams emanate from the goods. As with all unusual marks, research and attorney advice are required to see whether the mark is protectable.

307 COLOR MARKS

The single color of a product can sometimes act as a trademark. The U.S. Supreme Court upheld protection of a gold/green color of pads used in dry cleaning by professional cleaners. Owens-Corning has protection for the color pink, e.g., as applied to building insulation (U.S. Reg. No. 2,380,742). 3M Corporation has a registration for the color blue as applied to premium-quality masking tape (U.S. Reg. No. 2,176,916). How about brown for UPS trucks and uniforms? See, e.g., U.S. Reg. No. 2,131,693 for the color brown as applied to delivery trucks.

Note that even color marks can be unprotectably *descriptive* if they indicate the goods being sold, e.g., an orange color for oranges might not be protectable. Also, if the color serves a useful function it may not be protectable, e.g., a green color for farm implements. *Secondary meaning* is probably required to protect any such color mark. As mentioned *(Package Surface Designs, ¶ 283)*, the chosen color should be metaphorically appropriate for the product. For instance, cleaning materials are generally not brown nor emergency and alarm equipment typically green.

308 COLOR COMBINATIONS

Sometimes a mark comprises a combination of colors, with separate colors applied to different objects or parts of an object. For example, consider U.S. Reg. No. 2,436,265 for the VITTEL water bottle, covering the configuration of a square light blue bottle with rounded corners, a darker blue cap, and red and blue on the label.

VII Other Kinds of Marks & Devices

Often the color combination is linked to distinctively shaped objects such as stylized tablets. See, e.g., U.S. Reg. No. 2,567,799 for a mark consisting in part of stylized tablets colored pink, green, yellow, and blue. Cf. U.S. Reg. No. 1,623,869 for a configuration of five flavors of ice cream stacked on a cone, with a claim to the brown, pink, white, green, and orange colors of the flavors.

Typically, greater protection can be achieved only with *secondary meaning*. This kind of mark is best developed with an attorney's hands-on participation throughout the entire selection process.

309 LIQUID AND GEL COLORS

Makers of distinctively colored liquid products, for ingestion or household use, have had difficulty getting protection even though the public may strongly associate the coloring with a particular product. For instance, in one court case the original amber color of LISTERINE was not protected, and the same was true of the well-known pink of the PEPTO-BISMOL digestive remedy. The USPTO examination guide, however, indicates that colors of liquids are registerable subject matter; the example given in the PTO examination manual (TMEP ¶1202.05(d)(i)) is "fuchsia body oil," though full protection may depend on *secondary meaning*. Cf. U.S. Reg. No. 2,583,984 for a light blue gel containing blue speckles, for cleaning products. See also U.S. Reg. No. 2,427,697 for a bottle design featuring a dual-layered liquid, orange on top of white, for cleaning products. Even without legal protection, distinctive coloring can be a good marketing tool.

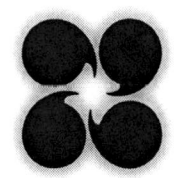

Marks consisting of scents should generally be readily recognizable, created with non-toxic and non-allergenic components, placed on or in association with the products, and maintain a consistent smell with little deterioration over a significant time period.

VII Other Kinds of Marks & Devices

310 POWDER AND PARTICLE COLORS

Like colors of liquids, powder and particle colors can sometimes enjoy protection, especially with *secondary meaning*. When clear containers are used, colored specks and particles are visible even before purchase and can become distinctive indicia of origin.

Obviously an orange powder for making an orange-flavored dessert will be hard to protect, so that *descriptive* and functional colors should be avoided if you want color protection. An example of particle color protection is U.S. Reg. No. 2,523,590 for mushroom spawn, where the mark comprises bright orange particles interspersed with the spawn. The PTO examination manual (TMEP ¶1202.05(d)(i)) gives as an example "red, white and blue granular washing machine detergent."

Though powder and particle color applications have not flooded the USPTO, companies selling liquid and powder products should not ignore protection for colored particles and specks.

311 PILL AND TABLET COLORS

Distinctive pill coloring has sometimes been protected. Pharmaceutical companies using distinctive coloring on famous trademarked products have been able to stop manufacturers of generic drugs from using the same colors. One argument is that the original manufacturers have higher quality products or at least better quality control procedures, and should be entitled to distinguish their original products from those of imitators. However, *secondary meaning* may be required before full protection is available. In some cases, protection may be available for a group of colors applied to capsules or tablets, e.g., as illustrated by U.S. Reg. No. 2,567,799 which covers a mark consisting in part of "stylized tablets in the colors pink, green, yellow and blue." See also U.S. Reg. No. 2,539,549 for detergent tablets, the mark consisting of "the total impression of a multitude of small tablets in the colors blue and white."

Naturally, colors should be selected with semantic, metaphoric, and emotional/visceral considerations in mind, particularly for medicines. As an example, in choosing a color for an anti-nausea pill one must not only consider point-of-sale reactions to the colors, if any, but also the color's effect when viewed before swallowing. Government agency regulations may also affect color selection for medicinal pills and tablets. *(Cf. Pill And Tablet Shapes, ¶ 299.)*

VII Other Kinds of Marks & Devices

312 WIRE, ROPE, AND THREAD COLORS

Distinctive strand colors in wires, ropes, and threads are sometimes protectable if not functional. See, e.g., U.S. Reg. No. 192,881 (Expired) covering manila rope and cable where the mark is an "elongated lineal compound yarn, thread, twine or the like, formed of separate yarns of blue and yellow in one of the threads of which the strands of rope or cable are composed." Also note U.S. Reg. No. 2,211,951 for "adjacent orange and white strands that are wound as a part of wire rope" and U.S. Reg. No. 1,552,475 for blue-and-yellow-stranded wire rope. As with other color marks, the goal is to establish *secondary meaning*, often with the use of *"look for" advertising*. Since the colors are typically intertwined, the most memorable marks are likely those with relatively few colors that highly contrast with each other.

As with colored pills and tablets *(¶ 311)*, practical, legal, metaphoric, and semantic considerations may apply. An obvious example is electrical wire for which certain colors have established significance. And don't count on getting protection for green gardening wire.

313 MISCELLANEOUS ORNAMENTS

Trademark law contemplates a wide variety of devices, not merely words, phrases, and 2-D designs. For instance, sewn-on ornaments for sneakers may be valid trademarks (see U.S. Reg. No. 1,465,556); so also might be small colored tabs sewn on back pockets of trousers (see U.S. Reg. No. 720,376). These non-verbal cues are capable of telling the customer where the goods come from. As with other marks, their use must be distinctive and relatively uniform so the customer perceives the device as an indication of origin and not merely an ornament. One way of finding whether a particular ornament can be a protectable mark is to search the USPTO TESS database using the "Structured Form Search (Boolean)" under the field "Description of Mark," though only your attorney can give final advice on this issue.

314 PRODUCT DISPLAYS

Other unusual marks are distinctive apparatus for displaying the products or distinctive displays of the products themselves. For instance, U.S. Reg. No. 2,165,090 for retail store services protects a design of a kiosk

VII Other Kinds of Marks & Devices

having display racks and display cases. U.S. Reg. No. 2,569,635 for candy distributed by Tootsie Roll Industries, Inc. covers a configuration of numerous lollipops wrapped together in the form of a bouquet. Though such marks often require *secondary meaning* to be registered on the *Principal Register,* for many products, particularly small items, the possibilities are endless for those using imagination. Unfortunately, many business owners don't know about developing and registering such display marks. As with miscellaneous ornaments *(¶ 313),* one way of seeing what kinds of displays have been registered is to search the USPTO TESS database under the field "Description of Mark," though only your attorney can give meaningful guidance on this issue.

315 LIVING MATTER MARKS

Theoretically, nothing prevents living materials from being shaped into "marks." For instance, if McDonalds Corporation arches can be protected, why not distinctively arranged or shaped entranceway trees, bushes, shrubbery, and flower arrangements, especially if *secondary meaning* could be achieved? However, a preliminary search of USPTO records did not reveal many efforts to register such "living" marks, which doesn't mean they don't or couldn't exist. Note U.S. Serial No. 75/216,993, an abandoned application for the shape of a poinsettia plant. Compare U.S. Reg. No. 3,238,974 for Anheuser-Busch's eight live horses hitched to a beer wagon and a companion USPTO application, Serial No. 77/389,674, for a live Clydesdale horse. Given that trademark protection has gradually expanded to more devices (e.g., sounds, fragrances, and moving images), someday soon "living matter" marks will probably walk the promenade.

316 TRADE DRESS

If distinctive, the product's overall appearance, packaging or presentation may become a protectable *trade dress.* For instance, the KODAK and FUJI packaging for film are good examples of distinctive trade dresses. Cf. U.S. Reg. No. 2,176,030 for IAM's purple trade dress packaging for "senior" animal food. Magazine covers may constitute protectable trade dress if the cover of every issue of the magazine has a commonly distinct appearance, even though the covers change somewhat from issue to issue. Even a restaurant's overall distinctive appearance, e.g., in terms of color scheme, layout, façade, and furnishings, can potentially be a trade dress. Cf. U.S.

VII Other Kinds of Marks & Devices

Reg. No. 2,172,961 for the red, white, and blue trade dress color scheme for AMOCO gas stations and convenience stores. Also note U.S. Reg. No. 2,254,662 for retail footware services, the mark comprising "inter alia, a microphone stand featuring games on the periphery, large shoe replicas, a center aisle leading to a center circle and the microphone stand, a checkered design with circles for signage, staggered display racks, seating pods, neon lighting on the signage featuring 'circus' lettering with the wording 'SHOE CARNIVAL,' 'FAMILY FUN,' 'NAME BRANDS,' and 'LOWEST PRICES,' and department signage in 'bullhorn' style lettering."

Though not always registerable, distinctive trade dress is often protectable. Sometimes a distinctive trade dress will be as or more important than the *house* or *product mark*. For instance, with supermarket goods, many customers immediately spot the product they want, not because of trademarks but rather because of trade dress; with some products, the consumer may not even know the trademark but easily recognizes the packaging. Note that legal protection for trade dress does not normally extend to the product's or packaging's functional features. ***(See Functional Marks, ¶ 320.)*** *"Look for" advertising* is typically critical to create customer recognition and enhance legal protection.

317 COLLECTIVE MARKS

In contrast to an ordinary trademark or service mark, a *collective mark* indicates a group or collective of individuals or entities as the products' source. Cf. PGA for golf services (U.S. Reg. No. 578,653) and the BETTER BUSINESS BUREAU logo for services relating to improving business and trade practices (U.S. Reg. No. 749,915). Even one registration for VIYELLA, the long-established fabric/clothing mark, shows a description as a "collective mark." (See U.S. Reg. No. 403,934.)

Typically collective marks need not be metaphoric, metonymic or otherwise very imaginative; it is usually enough if they are "solid" and conservative. One is not trying to create an imaginary experience or association with a product but usually an impression of strength, reliability, and integrity.

318 COLLECTIVE MEMBERSHIP MARKS

Collective membership marks indicate membership in an organized group, e.g., the AAA letters within an oval design indicating membership in the American Automobile Association (U.S. Reg. No. 645,541), or ROTARY

VII Other Kinds of Marks & Devices

INTERNATIONAL for membership in an international organization of business and professional leaders (U.S. Reg. No. 705,081). Cf. the design mark LEGIBUS ARMISQUE DEVOTI (meaning "devoted to law and arms") indicating membership in the U.S. Army Legal Services Agency (U.S. Reg. No. 1,409,041).

Because the membership mark will be used by individual members, an important consideration is the members' attitudes, reactions, and feelings about the mark. Thus, in selecting such a mark for an existing membership, polling the membership may be appropriate, especially for a trade or professional membership. Obviously, the mark selected should be one that members can proudly display.

319 CERTIFICATION MARKS

A *certification mark* certifies the quality or other characteristics of goods or services offered by somebody other than the mark's owner. A famous certification mark is "UL" owned by Underwriters Laboratory (U.S. Reg. No. 2,391,140) and affixed to various manufacturers' goods that have been safety-tested by Underwriters Laboratory. 100% PURE FLORIDA'S SEAL OF APPROVAL is another example (U.S. Reg. No. 1,430,705); so are the ROQUEFORT (for cheese) (U.S. Reg. No. 571,798) and "Union Label" certifications (e.g., U.S. Reg. No. 507,089). As with collective marks one is generally not seeking a very clever or imaginative mark. The certification mark is not used by your company to sell its own products but is usually a conservative mark designed to certify quality of other people's products. As such, you typically seek a mark that can be comfortably used by numerous licensees.

320 FUNCTIONAL MARKS

A color device or two- or three-dimensional design or shape may not enjoy trademark protection to the extent it is "functional." Functional devices are generally not protected as marks in order to allow competitors to fairly convey the same information using similar features and because functional elements are usually not distinctive indications of origin. A device is functional when it serves a useful purpose or conveys useful information other than the source of the product. For instance, the form, size, or shape of an article may be "functional" if it contributes to its utility, durability,

VII Other Kinds of Marks & Devices

effectiveness, or ease of use. But note that many seemingly functional shapes have been protected, e.g., a court upheld State trademark rights for the Rolls Royce car grill. See also U.S. Reg. Nos. 2,161,779 (a Chrysler Corp. SUV grill design) and 1,605,427 (a Volvo grill design). Cf. U.S. Reg. No. 2,268,107 for the configuration of a frame for bicycles.

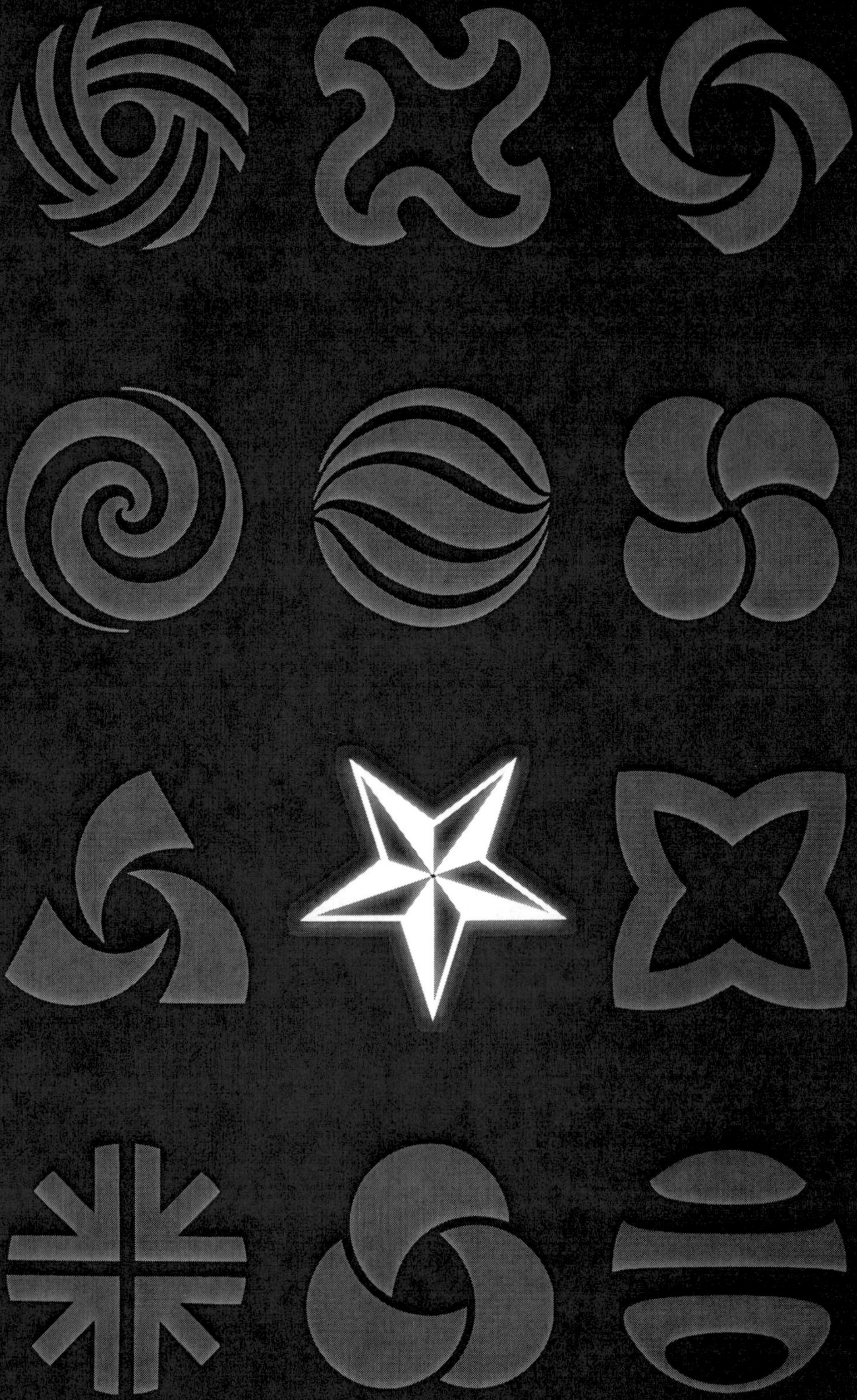

RESTRICTIONS THAT MAY AFFECT SELECTION

VIII Prohibitions

"Words calculated to catch everyone may catch no one."

ADLAI E. STEVENSON, JR.

Before starting selection,

review all restrictions and prohibitions relating to subject matter, including general prohibitions which affect all businesses and those which apply only to your industry. The following are some prohibitions and legal obstacles which affect trademark selection.

321 PROHIBITED STATEMENTS

IN CERTAIN REGULATED INDUSTRIES, marks embodying product claims may be prohibited. For instance, under laws administered by the U.S. Food and Drug Administration, the FDA may prohibit marks which make unauthorized health claims, so that someone marking their dietary supplement as DIABETES CURE would likely face an FDA enforcement action. Before selecting a mark that promises benefits, particularly health or safety benefits, one should seek legal advice. If international expansion is planned, that advice should extend to all planned territories.

322 MISDESCRIPTIVE MARKS

Avoid misdescriptive marks. Many deceptively misdescriptive marks are not registerable, especially at the USPTO, because a misdescriptive mark can mislead the public.

Hypothetically, TURKEY HEAVEN for canned chicken might be misdescriptive. SUPER SILK was held misdescriptive of clothes made from a synthetic silk-like fabric, CAFETERIA was denied registration for full service sit-down restaurant services, and SYRUP OF FIGS was once denied

VIII Prohibitions

full protection (i.e., injunctive relief denied) at a time when figs were not a material ingredient of that laxative product. Also, geographically misdescriptive marks may face problems, e.g., SWISSGOLD for watches made in China was denied USPTO registration, as TEXAS would be for products coming from Maine. Additionally, international treaty arrangements can bar registration of marks which, when used on wines or spirits, identify a place other than the origin of the goods. Even local laws ban marks that mislead as to the geographic origin of alcoholic beverages.

However, many successful marks convey impressions which don't match geographic origins or owners' backgrounds. For example, GEORGE KILLIAN'S IRISH RED may be brewed in the USA but is not misleading, especially when one considers the proverbial notion that there are more Irish in the USA than in Ireland. HÄAGEN DAZS products are not Scandinavian confections but originated in the Bronx. Also, an owner with a very ethnic name might use a more traditional British name to give a sense of respectability to the company or product. And some good *suggestive* marks don't match the products: e.g., GRAPE-NUTS breakfast cereal never contained either grapes or nuts, but its tiny nuggets may resemble grape seeds or grape "nuts," and similarly CHOCK FULL O'NUTS coffee didn't feature nuts even though coffee beans may be suggested by NUTS.

It's sometimes hard to tell the difference between suggestive marks which don't match the products and unregisterable misdescriptive marks. Perhaps the main difference is that the suggestive mark doesn't confuse or mislead consumers, while its purely misdescriptive cousin can.

323 INDECENT OR SCANDALOUS MARKS

Marks incorporating scandalous or indecent matter should be avoided. Though the user may have First Amendment rights to exploit the mark, by statute the USPTO may refuse registration and the mark may be hard to protect. For instance, the following marks, which might be relatively non-controversial today, were once refused registration or other protection: MADONNA for wines, BUBBY TRAP for bras, and SENUSSI (the name of a Muslim religious sect) for cigarettes. But BADASS for sound equipment was allowed; so was LIBIDO for perfume and ACAPULCO GOLD for suntan lotion, all of which would barely raise an eyebrow today. Also, marks like FCUK which are close to being swear words can sometimes be registered. Clearly, what is decent in one country/jurisdiction, may be indecent in

VIII Prohibitions

Theoretically, nothing prevents living materials from being shaped into "marks." For instance, if MCDONALD'S arches can be protected, why not distinctively arranged or shaped entranceway trees, bushes, shrubbery, and flower arrangements?

another, thus the need for connotation searches for certain marks.

324 MISLEADING OR DECEPTIVE MARKS

Marks which might mislead the public or incorrectly suggest a connection with living or dead persons, institutions, beliefs, or national symbols may be refused registration by the USPTO and generally should be avoided. The following were once denied registration: U.S. BICENTENNIAL SOCIETY (suggested government sponsorship), THE WASHINGTON MINT (suggested government connection, though THE WASHINGTON MINT, LLC is registered), and WESTPOINT for firearms (suggested connection with Military Academy, though registered for other products). But an image of the Statue of Liberty was held not a government symbol, and UNCLE SAM is a proper breakfast cereal mark.

Because words and symbols may have different connotations and shades of meaning in various countries/jurisdictions, it's conceivable that a mark may be misleading in one or more countries while perfectly acceptable everywhere else. Thus, whenever you intend foreign use, on the advice of counsel you should conduct a connotation search for any mark capable of differing connotations or meanings.

325 DISPARAGING MARKS

Marks which disparage living or dead persons, institutions, beliefs, or national symbols or bring them into contempt or disrepute may be refused registration by the USPTO and should generally be avoided. The same is true of marks reflecting religious, racial or political prejudice, though registration of JUNGLE JAP was allowed; so were registrations for the arguably-innocuous AMISH for cigars and JEW for entertainment services.

326 FLAGS AND INSIGNIAS

Marks which consist of or comprise the flag or coat of arms or other insignia of the United States or any State or municipality, or of any foreign nation, may be refused registration at the USPTO and should generally be avoided. Nevertheless, many businesses use flags and insignias on their products to indicate national origin, e.g., the insignia on SWISS ARMY watches or the American flag to indicate "Made in the U.S.A."

327 DECEASED PRESIDENTS

Marks which consist of or comprise the name, signature, or portrait of a deceased president of the United States during the life of his/her widow(er) may not be registered at the USPTO except with the widow(er)'s written consent.

328 SURNAME PROHIBITION

In the USA, marks which are "primarily merely surnames" are unregisterable on the Principal Register absent *secondary meaning*. This rule prevents unreasonable monopolies on surnames. The question is, what is "primarily merely a surname"? The detailed rules on this question are beyond the scope of this work, but some examples illustrate the prohibition.

The rarely used surname HACKLER was held not "primarily merely a surname" because it also exists as an ordinary word; the same result with BIRD. However, PICKETT and CHAPELL were held "primarily merely surnames" even though phonetic equivalents of "picket" and "chapel."

FAIRBANKS was allowed because it also has a geographic significance, though HAMILTON was barred since its geographic significance was held minor. Also if a surname identifies a famous historical person or place, it may be allowed, e.g., DA VINCI. Double surnames like SCHAUB-LORENZ will often not be considered "primarily merely surnames." Adding distinctive design elements can also escape the prohibition, as can adding extra words, as with HAMILTON PHARMACEUTICALS, NEWMAN'S OWN, and ALBERTO VO5 (VO5 reflecting the hairdressing's five vital emollients). But adding initials or titles (like "MR." or "MS.") or putting

VIII Prohibitions

the name in plural or possessive form (SMITHS or SMITH'S) usually does not circumvent the prohibition. If the surname is unusual, even if not equivalent to an ordinary word, it may sometimes escape a USPTO refusal. Consider BOSE, MAYTAG, and PRADA, founders' surnames, registered many times at the USPTO.

Similar prohibitions exist in other jurisdictions. Moreover, surname marks also may encounter practical obstacles in other countries. For example, in the United Kingdom, McDonalds Corporation had to deal with other people named McDonald in the food business. In Sweden when Coca-Cola Corporation tried to introduce a new drink called URGE, the Urge family objected.

329 LIVING INDIVIDUALS

Marks which consist of or comprise a name, portrait, or signature identifying a particular living individual (i.e., not the user of the mark) may be refused registration by the USPTO and should generally be avoided, unless written consent is procured, preferably in an attorney-drafted instrument. Failure to get consent to use someone else's personal attributes can also lead to liability, e.g., for invasion of privacy and violation of publicity rights.

330 DECEASED INDIVIDUALS

Even if one could register a deceased person's name or other personal attribute under USPTO rules, State publicity rights laws prevent unconsented commercial use of names, likenesses, voices, signatures, and photographs of the recently deceased. These laws could impose liability for using marks which comprise the personal attributes of dead people, and only an attorney familiar with publicity rights could help you determine whether such marks might be useable. Consent can sometimes be secured in writing from such dead persons' estates, often through agents who represent estates of deceased celebrities.

331 COPYRIGHTED IMAGES

Using someone else's drawing, illustration, photograph, or other artwork in your *design mark* could make you liable for copyright infringement. Remember that designs qualifying for trademark use may also be copyrightable. If unable or unwilling to develop your own original

VIII Prohibitions

design, then only consider certifiable public domain artwork or else images for which you can get written permissions, copyright transfers, or other applicable instruments from the design's creator(s) or other copyright owner(s), for which you will need the help of a copyright attorney.

332 FOREIGN PROHIBITIONS

As mentioned earlier *(Problems in Other Languages, et seq., ¶¶ 90 et seq.)*, what may be accepted in the USA may create problems in foreign countries. If MADONNA were once a problem for alcoholic beverages in the USA, imagine how difficult it might be for a Western company to use any sacred Muslim word or person (e.g., ALLAH or MOHAMMED) in an Islamic country. Typical prohibitions include marks that subvert the public order or are against established morals of the host country, and, in a few countries, marks that subvert government political objectives, e.g., marks that contravene a government's boycott policies. In some countries marks for alcoholic beverages are unregisterable, and every country has its own taboos and sacred cows.

333 MARKS PROTECTED BY STATUTE

A number of marks are specifically reserved and protected by statute, so they are usually "out of bounds" regardless of general rules governing conflicts and confusion. According to the USPTO, approximately 70 federal statutes prohibit the use of various words, names, symbols, etc. adopted by the U.S. Government or by particular national or international organizations. Examples of reserved marks are OLYMPIC, UNITED STATES OLYMPIC COMMITTEE, OLYMPIAD, PARALYMPIC, CITIUS ALTIUS FORTIUS, PAN-AMERICAN, AMERICA ESPIRITO SPORT FRATERNITE, RED CROSS, GENEVA CROSS, BOY SCOUTS, BOY SCOUTS OF AMERICA, GIRL SCOUTS, GIRL SCOUTS OF AMERICA, SMOKEY BEAR, and GIVE A HOOT, DON'T POLLUTE. Thus, if you wish to adopt the name or *slogan* of a quasi-official organization even for unrelated products, have your attorney check for statutory prohibitions.

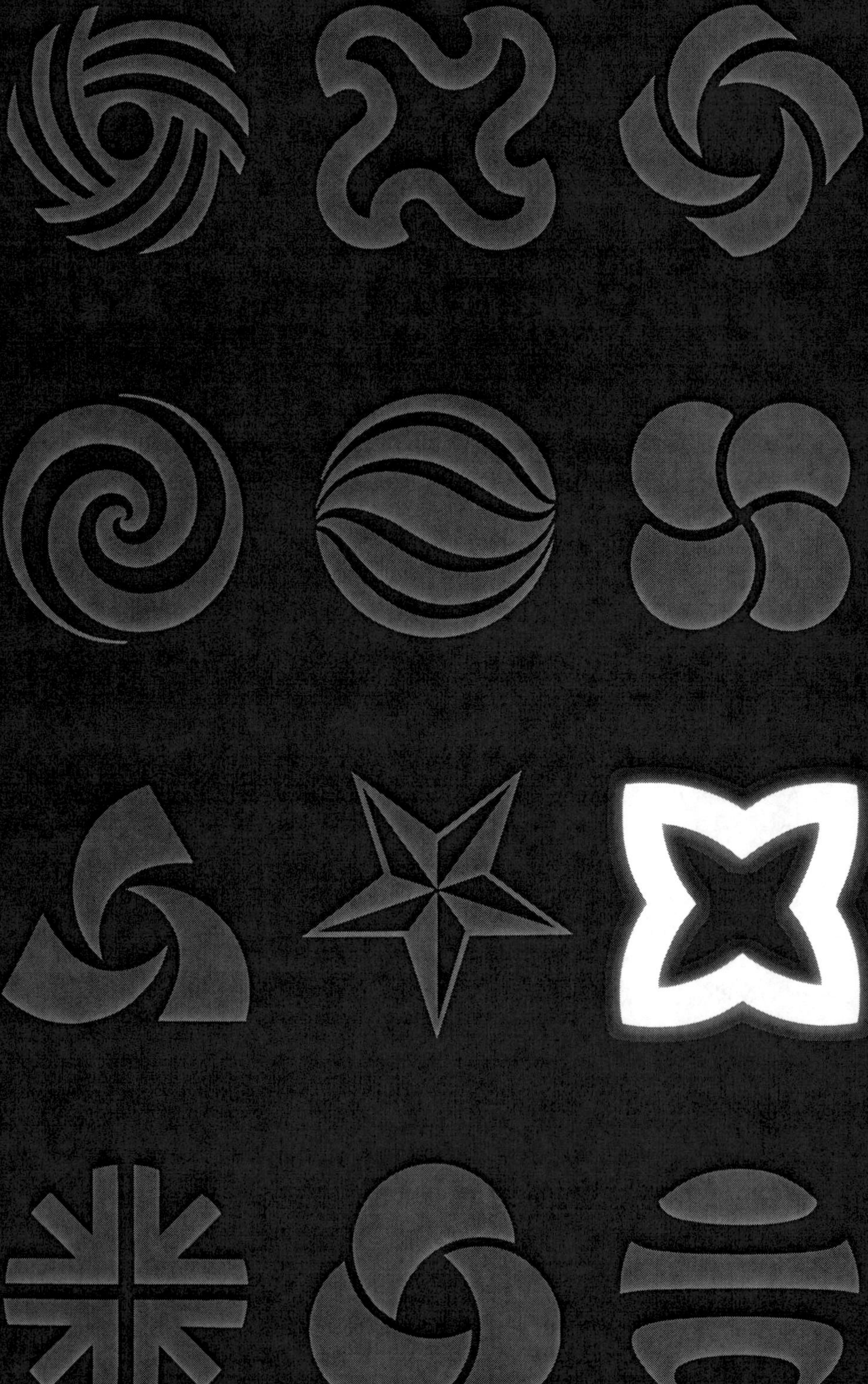

DEFINITIONS OF TRADEMARK-RELATED TERMS

IX Trademark Glossary

"Words are chameleons which reflect
the color of their environment."

JUDGE LEARNED HAND

The following abbreviated

trademark-related definitions are approximations only, and as the law changes, the definitions of these terms may change. For more current, accurate, and complete definitions, consult updated trademark treatises such as McCarthy on Trademarks and Gilson on Trademarks as well as Title 15, United States Code and the USPTO website at www.uspto.gov.

Arbitrary Mark: A mark comprised of existing word(s) having no ordinary relationship to the products offered with the mark, e.g., KIWI for shoe polish, APPLE for computers, and PENGUIN for books.

Brand: The expectations, perceptions, and memories about product(s) evocable by a trademark and its associated identifying devices, so that "branding" is the creation of expectations, perceptions, and memories about product(s) evocable by a trademark and its associated identifying devices.

Capricious Mark: *See "Fanciful Mark."*

Certification Mark: A mark used by a person or entity other than its owner to certify (1) regional or other origin, material, mode of manufacture, quality, accuracy, or other characteristics of such person's or entity's products, or (2) that the work or labor on the products was performed by members of a union or other organization. Examples of well known

IX Trademark Glossary

certification marks are UL (Underwriter's Laboratory) and the GOOD HOUSEKEEPING Seal of Approval.

Collective Mark: A mark used by members of a cooperative, association, or other collective group or organization to identify and distinguish their products, e.g., LURPAK used by the Mejeriforeningen Danish Dairy Board for butter and other spreadable dairy products from Danish producers (U.S. Reg. No. 2,638,403) and 3HO used by yoga instructors for yoga education services (U.S. Reg. No. 3,194,370).

Collective Membership Mark: A mark indicating membership in an organized group, e.g., the letters "AAA" within an oval shape, indicating membership in the American Automobile Association (U.S. Reg. No. 645,541) and 1% FOR THE PLANET, indicating membership in an association of businesses donating proceeds to environmental organizations (U.S. Reg. No. 3,233,020).

Color Mark: A mark comprised of one or more colors, often confined to a specific design or shape, e.g., the pink color of Owens-Corning building insulation (U.S. Reg. No. 2,380,742) the brown color used by United Parcel Service (UPS) (U.S. Reg. No. 2,901,090).

Descriptive Mark: A mark which describes the products or their functions or characteristics, e.g., SUPER BLEND for multi-viscosity oils (though registered with *secondary meaning*, e.g., U.S. Reg. No. 1,230,773 (expired)) or SUDSY for ammonia.

Design Mark: A mark consisting of a picture, design, or symbol, like the Baron Rothschild sheep's head used for wine (U.S. Reg. No. 3,073,740), also including stylized designs for words such as the IBM design (U.S. Reg. No. 1,205,090).

Dilution: Impairment of a famous mark's strength caused by unauthorized use of an identical or similar mark, trade name or other device, generally for unrelated products. Dilution can occur by "blurring" or by "tarnishment." A mark is diluted by blurring when its distinctiveness is impaired because of use of the other identical or similar device. A mark is diluted by tarnishment when its reputation is impaired because of unsavory or unflattering use of

IX Trademark Glossary

the other identical or similar device. E.g., the owner of BUDWEISER for beer brought an anti-dilution action against BUTTWISER for T-shirts, an alleged blurring, and TOYS "Я" US for children's toys encountered ADULTS "R" US for sexual devices, an alleged tarnishment.

Family of Marks: A group of marks, owned by one person or entity, which all have a common element. Typically the family of marks is applied to related products to indicate a single source for all the products. The "MC" device used in McDonalds Corporation trademarks creates a family of marks, e.g., MCDONALD'S, MCNUGGETS, and MCSNACK; so does "CITI," as in marks such as CITIPRIVILEGES, CITITREASURY, and CITIINSURANCE.

Fanciful Mark: A mark comprised of coined "word(s)" having no meaning in any language, e.g., KODAK for film, EXXON for petroleum products, and PROZAC for anti-depressant medications.

Federal Registration: A registration at the United States Patent and Trademark Office (USPTO) in Alexandria, Virginia, which enhances protection under Federal law.

Foreign Registration: A registration in any jurisdiction outside the U.S.A.

Generic Designation: A designation which is a common name of the products being provided, such as TELEPHONE or ESCALATOR. An improperly used distinctive mark can become generic, and therefore no longer protectable, especially when used improperly as a noun, as with ASPIRIN or CELLOPHANE.

House Mark: A mark designed to identify an entire business which may offer multiple products. MICROSOFT is a house mark for Microsoft Corporation which offers numerous products under individual product marks such as WINDOWS, WORD, ENCARTA, and EXCEL. Similarly, HONDA is a house mark under which resides product marks like ACCORD, CIVIC, and ACURA.

Ingredient or Component Mark: A mark indicating the source or origin of an ingredient or component of the product but frequently not owned by the product's manufacturer or distributor. Examples are INTEL INSIDE, DOLBY, GORE-TEX, and NUTRASWEET.

IX Trademark Glossary

International Registration: A registration at WIPO (World Intellectual Property Organization), headquartered in Geneva, Switzerland, procured through the Madrid Agreement or Madrid Protocol. At the time of first publishing this work, the USA was only a party to the Madrid Protocol.

"Look For" Advertising: Advertising that encourages the consumer to "look for" the color, seal, medallion, sticker, or other device which the sponsor wants to establish as a protectable mark or *trade dress*. Examples are "Just look for the blue, white and red State of Maine trademark the next time you're shopping for potatoes" and the International Ladies' Garment Workers' Union song and *slogan* "Look for the Union Label."

Olfactory Mark: A mark consisting of a distinctive scent, often applied to goods or containers or displays for the goods. The first such mark registered at the USPTO was a floral fragrance applied to thread and yarn (U.S. Reg. No. 1,639,128). See also, e.g., U.S. Reg. No. 3,143,735 for a vanilla scent applied to office supplies.

Principal Register: The Register maintained by the USPTO listing marks which are or have become distinctive, i.e., capable of distinguishing the products of the owner from those of others. Marks registered on the Principal Register enjoy greater protection than those on the *Supplemental Register*. Excluded from this Register are non-distinctive subject matter such as *descriptive* designations, marks "primarily merely surnames," and certain misdescriptive marks.

Product Mark: A mark associated with a particular product, as distinguished from a house mark which relates to the entire business. Product marks include TERCEL, AVALON, COROLLA, and CAMRY, which reside under the TOYOTA house mark.

Secondary Meaning: The additional significance that a word, slogan, design, or other device achieves as an indication of source or origin, in contrast to its primary significance as *descriptive* or other non-distinctive subject matter. Secondary meaning is attained when, after extensive use and advertising, the public perceives the otherwise non-distinctive device as an indication or source or origin. TASTY for foods was registered at the USPTO with secondary meaning (U.S. Reg. No. 2,092,872); so was DIGITAL

IX Trademark Glossary

for computer equipment (U.S. Reg. 2,353,022 (expired)). Secondary meaning is also referred to as "acquired distinctiveness."

Service Mark: A word, name, symbol, or device, or any combination thereof, used by a person or entity to identify and distinguish the services of one person or entity from the services of others and to indicate the source of the services, even if that source is unknown. Most insurance marks like GEICO and TRANSAMERICA are entirely or primarily service marks rather than trademarks since the owners are exclusively or primarily offering services rather than goods. For these purposes a "service" is a real activity performed to the order of, or for the benefit of, someone other than the user of the mark, which activity must be qualitatively different from anything necessarily done in connection with the sale of the user's goods or the performance of another service.

Slogan: A phrase or statement that helps promote interest in a company or its products, frequently *descriptive* or highly *suggestive*, directly touting a specific quality or benefit, often intended for short term use, and typically longer than a *tagline*. Examples are the British Airways slogan THE WORLD'S FAVOURITE AIRLINE and the New York Times slogan ALL THE NEWS THAT'S FIT TO PRINT.

Sound Mark: A mark comprised of a distinctive sound or of a combination or series of sounds, e.g., the NBC chimes (U.S. Reg. No. 916,522) or the Twentieth Century Fox musical phrase (U.S. Reg. No. 3,141,398).

State Registration: A registration at a State trademark registry in any of the 50 States in the U.S.A.

Suggestive Mark: A mark which intimates or suggests the goods or services, or their characteristics, without being *descriptive*, so that the underlying connection between the mark and the goods or services only appears upon reflection or upon exercise of the customer's knowledge or imagination, e.g., MOUSE SEED for rodent poison or SUNKIST for fruits.

Supplemental Register: The Register maintained by the USPTO which lists marks potentially capable of distinguishing the owner's products from those of others but not registerable on the Principal Register. E.g.,

IX Trademark Glossary

descriptive or geographically descriptive marks as well as surnames are possibly registerable on the Supplemental Register. Supplemental Register registrations provide fewer benefits than those on the *Principal Register.*

Tagline: A very short phrase or other short combination of words that reflects the tone, essence or premise of a company or its products, frequently two to four words in length, *arbitrary* or remotely *suggestive*, metaphoric or imaginative, and designed for long term use. Examples are the NIKE tagline JUST DO IT and IMPOSSIBLE IS NOTHING associated with ADIDAS.

Trade Dress: The distinctive, non-functional appearance of a product, its packaging or presentation, arising from features such as size, shape, colors, arrangement, texture, and graphic design. The packaging for KODAK and FUJI film are trade dresses; so would be the decorations, interior arrangements, and color schemes of the TACO CABANA restaurants.

Trade Name: The name used by a person or entity to identify his/her/its business, as distinct from a *trademark* or *service mark*, e.g., Eastman Kodak Company as distinct from KODAK, Xerox, Inc. as distinct from XEROX, and Atlantic Richfield Company in contrast to ARCO.

Trademark: A word, name, symbol, or device, or any combination thereof, used by a person or entity to identify and distinguish his/her/its goods from those manufactured or sold by others and to indicate the source of the goods, even if the source is unknown.

Word Mark: A mark comprised of text, consisting of letters or other typographical elements, or both, e.g., MINOLTA, COBRA, 7-ELEVEN, W3C, BLACK & DECKER, VICTORIA'S SECRET, and M@DNOYZ.

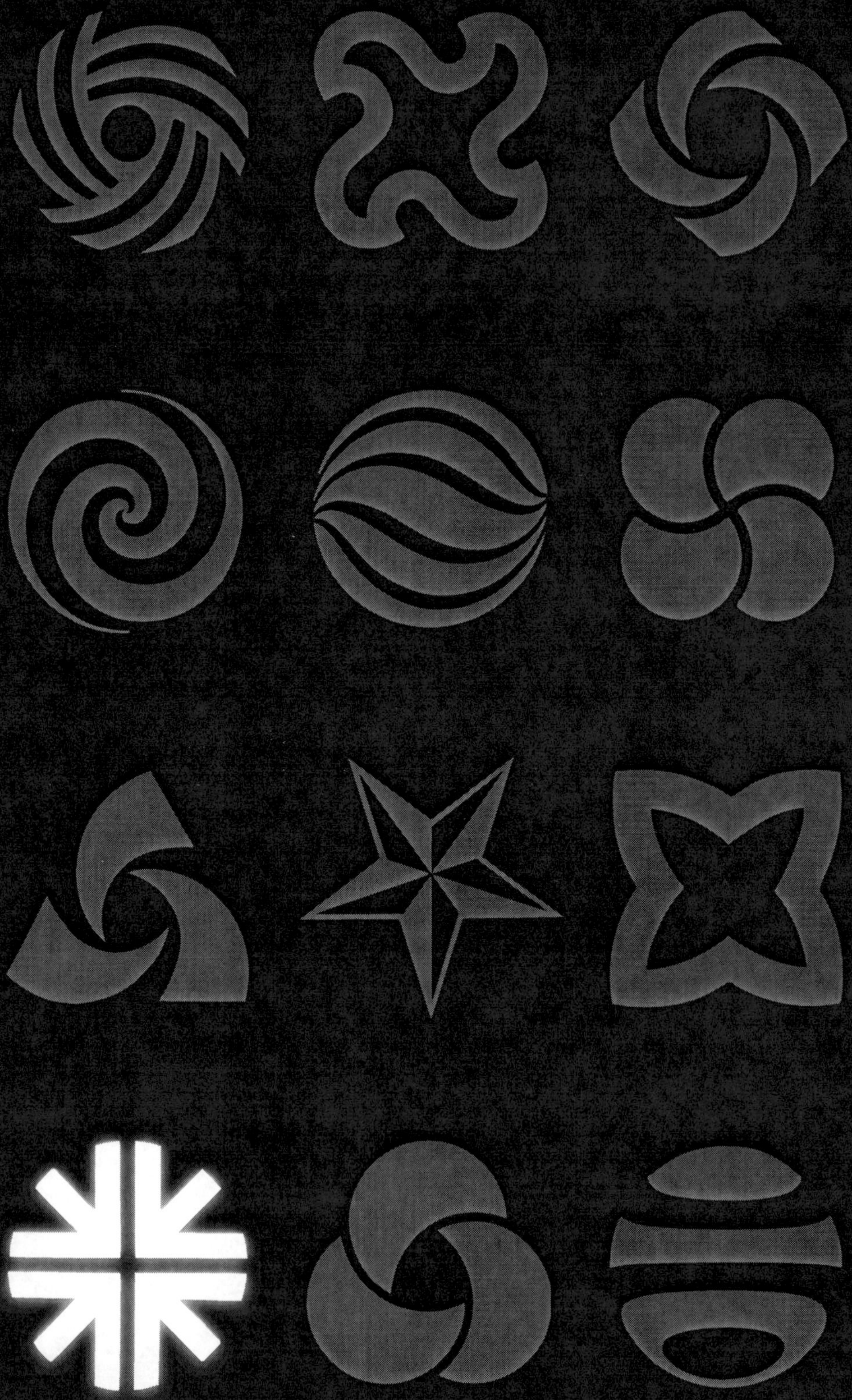

DEFINITIONS OF LINGUISTIC TERMS

X Linguistic Glossary

✺

"In real life, unlike in Shakespeare, the sweetness of the rose depends upon the name it bears. Things are not only what they are. They are, in very important respects, what they seem to be."

HUBERT H. HUMPHREY

The following abbreviated linguistic

definitions are approximations only, especially because many of these linguistic terms have been defined so differently by various authorities. Discussion of these terms can be found online at www.wikipedia.org and via searches for "linguistic terminology."

Abbreviation: A word or combination of words formed by clipping or curtailment, e.g., MATH rather than MATHEMATICS or PHONE rather than TELEPHONE. Trademark examples are CLUB MED(iterranean) and PAN AM(erican).

Acronym: A word formed from the initial letters of a multi-word name, e.g., WIPO (World Intellectual Property Organization) and NATO (North Atlantic Treaty Organization). Trademark examples are MADD (Mothers Against Drunk Driving) and GEICO (Government Employees Insurance Corporation).

Alliteration: A linguistic device consisting of two or more successive or slightly separated words starting with the same sound, as in LEAPING LIZARDS or WICKED WIZARD OF WALES. Trademark examples are BOB'S BIG BOY and REYNOLDS WRAP.

Anagram: A word or combination of words having the same letters as another but arranged differently, as per LISTEN in relation to SILENT and ALEC GUINESS in relation to GENUINE CLASS. Trademark examples are CAMRY (MY CAR) and SPANDEX (EXPANDS).

X Linguistic Glossary

Anglicization: The transformation of a foreign word or word combination into an English sounding, English looking, or otherwise English-compatible word or word combination, as with BEAUCHAMPS into BEACHAM or CRISTOFORO COLOMBO into CHRISTOPHER COLUMBUS. Trademark examples are NUVO from "nouveau" and BOO-KU from "beaucoup."

Antonym: A word having an opposite meaning to another, e.g., BLACK in relation to WHITE or GOOD in relation to EVIL. Trademark examples are INFINITI and ZERO as used for car parts (marks which are antonyms in relation to each other) and PRO & CON (antonyms within a mark) for political and public interest publications and databases.

Aphesis: *See Decapitation.*

Apocope: The omission of the last letter, syllable, or part of a word, achieving results like MADAM derived from the French MADAME or the American CATALOG in relation to the British CATALOGUE. Trademark examples are MOBIL and ZIPLOC.

Aptronym: A name which matches, complements, or suggests a person's character or occupation, e.g., JOHNNY APPLESEED, planter of apple trees, or MARGARET COURT, tennis player. Trademark examples are BETTY CROCKER which strongly suggests a homemaker and SCHUMACHER (German for "shoemaker") for shoes.

Assonance: Vowel repetition in the same stressed syllables of two or more successive or slightly separated words, achieving a quasi-rhyme or vowel alliteration effect, as in ROCK 'N ROLL, also featuring consonant alliteration, and MAD AS A HATTER. Trademark examples are HARMAN/KARDON and LOCK & LOAD.

Back-Formation: A means of developing new words by assuming that a word's earlier form was a derivation and reconstructing the supposed original form by removing a suffix, prefix or other part from the earlier form. Examples are BURGLE derived from BURGLAR and DIPLOMAT created from DIPLOMATIC. Trademarks containing "back-formed" words are BURGER KING since BURGER was backwardly formed from "hamburger" (from the city of Hamburg) and INTUIT, derived from "intuition."

X Linguistic Glossary

Bacronym aka Backronym: The reverse of an acronym, namely a word or combination of words whose sounds or meaning mimic, evoke, or reflect an earlier-developed shorter word or acronym, such as PORT OUT, STARBOARD HOME for POSH or SAVE OUR SHIP for SOS. Trademark examples are ESSO, derived from S.O., the initials of Standard Oil, and JEEP, derived from G.P., the initials of General Purpose vehicle.

Cachet: The condition of enjoying prestige, respect, or admiration, like that possessed by the Nobel Prize or by a prestigious university such as Harvard. Trademark examples are ROLLS-ROYCE and MERCEDES-BENZ.

Cacophony: The opposite of euphony, i.e., the unpleasant, harsh, rough, or discordant quality of sound in a word or combination of words, as exemplified by BLOG and CACKLE. Trademark examples are ABERCROMBIE & FITCH and MITSUBISHI.

Capitonym: A word changing its meaning, and sometimes its pronunciation, when capitalized, e.g., Job, the Biblical character vs. "job," the task or occupation, and August, the month vs. "august," the adjective. Trademark examples are "RAINIER," pronounced like the surname or the name of the mountain, vs. "rainier," the adjective, and READING, pronounced as "redding" like the English city Reading, vs. "reading," the gerund of "read."

Chiasmus: A rhetorical device, often expressing wit or humor, in which the word order in two otherwise parallel phrases is reversed. Examples are Samuel Johnson's critique, "YOUR MANUSCRIPT IS BOTH GOOD AND ORIGINAL, BUT THE PART THAT IS GOOD IS NOT ORIGINAL; AND THE PART THAT IS ORIGINAL IS NOT GOOD" or Winston Churchill's remark on drinking, "ALL I CAN SAY IS THAT I HAVE TAKEN MORE OUT OF ALCOHOL THAN ALCOHOL HAS TAKEN OUT OF ME." Trademark examples of implied or semi-chiasmus are "YOU'LL SEE IT WHEN YOU BELIEVE IT" (the converse of "you'll believe it when you see it") for weight reduction programs, and MOTHER THE NECESSITY OF INVENTION (contrasting with "necessity, the mother of invention") for backpacks and travel bags.

X Linguistic Glossary

Consonance: The repetition of consonant sounds within words, as in SLALOM and FEBRUARY. Trademark examples are PRIORY and PARALLELS.

Consonant: An alphabet letter or cluster of letters which symbolizes a speech sound made by blocking the flow of air from the lungs, thus representing the containment of energy. Consonants in English are B, C, D, F, G, H, J, K, L, M, N, P, Q, R, S, T, V, W, X, Z, and, depending on usage, Y, as well as some digraphs such as CH, SH, and TH.

Consonant Cluster: A clump of consonants in a word, as per the NGSTR in "angstrom" or the LCH in "mulch." Examples of trademarks having such clusters are GROLSCH and SCHLAGE.

Contraction: A word or combination of words with letters omitted but still giving the impression of the original word or word combination, such as CAN'T for CANNOT and YOU'D for YOU WOULD. Trademark examples are FLICKR and NVIDIA.

Contronym: A word or combination of words having two opposite meanings, e.g., BOLT connoting both "flee" and "tie down" and TRIM connoting both "addition" and "excision." Trademark examples are SCREEN connoting both "hide" and "show" and TRIP connoting both "stumble" and "move with agility."

Decapitation: The excision of a word's first letter, syllable, or part as occurred with NADDER, the snake, which is now called ADDER, and with ESCAPE GOAT, which morphed into SCAPEGOAT. Trademark examples are ARMONY from "harmony" and ITANIUM from "titanium." A special kind of decapitation is aphesis, the loss of an unstressed vowel at the beginning of a word. Trademark examples are WILD 'BOUT BERRIES and ROBIN HOOD (E)SQUIRE.

Diacritical Mark: A symbol applied to a letter to indicate its pronunciation, e.g., the umlaut in NAÏVE or the tilde in BAÑO. Trademark examples are HÄAGEN DAZS and ERTÉ.

Digraph: A cluster of two letters such as PH or TH used to express a single sound or a sequence of sounds not ordinarily corresponding in sound to the sequence of letters. Trademark examples are SHELL and CHANEL.

X Linguistic Glossary

Diminutive: A word or combination of words formed from another, usually by adding a suffix, to express a smaller version of its kind, e.g., KITCHENETTE or DUCKLING. Trademark examples are WHEATIES and NACHITOS.

Double Entendre: A combination of words having two meanings, e.g., JUST DESSERTS, which refers to cuisine but connotes deserved consequences, or PART COMPANY, which could refer to a departure or a company selling parts (or is perhaps a triple entendre since it might denote a talent agency). Trademark examples are HEALTHYSELF for medical services, which is either HEAL + THYSELF or HEALTHY + SELF, or THE SOFT PUNCH for noncarbonated soft drinks.

Endonym: An endonym is a place name used by local inhabitants instead of the name used by foreigners, such as London vs. Londres and Roma vs. Rome, and the opposite of an "exonym," the place name used by foreigners rather than by locals, such as Munich vs. München and Turin vs. Torino. Trademark examples are BOMBAY, an exonym for "Mumbai," and O-TOWN, an endonym for "Orlando."

Eponym: The name of a discovery, principle, place, product, or other thing which originated from the name of a real or fictitious person, e.g., DIESEL or POINSETTIA. Trademark examples are STETSON and MARTINIZE.

Euphony: The opposite of cacophony, i.e., pleasing, sweet, smooth, or harmonious quality of sound in a word or phrase, as exemplified by SOVEREIGN and CELLAR DOOR. A euphonious word could be called a "harmonym" or "euphonym." Trademark examples are MAYBELLINE and YAMAHA.

Exonym: *See Endonym.*

Extraction: A word or combination of words formed by extracting relatively few letters from a longer word or a few words from a phrase, e.g., I'D from I WOULD (a contraction often being an extraction) or FWD from FORWARD (a text messaging shortcut as a kind of extraction). Trademark examples are TEFLON from "polyTEtraFLuOroethyleNe," its chemical name, or PEZ from "Pfefferminze," German for "peppermint."

X Linguistic Glossary

Fossil Word: A obsolete word or combination of words which survives in a language only as part of an idiomatic expression, such as FETTLE which survives within "in fine fettle" and LOGGERHEADS which inhabits "at loggerheads with." Trademark examples are KITH from "kith and kin" and SPIC AND SPAN.

Function Word aka Functor: A word with little meaning whose primary function is to express grammatical relationships with other words in a phrase or sentence, such as prepositions like OF and FOR, conjunctions like AND and BUT, and articles like A and THE. Examples of trademarks that include function words are FILL IT TO THE RIM WITH BRIM and IT'S ALL IN THE GAME.

Genitive: The possessive case/form of a noun or pronoun, as per BOOK'S or PILOTS', which generally indicates that the noun or pronoun is the possessor of another noun, e.g., "The book's first chapter" or "The pilots' union." Trademark examples are MRS. PAUL'S and WENDY'S.

Heteronym: A word or combination of words having the same spelling as another but a different meaning and pronunciation, as per LEAD, the verb and the metal, and BUFFET, the blow and the food service. A heteronym is a special kind of homograph. Trademark examples are BASS, the fish and the sound range, and DOVE, the bird and the past tense of "dive," though each usually having only one pronunciation when used as a mark.

Heterophone: A word or combination of words whose sounds are different from those of another, often referring to words whose sounds are somewhat similar, like "parson" vs. "person" or "fakir" (pronounced "fakeer") and "faker." Trademark examples are HONDA and HYUNDAI or HINT O' HONEY and HIDDEN HONEY.

Holonym: *See Meronym.*

Homograph: A word having the same spelling and sound as another but a different meaning, as per RUN connoting "movement" but also "tearing" or TAP connoting an "outlet" but also a "touch." Trademark examples are VAULT, connoting both "leap" and "valuables' storage space," for

X Linguistic Glossary

magazines on offshore investing, and PARTS UNKNOWN, which could conceivably be associated with "travel," "barbering," "warehousing" or "talent scouting" but is used for clothing.

Homonym: A word or combination of words having the same sound as another but a different spelling, as per BEAR and BARE or PEEK and PEAK. Examples of trademarks which rely on the effects of homonyms are MINUTE MAID ("made") for frozen juices and JOOST ("juiced") for computerized entertainment services.

Hypernym: *See Hyponym.*

Hyponym: A hyponym is a word more specific in meaning than a related word, e.g., SEDAN vs. CAR or HAMMER vs. TOOL. The opposite is a hypernym, a word more general in meaning, such as TREE vs. MAPLE or BIRD vs. PIGEON. Trademark examples are TERCEL, a hyponym of "hawk" because a "tiercel" is a male hawk, and "antelope," a hypernym of REEBOK since a "rhebok" is a kind of antelope.

Idiom: A combination of words whose typical meaning is different than its literal meaning, such as HIT THE ROAD ("get started" vs. "strike the pavement") or BOUGHT THE FARM ("died" vs. "purchased the agricultural property"). Trademark examples are LET IT RIP and CUT TO THE CHASE.

Jargon: Vocabulary peculiar to a particular trade, industry, occupation, profession, or similar group, often not understood or used by others, as per the legal term SUA SPONTE (meaning "on his/her own volition" in Latin) or the military term ALPHA STRIKE. Trademark examples are FORCE MULTIPLIER and EVENT HORIZON.

Lexeme: A fundamental unit of the lexicon of a language and whose members represent its various forms. Members of the lexeme GO include, e.g., GOES, GONE, GOING, and WENT, and members of the lexeme FINE include, e.g., FINER, FINEST, FINELY, FINENESS, and FINERY. Trademark examples include former marks like MIMEOGRAPH that went generic after the mark became a lexeme with various members (e.g., MIMEOGRAPH, MIMEOGRAPHER, and MIMEOGRAPHING), and by analogy a *family of marks* whose quasi-lexeme members are owned by one company (e.g., the marks CITIBANK, CITICARDS, and CITITREASURY).

X Linguistic Glossary

Malapropism: A funny use of a word or combination of words, typically because of unintended meaning, confusion with similar sounding word(s), or erroneous spelling, as in "He's a wolf in cheap clothing" and "The doctor felt the man's purse and said there was no hope." Trademark examples are MYLANTA, "lant" being stale urine used to scour wool, and DRECK, "dirt" in German, used for leather preservatives.

Matronym aka Metronym: A name originating from a mother's name, as per MEGSON, son of Meg, or HILLIARD from Hildegard. Trademark examples are ANSON, from Ann(e) (though sometimes also a decapitation of Hanson) and TILLOTSON, derived from a diminutive of Matilda.

Meronym: A meronym is word or combination of words that designates a thing or concept which is part of some other thing or concept, as per PETAL, a meronym in relation to FLOWER. A holonym is a meronym's opposite, namely a word or combination of words that designate a thing or concept which includes some other thing or concept, as per ATOM, a holonym in relation to PROTON. Trademark examples are NEWSDAY in relation to NEWSWEEK, and SAKS FIFTH AVENUE in relation to its hypothetical alternatives SAKS MANHATTAN or SAKS NEW YORK.

Metaphor: A word or phrase suggesting a concept which it directly would not, thus creating an imaginative comparison between the new concept and the concept ordinarily denoted, e.g., THIS BUD OF LOVE, comparing love to a flower, or SURFING THE WEB, watersport and spider's craft encountering the electronic frontier. Trademark examples are CHICKEN OF THE SEA for canned tuna and FRUIT OF THE LOOM for underwear.

Metaphrase: A word-for-word translation, often lacking proper idiomatic meaning, e.g., MY WAY OR THE HIGHWAY literally translated into Spanish as MI MANERA O LA CARRETERA, entirely losing its idiomatic meaning, or SABER ES PODER, literally translated from Spanish into English as TO KNOW IS TO BE ABLE, partially losing its idiomatic meaning. Trademark examples are KFC's slogan FINGER-LICKIN' GOOD literally translated into Chinese so that it came out as EAT YOUR FINGERS OFF and PURE LIFE for bottled water which would be literally translated in Spanish markets as VIDA PURA, so the owner adopted a more appropriate PUREZA VITAL.

X Linguistic Glossary

Metonym: A word or combination of words ordinarily denoting one concept but used to identify another, e.g., BOTTLE denoting "drinking" and KREMLIN denoting the former Soviet government or the current Russian government. Trademark examples are RED LOBSTER for fish restaurants and STAPLES (if meaning fastening devices) for office supplies.

Morpheme: A unit of meaning, consisting of a word or part of a word, that cannot be divided into smaller units of meaning, e.g., NOX in "equinox" refers to "night" and DECK, a whole word having no smaller units of meaning. Trademark examples of morpheme construction are COMPILEX for computerized database services for personal injury lawyers (COMP + PI + LEX and COMPILE) and VASELINE for an oil/water emulsion (from "Wasser," pronounced "vahser," German for water, and "elaion," Greek for oil).

Neologism: A new word first coming into the language. Years ago GEEK was such a new word; GINORMOUS is a more recent creation. Trademark examples are GOOGLE, a distinctive trademark, but also sometimes colloquially used *generically* as a verb to express doing an online search, and XEROX, also a distinctive trademark but colloquially once used generically as a noun, verb, and adjective in connection with photocopies.

Nomenclature: A system of names or a method for assigning names in an art, science, trade, or other field, as per a botanical or astronomical nomenclature. Trademark examples are trademark nomenclature guidelines prescribed by the U.S. Food & Drug Administration designed to prevent confusion in dispensing pharmaceuticals and naming conventions for proprietary and licensed products proclaimed by big companies like Microsoft Corporation.

Nominative: The subjective case/form of a noun or pronoun which generally indicates that in a phrase or sentence the noun or pronoun is the active subject of a verb, not its object, e.g., "The BOOK is both good and original" or "The PILOTS flew many flights." Real word trademarks that contain or comprise nouns or pronouns typically show them spelled in the nominative case/form rather than in the genitive (e.g., WENDY'S) or objective case/form (HIM).

X Linguistic Glossary

Nonce Word: A word created for a special occasion or intended to be used only "once" (though sometimes surviving in the language), like QUARK created by James Joyce for Finnegans Wake or SUPERCALIFRAGILISTICEXPIALIDOCIOUS from the "Mary Poppins" musical. Trademark examples are TORINO 2006 developed for the Torino winter Olympic Games and THREE-PEAT created by basketball coach Pat Riley to reference winning a basketball championship three times in a row.

Onomatopoeia: The linguistic phenomenon of a word sounding like the thing it denotes, e.g., MEOW or HICCUP. Trademark examples are SCHWEPPES, mimicking the sound of carbonated beverages, and FERRARI, reminiscent of a car engine's roar.

Oronym: A word or combination of words sounding like another word or combination of words, e.g., ICE CREAM vs. I SCREAM or WHITE SHOES vs. WHY CHOOSE. Trademark examples are BEEFEATER ("bee feeder") and ARM & HAMMER ("Armand Hammer," the industrialist).

Oxymoron: A combination of two or more words that might be perceived as incongruous, e.g., JUMBO SHRIMP or ACCURATE ESTIMATE. Trademark examples are BLACK SUN and LIQUID DIAMOND.

Palatability: The acceptability of a word or combination of words across language and cultural boundaries. Words like OKAY and, more recently, EMAIL are palatable and widely accepted around the world. Examples of highly palatable trademarks are SONY and NOKIA.

Palindrome: A word or combination of words which spells the same thing both forwards and backwards, e.g., DEIFIED and SO MANY DYNAMOS. Trademark examples are ZOONOOZ and ROTAVATOR.

Parody: In relation to wordplay and trademarks, a word or combination of words which by its use and similarity mocks, satirizes, or humorously references an established name, *slogan*, mark, or title, e.g., the trademarks CHEWY VUITON for dog accessories which parodies LOUIS VUITTON or VICTOR'S LITTLE SECRET for adult products which parodies VICTORIA'S SECRET.

X Linguistic Glossary

Patronym: A name originating from a father's name, as per SAMSON, son of Sam(uel) or FITZPATRICK, son of Patrick. Trademark examples are MCDONALD'S and ALBERTSONS.

Petronym: A word or combination of words "set in stone," like VISA and KNIFE EDGE, whose meaning is relatively singular, long lasting, and constant even if capable of many metaphoric uses, and somewhat the opposite of a pteronym. Trademark examples are ORACLE and AJAX.

Phoneme: The smallest phonetic (sound) unit of language that can convey a distinction in meaning, e.g., the "S" sound in "set" as distinguished from the "J" sound in "jet" or the "W" sound in "wane" vs. the "V" sound in "vein." Trademark examples are the "S" sound in SONIQUE vs. the "M" sound in MONIQUE and the "I" sound in TRUSS-SKIN vs. the "O" sound in TRUSCON.

Phonosemantics aka Sound Symbolism: The semantics of sound, or the study of the meaning of sounds, e.g., whereby one may surmise the semantics of individual letter sounds. For instance, the dispersed energy of the "W" sound accounts for wispy words like "whimper," "whisper," and "wallow," whereas the highly focused energy of the "T" sound spawns tight words like "taut," "tense," and "terse." Trademark examples might be the boisterous "B's" in BOB'S BIG BOY and the spiritual "A's" in AVAYA.

Portmanteau: A word created by blending recognizable components of two or more other words, like SMOG from "smoke" and "fog" or BRUNCH from "breakfast" and "lunch." Trademark examples are SPAM from "spiced" and "ham" and WATSU from "water" and "shiatsu."

Pteronym: A "winged" word or combination of words, like SET and FILE, whose meaning tends to move, evolve, splinter, and mutate over time, somewhat the opposite of a petronym. Trademark examples are LONGS, connoting a surname, physical and temporal length, yearning, etc., and DR. PEPPER, with PEPPER connoting a surname, tree, condiment, verb, etc.

Pun: A play on words by which a word is replaced with a similar word, like a homonym or similar heterophone to achieve a clever or humorous new meaning, e.g., NOTHING RISQUE, NOTHING GAINED and A PUN

X Linguistic Glossary

IS ITS OWN REWORD. Trademark examples are FIG NEWMAN, a pun on FIG NEWTON, and FROOGLE, the former GOOGLE name for its shopping search engine.

Rebus: Pictures, symbols, letters, or numerals, or a combination of such elements which by sound or symbolism suggest a word or phrase, e.g., Q8 is a rebus for "Kuwait" and 4N6 a rebus for "forensics." Trademark examples are TOYS "Я" US and T42.

Retronym: A new word or combination of words used for an old thing or concept whose original name is no longer appropriate or is used for something else, usually formed by adding an adjective to the original noun, as in DIRT ROAD (originally just ROAD before roads were generally paved) and AM RADIO (just RADIO before the FM band was introduced). Trademark examples are COCA-COLA CLASSIC for the original-flavor drink and G1 TRANSFORMERS for the original toy action figures.

Reversal: A word which spells another word backwards, e.g., STRESSED and DESSERTS or REVEL and LEVER. Trademark examples are HARPO, a reversal of "Oprah" (Winfrey), and SERUTAN, "natures" reversed.

Rhyme: The identity of sound between two or more words from the last stressed vowel to the end of each word, the consonant or consonant group preceding the last stressed vowel being different for each word, as in TANGO and MANGO or GUESS and CARESS. Trademark examples are FAMOUS AMOS (rhyme within a mark) and GO-GURT yogurt (rhyme with the product name).

Ricochet Word: A word, usually hyphenated, formed by reduplicating the first component, but with the second component either having a different first consonant sound or a different first vowel sound, e.g., CHIT-CHAT or ROLY-POLY. Trademark examples are KIT KAT and TUSH-CUSH.

Slang: Very informal, often ephemeral words or combinations of words that are typically striking, vivid, colorful, idiomatic, metaphorical, or vulgar, though sometimes formally accepted into a language following widespread, long term usage. GIZMO was once slang as was HELL'S BELLS. Trademark examples are JEEPERS and DEAD PRESIDENTS (money in bills).

X Linguistic Glossary

Syncope: The omission of an interior letter, syllable, or other part of a word, as per the contraction CAN'T in relation to CANNOT and the American ALUMINUM compared to the British ALUMINIUM. Trademark examples are CUISINART vs. CUISINE ART and TINACTIN vs. TINEA ACTION.

Synonym: A word or combination of words having the same meaning as another, as per BLACK and EBONY or CARELESS and NEGLIGENT. Trademark examples are TUCKS, a kind of inserts when used for suppositories, thus matching the mark to the product, and GARDEN OF LIFE for nutritional supplements, substantially synonymous with EDEN, another nutrition mark.

Tautonym: A word or term comprising two or more identical components, as per COUSCOUS and BERI BERI. Trademark examples are MIU MIU and TOMTOM.

Telescoped Word: A composite word formed by joining two or more words that share letters, as in CINEMADDICT and GUESSTIMATE. Trademark examples are TRAVELODGE and WORMIX.

Theronym: A name, particularly a product name, derived from an animal's name, e.g., CAT'S EYE or HOT DOG. Trademark examples are CATERPILLAR and DODGE RAM.

Toponym: A place name for a locality, region, or other part of the Earth's surface such as EVEREST or LOCH NESS. Trademark examples are EVIAN and YUKON.

Translation: A word or combination of words from one language whose meaning is expressed in another language, e.g., VERDE (Spanish for "green") translated as GRÜN in German, or CAVE CANEM from Latin translated into BEWARE THE DOG. Trademark examples are MEIRYO, meaning "clear," "lucid," or "plain" in Japanese, for font-related software, and FACILPAGO, connoting "easy payment," used by the Home Shopping Network.

X Linguistic Glossary

Transliteration: A word or combination of words from one alphabet or script, expressed in another alphabet or script, usually preserving the sound or concept, or both, of the word or combination of words from the original alphabet or script. Trademark examples are CARTIER, phonetically transliterated into Chinese characters to sound like KA DI YA, and PEPSI COLA, phonetically and conceptually transliterated into Chinese characters to sound like BAI SHI KE LE, which means "everything makes you happy."

Trigraph: A cluster of three letters such as SCH or EAU used to express a single sound or sequence of sounds not ordinarily corresponding in sound to the sequence of letters. Trademark examples are BEAU and SCHLAGE.

Vowel: An alphabet letter which symbolizes one or more speech sounds made without blocking the flow of air from the lungs, thus representing the free flow of energy. Vowels in English are A, E, I, O, and U, and, depending on usage, Y.

Word: The smallest unit of syntax in a phrase or sentence, though not to be fully identified with a *word mark* which is defined in relation to typography in the Trademark Glossary.

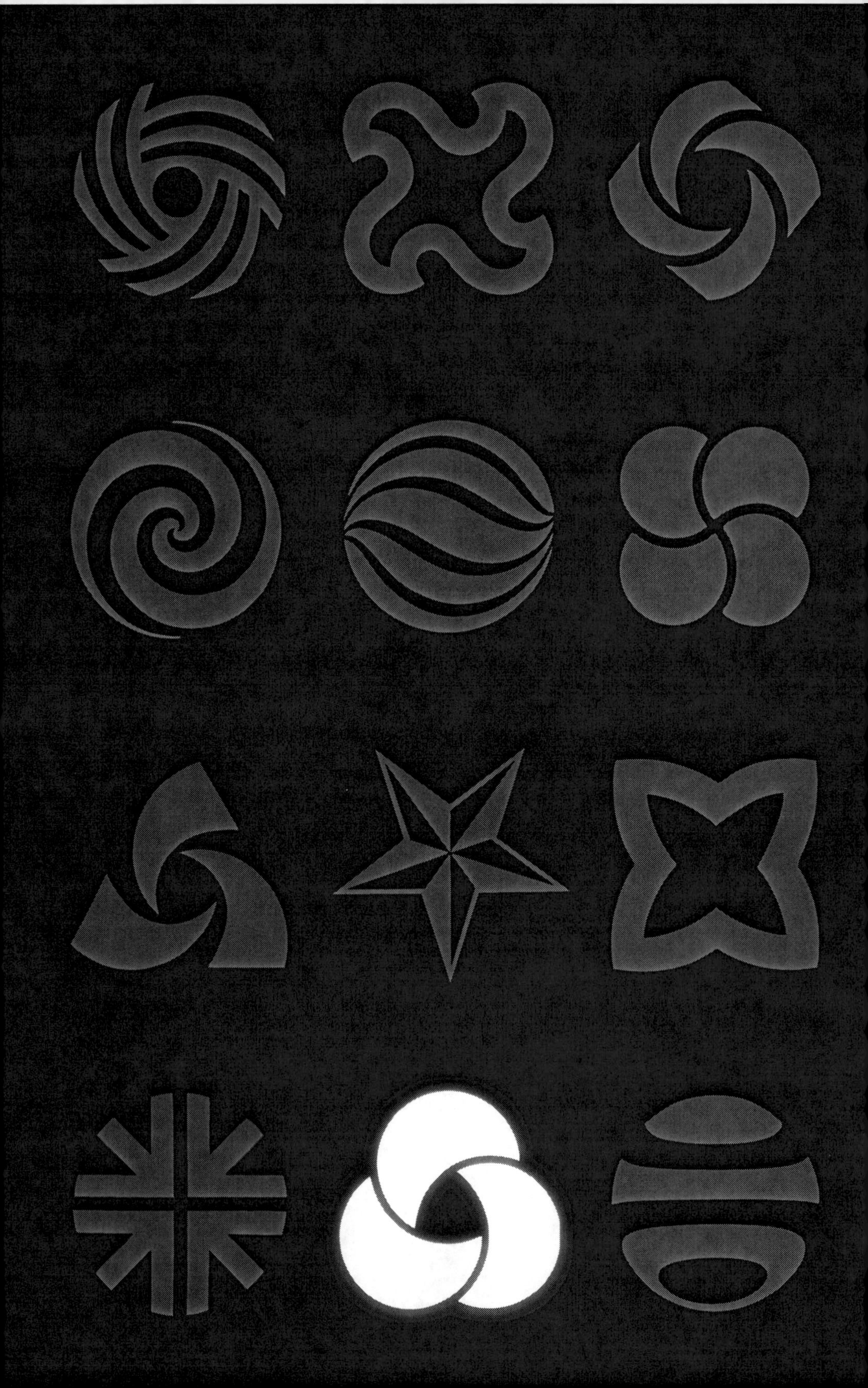

LOCATIONS OF WORD MARKS IN TEXT

XI Index of Word Marks

"From antiquity, people have recognized the connection between naming and power."

CASEY MILLER AND KATE SWIFT

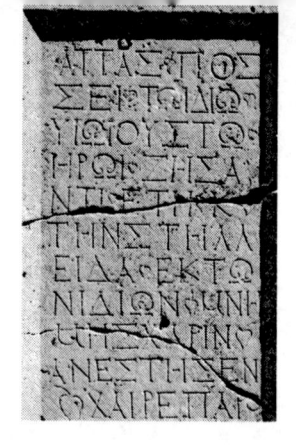

This Index shows the paragraph
numbers where word marks appear in the paragraphs numbered 1 through 333.

WORD MARK	PARAGRAPH NUMBER	WORD MARK	PARAGRAPH NUMBER
66.	184	A TO Z	221
76.	184	AAA	97
409	184	AAMCO	128
501	184	ABBA	183
727	184	ABBOTT & COSTELLO	58
737	184	ABC	234
747	184	ABERCROMBIE & FITCH	58, 66
757	184	ABRACADABRA	52, 203
767	184	ACAPULCO GOLD	323
777	184	ACCENTURE	18
787	184	ACCORD	105, 109
4711	115, 139, 184	ACURA	91, 105
100% PURE FLORIDA'S SEAL OF APPROVAL	319	ADIDAS	30, 51, 93, 95, 188, 229
1-800-HOLIDAY	115	ADOBE	209
1-800-PICK-UPS	115	AETNATEC	186
1 + 1 = 3	184	AIDA	149
37SIGNALS	184	AIM	171
3M	55	AIRBRUSH	142
4N6	172, 182	AIRBUS	74
4N6PRT	172	AJAX	152
7-ELEVEN	184, 201	AKAI	206
		ALBERTO VO5	328

250

XI Index of Word Marks

WORD MARK	PARAGRAPH NUMBER
ALBERTSONS	101
ALCATRAZ	140
ALDI	176
ALEXIS	37
ALFA ROMEO	149
ALKA	156
ALLSTATE	29, 225, 228
ALPHA TO OMEGA	221
ALTAVISTA	192
ALWAYS CLOSED	135
AMANA	67
AMAZON.COM	122, 189
AMBIEN	67, 103, 164
AMD	79
AMERICA ESPIRITO SPORT FRATERNITE	333
AMERICAN APPAREL	95
AMERICA'S ROAST BEEF, YES SIR	155
AMINO FUEL	108
AMISH	153, 325
AMOCO	156
AMWAY	125, 127, 156
ANACIN	160
ANOMALY GAMES	179
ANSON	101
ANTISENILIN	222
ANUSOL	225
AOL	155
APPLE	37, 62, 71, 75, 108, 116, 133, 215, 233
ARBY'S	155
ARCH REST	134
ARCO	156

WORD MARK	PARAGRAPH NUMBER
ARM & HAMMER	46, 62, 150, 225
ARMANI	98
ARMONY	164
ARTHRITICARE	175
ASE	192
ASPIRIN	86, 116, 142, 160
ATLAS	150
AUDI	39, 191, 192
AUNT JEMIMA	41, 81
AVALON	105, 138, 152
AVAYA	78
AVIS	226, 228
AVON	233
AZANTAC	13, 94
AZTEC	153
B OF A: BANKING ON AMERICA	64
B4UP	172
B9	172
BABELFISH	125
BADASS	323
BAGEL NOSH	192
BAGZILLA	200
BAKER STREET	139
BALI	170
BALLPARK	211
BANANA REPUBLIC	57, 66, 68, 102, 112
BAND-AID	59, 159, 160
BANTAM	45, 202
BARBARA ARDEN	53
BARBIE	232
BASKIN 31 ROBBINS	184
BASS	224

XI Index of Word Marks

WORD MARK	PARAGRAPH NUMBER
BAYER	93
BAZOOKA	68, 116, 211
BEACHAMS	194
BECK'S	202
BECK'S BEER	46
BEEFEATER	46, 48
BEETLE	209, 226
BEN & JERRY'S	144
BENADRYL	74
BENTLEY	105
BEST	141
BEST FOODS	141
BEST WESTERN	141
BETHESDA SPRING	118, 138
BETTER HOMES	135
BETTER HOMES AND GARDENS	135
BETTER MONEY. LIFE TAKES VISA	186
BETTY CROCKER	5, 146, 232
BIC	80, 96, 100, 105, 170
BIG BEN	140
BILL BLASS	146
BILLABONG	127
BIRD	328
BIRDS EYE	143, 202
BISMARCK	148
BK	97
BLACK & DECKER	58, 78
BLACK CRACKER	53
BLACK SUN	218
BLAUPUNKT	5, 206
BLITZ	46
BLOCKBUSTER	78

WORD MARK	PARAGRAPH NUMBER
BLUE	215
BLUE CROSS	206
BLUE LICK WATER SPRINGS	138
BLUE MOON	157
BLUE SKY	233
BLUESTONE	177
BMW	97, 109
BMW 318	109
BMW 323	109
BMW 328	109
BMW 528	109
BMW 540	109
BOB'S BIG BOY	102, 202
BOLT	223
BOMBAY	138
BON AMI	192
BOO-KU	194
BOOST	231
BOSCO	143
BOSE	328
BOY SCOUTS	333
BOY SCOUTS OF AMERICA	333
BRAHMA	125
BRAUN	93
BRAVES	81
BREAD OF LIFE	227
BRIDGESTONE	39
BRILLO	132
BROADWAY	139
BROOKS	171
BROOKS BROTHERS	202
BROTHER	215
BROWN COW	206, 226

XI Index of Word Marks

WORD MARK	PARAGRAPH NUMBER
BUBBY TRAP	323
BUD	65, 170
BUDWEISER	65, 112
BUFFERIN	160
BUG	209
BUGS BUNNY	23
BUMBLE BEE	133
BURGER KING	41, 58, 93, 126, 212
BURNSIDE	180
BURT'S BEES	202
BUSCH	112
CAFETERIA	322
CALVIN KLEIN	146
CAMAY	194
CAMELOT	138, 152
CAMPBELL'S	194
CAMRY	105, 181
CANON	5, 61, 202
CANOPUS	151
CANOSCAN	204
CARL'S JR.	158
CARMEN	149
CARNIVAL	67
CASIO	91
CATERPILLAR	134, 226
CB4UP	172
CBS	234
CELERON	79
CELESTIAL SEASONINGS	80
CELLOPHANE	142
CEMEX	132
CENTURY 21	173, 184
CHAMPION	141

WORD MARK	PARAGRAPH NUMBER
CHANEL NO. 5	184
CHAPELL	328
CHARLIE THE TUNA	226
CHARMIN	163
CHEERIOS	67, 209
CHEROKEE	109, 153
CHEVROLET	66, 143
CHEVROLET SILVERADO	30
CHEVRON	62
CHEVY	65, 66
CHEWY VUITON	28, 200
CHEYENNE	153
CHICKEN OF THE SEA	71, 226
CHICLETS	173, 210
CHIEFS	81
CHIPPEWA	153
CHIQUITA	203
CHOCK FULL O'NUTS	71, 322
CHOICE	141
CHROMAX	160
CHRONICLE	29
CHRYSLER	109
CINGULAR	122, 166
CIRRHUS	79
CISCO	79
CISCO SYSTEMS	202
CITI	108
CITIBANK	108
CITIUS ALTIUS FORTIUS	333
CITY	215
CIVIC	105, 109, 183
CLARITIN	160
CLASSIC XII	184

253

XI Index of Word Marks

WORD MARK	PARAGRAPH NUMBER
CLEOPATRA	148
CLIX	185
CLOROX	160, 207
CLUB	136
CLUB MED	58, 156
COBRA	226
COCA-COLA	18, 65, 91, 93, 98, 203, 204, 208
COCA-COLA CLASSIC	107
CODE*SMART	186
COHIBA	192
COKE	19, 49, 65, 98, 142
COLD STONE	58
COLORA	165
COMANCHE	153
COME ON IN	217
COME ON STRONG	217
COMPAQ	56, 163
COMPILEX	40, 174
COMPLETE IDIOT'S GUIDE	41
CONCEPT XXI	185
CONOCO	156
CONSTITUTION	29
CONVERSE	30, 224
COODJU	136
COPPER TAN	46
COPPERTONE	46, 118
COUP DE GRASS	198
COURTYARD	111
COW AND GATE	226
CRACKER JACK	205
CRAIG'S LIST	221
CRAYOLA	176
CRAZYLEGS	145

WORD MARK	PARAGRAPH NUMBER
CREAM OF WHEAT	71
CREATIVE RECREATION	30
CROAKIES	30, 210, 213
CUISINART	163
CURE!	186
CUT TO THE CHASE	196
CUZN	182
CWM	192
CYCLONE	46
CYLIX	197
DA VINCI	148, 328
DAEWOO	118
DAIRY QUEEN	41, 57, 58, 124, 126
DANNY'S	166
DATASTORM	218
DAUNOXOME	103
DEIFIED	183
DELL	143
DENNY'S	144, 166
DEPEND	214
DHL	79, 97, 155
DIAMANTE	62
DIEHARD	59, 134
DISALCID	104
DISCOVER	214, 228
DISNEY	112, 120
DISPATCH	29
DIXIE	61
DKNY	82, 155
DODGE CARAVAN	174
DODGE RAM	30
DOG FARTS	70, 80
DOGPILE	70

XI Index of Word Marks

WORD MARK	PARAGRAPH NUMBER
DOLE	171
DOLOMITE	160
DOMINO'S	209
DON'T SAY GLUE, SAY YOOHOO!	201
DOS EQUIS	192
DOVE	224
DOWNING STREET	139
DQ	97
DR. PEPPER	173
DRANO	187
DREAMLINER	16
DRECK	90
DRIVERS WANTED	228
DUDS	135
DUM DUMS	204
DUNES	171
DUPONT	66, 143
DURANGO	138
DWARF	168
DYANSHINE	175
EBAY	75, 122, 160
ECCO	166
ECOPOWER	230
EDEN	39, 221
EDSEL	8, 25
EHARMONY	75
EIFFEL TOWER	140
ELEPHONE	164
ELF	155
EMINEM	204
ENCARTA	107
ENERGIZER	212

WORD MARK	PARAGRAPH NUMBER
ENFORCER	212
ENGELBERT HUMPERDINCK	146
ENGLISH LEATHER	134
ENQUIRER	29
ENRON	160
ENSURE	214, 231
EREWHON	138, 178
ERTÉ	187
ESCALATOR	74, 142
ESPRIT DE CORP	89
EVENT HORIZON	197
EVEREADY	134, 163
EVIAN	118, 138, 178
EX BIER	46
EXAMINER	29
EXCEL	107
EXCITE	214
EXPLORER	212
EXXON	37, 38, 49, 55, 56, 132, 160, 162, 165
EYEFUL	220
EZ FLO	169
EZT	172
FABER-CASTELL	100
FACILPAGO	193
FAIRBANKS	328
FAIRY	126
FALSTAFF	149
FAMOUS AMOS	201
FARMERS	29
FAST	216
FAT BOY	209
FCUK	70, 323

XI Index of Word Marks

WORD MARK	PARAGRAPH NUMBER
FEDEX	79, 129, 156, 228
FENDI	105
FERRARI	207
FIDELITY	125
FIG NEWMANS	23, 198, 200
FIG NEWTONS	198, 200
FIGARO	149
FILL IT TO THE RIM WITH BRIM	64, 69
FI'ZI:K	136
FLICKR	163
FLINTSTONES	23
FLOMAX	104
FLONASE	104
FOR DUMMIES	41
FORCE MULTIPLIER	197
FORD	120, 143
FORD F-150	30
FORMICA	142
FRIGIDAIRE	116, 165, 175
FROOGLE	169
FRUIT OF THE LOOM	71, 80, 125
FUJI	138
G1 TRANSFORMERS	107
GAP	96, 98, 102, 112
GARDEN OF LIFE	39, 221
GATORADE	160
GAZA	192
GENETEK	51
GENEVA CROSS	333
GENTLY	216
GEORGE KILLIAN'S IRISH RED	322
GEORGIO ARMANI	98, 146

WORD MARK	PARAGRAPH NUMBER
GERPLUNK	207
GET A GRIP	227
GHOSTHUSTLERS	198
GILBERT & SULLIVAN	58
GIRL SCOUTS	333
GIRL SCOUTS OF AMERICA	333
GIVE A HOOT, DON'T POLLUTE	333
GLAD	221
GLEAM	171
GLOBE	29
GO	214
GODZILLA	200
GO-GURT	201
GOLDCLAD	175
GOOD & PLENTY	141
GOOD GUYS	80
GOOD HUMOR	80
GOOD SAMARITAN	227
GOOD TASTE. NO WAIST	201
GOODYEAR	59
GOOGLE	49, 54, 70, 148, 169
GOO-GOO	196
GORE-TEX	113
GOT MILK?	214
GRAHAM WEBB	101
GRAPE-NUTS	322
GRATEFUL DEAD	218
GREEN & BLACK'S	206
GREEN GIANT	124, 206
GREMLIN	126, 209
GROLSCH	52
GRUBB	222
GUARDIAN	29

XI Index of Word Marks

WORD MARK	PARAGRAPH NUMBER
GUCCI	66, 105
HÄAGEN-DAZS	50, 132, 187, 192, 322
HACKLER	328
HAIREM	169
HAMILTON	328
HAMILTON PHARMACEUTICALS	328
HANAFORD'S HOME RUNS	224
HANDSPRING	225
HANG TEN	62, 63, 214, 225
HARCOURT BRACE	58
HARD PLACE	157
HARD ROCK	58
HARLEY-DAVIDSON	65
HARMON/KARDON	53, 170, 201, 205
HARMONY	164
HARRODS	158
HARRY AND DAVID'S	58, 144
HARVEYS BRISTOL CREAM	39
HASBRO	66
HEAD	96, 171
HEAD & SHOULDERS	225
HEALTHYSELF	177
HEBREW NATIONAL	153
HERALD	29
HERE'S JOHNNY	28, 200
HERSHEY'S	143
HITACHI	192
HOG	65, 66
HO-JO	66
HOLIDAY INN	115
HOME DEPOT	102, 105, 217

WORD MARK	PARAGRAPH NUMBER
HOME EXPO	102, 105
HONDA	109, 143
HOPE SPRINGS	157
HORCH	39
HOSPIRA	5
HOW	216
HOWARD JOHNSON	66
HOWDY DOODY	203
HUMMER	105, 170
HUSH PUPPIES	133, 159, 209, 210, 213
HYPERION	75, 151, 191
IBM	48, 60, 93, 95, 97, 120, 228
IHOP	97, 98, 155
IKEA	166
I'M LOVIN' IT	229
IMAX	225
IMPALA	226
IMPOSSIBLE IS NOTHING	229
IMPROV	56
INcENT$	167
INCA	153
INFINITI	109, 166
INFINITI I30	109
INFINITI J30	109
INFINITI Q30	109
INFINITI QX4	109
IN-N-OUT BURGER	102, 231
INNOVIII	172
INTEL	79, 104, 105, 134, 170
INTEL INSIDE	113, 191
INTERNATIONAL HOUSE OF PANCAKES	97, 98, 155
INTUIT	212

XI Index of Word Marks

WORD MARK	PARAGRAPH NUMBER
IO	151
iPHONE	75
iPOD	75, 110
IRON BUTTERFLY	218
IROQUOIS	153
ISKOOLA POTA	193
IT PAYS TO DISCOVER	228
ITANIUM	164
IT'S A JUNGLE OUT THERE	227
IT'S NOT JUST A DEAL, IT'S A DELL!	64
IUNIVERSE	160
IVORY	136
JABRA	123
JACK DANIELS	146
JACK IN THE BOX	62, 102, 124, 126
JAGUAR	62, 209, 226
JAM	224
JANTZEN	49
JAZZERCISE	163, 176
JEEP	49, 96, 155, 168, 172
JELL-O	49, 160, 207
JETTA	55, 72, 88, 132
JEW	325
JEZTERZ	136
JIMMY	144
JOB	224
JOHNSON & JOHNSON	120, 143, 204, 217
JONES LOCKER	157
JORDACHE	28, 40
JOURNAL	29
JOY	96
JUAN VALDEZ	146
JUNGLE JAP	325

WORD MARK	PARAGRAPH NUMBER
JURASSIC PARK	190
JUST DESSERTS	199
JUST DO IT	229
JUSTERNINI & BROOKS	58
K9	172
KABC	234
KABOOM	207
KAOPECTATE	208
KASHI	136, 166
KEDS	30
KELLOGG'S	143
KELVINATOR	154
KENTUCKY FRIED CHICKEN	98, 155
KEROSENE	74, 86
KERPLUNK	207
KEY	46
KFC	98, 155
KINDLEKIN	204
KING ARTHUR	152
KINKO'S	168, 232
KIT KAT	205
KITCHENAID	160
KIWI	37, 88, 233
KIX	96, 99, 169
KLEENEX	60, 116, 142, 168
KLUTZ	196
KMART	37
KODAK	37, 54, 91, 132
KOOL-ADE	160
KOTEX	178
KPBS	234
KQED	234
L'EGGS	169

258

XI Index of Word Marks

WORD MARK	PARAGRAPH NUMBER
LA ROSA	192, 203
LA YOGURT	195
LADY GODIVA	148
LAKE WOBEGON	138
LAKOTA	153
LAND O'LAKES	233
LAND ROVER	212
LANDS' END	233
LAREDO	109, 138
LE CASE	195
LECTRONIC	207
LED ZEPPELIN	218
L'EGGS	38, 255
LEGO	194, 225
LEO9	172
LEPTOPRIN	42
LET IT RIP	196
LEVI STRAUSS	98
LEVI'S	98
LEXIS NEXIS	201
LEXUS	37, 105
LIBIDO	323
LIBRIUM	74
LIFE	215
LIFE SAVERS	209
LIFEBUOY	209
LIGHTNIN'	46
LINUX	166, 232
LIQUID DIAMOND	218
LISTEN	181
LISTERINE	154, 160
LIV	185
LIZ CLAIBORNE	146
LOCH NESS	138

WORD MARK	PARAGRAPH NUMBER
LOCK AND LOAD	201
LOCKHEED MARTIN	58
LOGITECH	89
LOJACK	222
LONG JOHN SILVER	149
LOOK	214
L'OREAL	89
LOUIS VUITTON	28, 200
LOUIS XIV	185
LUNESTA	67
LYCOS	18, 38, 134, 191
LYCRA	170, 213
M & M 'S	155, 204
M@DNOYZ	50, 167
MA%I-FUND	167
MAC	108
MAC & JAC	58, 144, 201
MACINTOSH	108
MAD	171
MADD	155
MADONNA	323, 332
MAGNAVOX	191, 192
MAID IN THE SHADE	220
MAIL	29
MALTED MILK	142
MARATHON	191
MARIMEKKO	138
MARK IV	184, 185
MARKS & SPENCERS	58
MARRIOTT	111
MARS	150, 151, 205
MARTHA STEWART	146
MARTINELLI'S	158
MARTINIZE	154

259

XI Index of Word Marks

WORD MARK	PARAGRAPH NUMBER
MARVEL	126, 214
MASTERCARD	59, 188
MAUI	76
MAXELL	163
MAYA	153
MAYTAG	82, 143, 328
MAZDA	125
McDONALD'S	101, 108, 124, 229
McDONELL DOUGLAS	58
MCI	185
MEIRYO	193
MEN ARE FROM MARS, WOMEN ARE FROM VENUS	190
MENNON	178
MERCEDES BENZ	58
MERCURY	29, 83, 150
MET	156
MICHELOB	56, 112
MICROSOFT	45, 107, 118
MIDAS	75, 83, 150
MIDOL	90
MINOLTA	192
MINUTE MAID	220
MIRAMAX	5, 90, 191, 232
MIST STICK	90
MITSUBISHI	62, 96, 120
MIU MIU	129, 204
MOBIL	163
MOHAWK	153
MONSTER.COM	80, 189
MONTGOMERY WARD	58
MOTEL 6	184
MOTHERS AGAINST DRUNK DRIVING	230
MOTOROLA	176
MOUNTAIN DEW	71, 211
MR. CLEAN	173, 222
MR. COFFEE	41
MRS. PAUL'S	158, 173
MRS. TEA	41
MUPPETS	176
MUSTANG	226
MUTUAL OF OMAHA	83
MYLANTA	78, 82
MY-T-FINE	186
NABISCO	107, 114
NACHITOS	210
NAIR	163
NAPOLEON	148
NATIONWIDE IS ON YOUR SIDE	201
NATURES	178
NEIMAN MARCUS	58, 61
NEONETTE	222
NEONYM	129, 134
NETSCAPE	218
NEUMATIC	164
NEW BALANCE	30
NEWMAN'S OWN	173, 328
NEWS	29
NEWTON	148
NIKE	75, 120, 191, 229
NINE TAILS	157
NINTENDO	66
NISSAN	95
NITTY GRITTY	196
NO-D-KA	135, 169
NOKIA	66, 91, 138, 232
NON SEQUITUR	89

XI Index of Word Marks

WORD MARK	PARAGRAPH NUMBER
NOVA	90
NOVARTIS	163
NOW	155
NOW, THAT'S BETTER	186
NUNN BUSH	171
NUTRASWEET	113
NUVO	194
NVIDIA	37, 163
NYLON	116, 160
NYQUIL	54, 67, 174
OBELUS	197
OCEAN SPRAY	233
OCULAX	67
ODYSSEY	152
OLD FAITHFUL	140
OLD NAVY	102, 105, 112
OLD REPUBLIC	83
OLYMPIAD	333
OLYMPIC	333
ONE-A-DAY	186, 231
ORACLE	125, 191
ORANGE	37, 186, 215, 233
OREO	157
ORION	151
ORO FINO NUGGET	193
ORVILLE REDENBACHER	96
OUST	214
OVALTINE	157, 160
OXO	97, 122, 155, 183
PAC BELL	156
PACITAXELINE	103
PACKARD BELL	58
PALL MALL	205
PALM	225

WORD MARK	PARAGRAPH NUMBER
PALMOLIVE	59, 170, 175, 176
PAM PAM	129, 204
PAN-AM	156
PAN-AMERICAN	333
PARALYMPIC	333
PART COMPANY	199
PARTS UNKNOWN	224
PAUL MITCHELL	99
PAVAXIN	42
PAX WORLD FUND	230
PAYPAL	46, 86
PELICAN	45
PENGUIN	45, 133
PENNYWISE	157
PENTIUM	6, 75, 101, 191
PEP BOYS	145
PEPPERIDGE	175
PEPSI	49, 67, 98, 208
PEPSI COLA	98
PEPTO-BISMOL	208
PETERBILT	125, 127, 144
PETSMART	177
PEZ	157
PGA	317
PHENTERCOT	104
PHOS FUEL	108
PICASA	148, 176
PICKETT	328
PICTURE IT!	214
PIERRE CARDIN	146
PIGGLY-WIGGLY	201
PILATES	154
PIMM'S	171
PINAUD	50, 192

XI Index of Word Marks

WORD MARK	PARAGRAPH NUMBER
PINK FLOYD	218
PINTO	162
PIXAR	207
PLANET HOLLYWOOD	57
PLANTERS	202
PLATO	148
PLATYPUS	88, 132
PLAY IT AGAIN SAM	70, 227
PLAYRIGHT	220
PLAYRITE	220
PLAYWRIGHT	220
PLAYWRITE	220
POCONO OVAL	53
POKEMON	23
POLARTEC	76, 104
POLLONAISE	40
POLO	62, 105
POPSICLE	142
POST	29
POSTAL PLUS	39
POWERPOINT	107
PRADA	100, 105, 328
PRANA	71
PRELUDE	109
PRENTICE-HALL	58
PRESENTATI*N PLATES	167
PRO FORMA	89
PRODUCT 19	184
PROZAC	37, 54, 123, 132, 162
PRUDENTIAL	29, 83, 102
PUMA	30
PURE LIFE	193
PUREZA VITAL	193
PURITAN	153

WORD MARK	PARAGRAPH NUMBER
PYTHON	226
Q8	172
QANTAS	37, 163, 168
QD QUAQUE DIE ONLINE	193
Q-TIPS	159, 168, 207
QUAKER	153
QUALCOMM	55, 56
QUICKEN	214
QUICKLY	216
QUILL	75
QVC	97, 120, 155
RABBIT	209
RAINFOREST	230
RAINIER	224
RAISE YOUR HANDS IF YOU'RE SURE	64
RALEIGH	194
RALPH LAUREN	105
RAM	226
RAMSES	70, 83, 122, 148
RAYON	160
REACH	231
READING	224
RED BULL	195, 206
RED CROSS	206, 333
RED HOTS	68
RED LOBSTER	219
REDFIELD	194
REDSKINS	81
REEBOK	30, 134, 226
REEF	127
REGAL	183
REI	155
RELIANCE	29, 102

XI Index of Word Marks

WORD MARK	PARAGRAPH NUMBER
REMBRANDT	83
RENAISSANCE HOTELS & RESORTS	111
RESIDENCE INN	111
REVEL LEVER	179
REYNOLDS WRAP	202
RIGOLETTO	149
RIN TIN TIN	203
RINGLING	207
RITZ	107, 114, 215
RITZ-CARLTON	111
RITZY	215
ROBIN HOOD	152
ROBINSONS-MAY	158
ROCKET POPS	209
ROGAINE	103
ROLEX	72, 105
ROMAN MEAL	75
RONZONI	201, 203
ROOSEVELT	194
ROQUEFORT	137, 319
ROSENFELD	194
ROTARY INTERNATIONAL	318
ROTAVATOR	183
ROTO-ROOTER	202
ROZEREM	67
RUB-A-DUB	203
RUBBERMAID	178
S.O.S	155
SABLE	226
SAFEWAY	59, 80
SAKS FIFTH AVENUE	58, 115, 139
SALT OF THE EARTH	227
SALVATORE FERRAGAMO	52, 96, 146

WORD MARK	PARAGRAPH NUMBER
SANDOZ	67
SANKA	86, 142, 174
SANYO	118, 233
SARA LEE	18, 72, 146, 232
SATURN	125, 151
SBC	155
SCHAUB-LORENZ	328
SCHICK	202
SCHLAGE	52, 168
SCHUMACHER	146
SCHWEPPES	207
SCOTCH	153
SCRABBLE	166, 168
SCREEN	223
SCRIPTEASERS	198
SEARS	61, 98
SEARS ROEBUCK	98
SEBASTIAN	101
SECOND LIFE	95
SEEDS OF CHANGE	227
SELECT	141
SEMPRON	79
SENTINEL	29
SENUSSI	323
SERUTAN	178, 183
SERUTAN IS NATURES SPELLED BACKWARDS	69
SHAKE 'N BAKE	205, 214
SHARPER IMAGE	141
SHELL	62, 93, 133
SHREDDED WHEAT	142
SHRINKRAP	199
SIERRA	138
SILK	163

XI Index of Word Marks

WORD MARK	PARAGRAPH NUMBER
SILVER SHADOW	206
SIMON & SCHUSTER	57
SIR SPEEDY	173
SIRIUS	151
SKECHERS	30
SKIL	169, 170
SKY	215
SLIM-FAST	59, 175
SLINKY	213
SMIRNOFF	143
SMITH & SMITH	217
SMITH & WESSON	58
SMITH BARNEY	58
SMOKEY BEAR	226, 333
SMUCKERS	68
SNAP CRACKLE POP	99
SNAPPLE	176, 207
SNICKERS	49, 166
SOLUTIONS FOR A SMALL PLANET	228
SONY	54, 91, 93, 191
SOUP TO NUTS	221
SPACKLE	220
SPAM	176, 201, 205
SPANDEX	181
SPANKY'S	145
SPEEDO	160
SPIC AND SPAN	197, 205, 227
SPRINGHILL SUITES	111
SPRINT	134, 186, 214
SPRITE	49
SQUAW	81
ST. GEORGE	152
STANDARD	141

WORD MARK	PARAGRAPH NUMBER
STAPLES	136, 219
STAR	39
STARBUCKS	38, 149
STARDUST	126
STATE FARM	29
STEINWAY & SONS	143
STETSON	154
STINKY FEET	80
STRONGHOLD	134, 175
SUBARU	62
SUDAFED	156, 169
SUGAR BEAR	99
SUN	29, 151
SUN-MAID	220
SUNSET BOULEVARD	139
SUPER SILK	322
SUPERMAN	60
SWISS ARMY	326
SWISSGOLD	322
SYRUP OF FIGS	322
T42	172, 182
TAB	5, 74
TABASCO	138
TACO BELL	62
TACOMA	138
TAHOE	138
TAJ MAHAL	140
TASTY	38
TAURUS	191
TCBY	155, 201
TEAM FROG	58
TEFLON	132, 157, 160
TELEGRAPH	29
TELEPHONE	74

XI Index of Word Marks

WORD MARK	PARAGRAPH NUMBER
TENDER MERCIES	227
TERCEL	134, 226
THE COUNTRY'S BEST YOGURT	155
THE FUTURE'S BRIGHT, THE FUTURE'S ORANGE	186
THE GREATEST SHOW ON EARTH	46, 200
THE GREATEST SNOW ON EARTH	46, 200
THE REPUBLIC OF TEA	57
THE SOPRANOS	218
THE WASHINGTON MINT	324
THE WASHINGTON MINT, LLC	324
THE WORLD ON TIME	228
THE WORLD'S FAVOURITE AIRLINE	228
THERMOS	18, 116, 191
THIS CAN'T BE YOGURT!	155
THREE MUSKETEERS	149
TIC TAC	205
TIDE	71
TIFFANY	66
TILLOTSON	101
TIMBERLAND	233
TIME	71, 171
TIMES	29
TIMEX	173
TINACTIN	160, 163, 204, 174
TOM & JERRY	58
TOMTOM	204
TONDO	197
TONY THE TIGER	226
TORINO 2006	73
TORNADO	46
TORO ROJO	195

WORD MARK	PARAGRAPH NUMBER
TOSHIBA	49
TOUCHSTONE	112
TOWNEPLACE SUITES	111
TOYOTA	192
TOYS "Я" US	169, 179, 186
TOYS, ETC.	173
TRADITIONAL MEDICINALS	203
TRAVELERS	102
TRAVELOCITY	165, 177
TRAVELODGE	59, 163, 175, 176
TRIBUNE	29
TRIM	135, 223
TRINITY	125
TRIP	223
TROJAN	83, 153
TROPICANA	233
TRUE LIES	218
TRUESTE	165
TUCKS	221, 225
TUMBLEBEAD	198
TUMBLEFEED	198
TUMBLESEED	198
TUMBLESTEED	198
TUMBLESTEEDS	198
TUMBLEWEED	198
TUSH-CUSH	201, 205
TWININGS	168
TWINKIES	168, 210, 213
TWINLAB	108
TWIX	49, 163, 168
TY	192
U.S. BICENTENNIAL SOCIETY	324
UBS	97, 155
UBUNTU	62

XI Index of Word Marks

WORD MARK	PARAGRAPH NUMBER
UHU	207
UL	106, 319
UNCLE BEN'S	41
UNCLE SAM	324
UNCOLA	222
UNDERNEATH IT ALL	227
UNI-BALL	100, 105
UNION	29
UNITED PARCEL SERVICE	97
UNITED STATES OLYMPIC COMMITTEE	333
UPC	135
UPS	97
URBAN	215
URGE	328
V-8	134, 155, 184, 186
VALIUM	74, 208
VALVOLINE	134
VASELINE	142, 176
VAULT	224
VEGA	151
VELCRO	30, 43, 49, 69, 74, 132, 162, 170, 213
VELUX	201
VERIZON	129, 176
VIAGRA	123
VICHY	118, 138
VICODIN	208
VICTOR'S LITTLE SECRET	28
VICTORIA'S SECRET	28, 101
VICTORINOX	5, 232
VIDA PURA	193
VIDAL SASSOON	99
VINEYARD	219

WORD MARK	PARAGRAPH NUMBER
VIRAGO	101, 197
VIRUPEL	42
VIRUSSCAN	59, 188
VISA	71
VISA GOLD	206
VISCONTI	100, 105
VISINE	79
VIYELLA	317
VODAFONE	157
VOLKSWAGEN	192, 202
VOLVO	191, 202
VOYAGER	13, 212
VULCAN	170
VW	228
WACKO	196
WALKMAN	134, 215, 225
WALL STREET	139
WARNER BROTHERS	143
WATSU	176
WAUSAU	29
WCBS	234
WE TRY HARDER	228
WEDGWOOD	154
WELLBUTRIN	111
WENDY'S	19, 126, 144, 232
WESSEX	138
WESTPOINT	324
WGBH	234
WHEATETTES	210
WHEATIES	210
WHERE THERE'S LIFE... THERE'S BUD	46, 200
WHERE THERE'S LIFE... THERE'S BUGS	46, 200

XI Index of Word Marks

WORD MARK	PARAGRAPH NUMBER
WHIRLPOOL	136
WHISK	214
WHISKAS	134
WHLO	234
WHOLE FOODS	221
WIKIPEDIA	176
WILD OATS	233
WINDEX	160, 207
WINDOWS	107
WIRED	75, 181
WISHY WASHY	196
WISK	214
WITH A NAME LIKE SMUCKERS, IT HAS TO BE GOOD	64
WOOLITE	60
WORD	107
WORDPERFECT	188
WORLD	29
WORLD$NET	118, 165, 167
WORMIX	163
WRANGLER	109
WURLITZER	25
X-ACTO	160
XANAX	183

WORD MARK	PARAGRAPH NUMBER
XEROX	75, 89, 120, 134, 142, 168, 183, 191, 192
XPERT	164
YAHOO!	49, 70, 149
YALE	143
YAMAHA	49, 168, 192
YAMMIT	208
YOO-HOO	196, 201
YOU'RE IN GOOD HANDS	228
YOUTUBE	74
YO-YO	116, 142
YUKON	138
ZANTAC	19, 94, 165, 168
ZANTE	197
ZENITH	79, 168
ZEST	67
ZICAM	42
ZILLOW	176
ZINMAX	208
ZIPLOC	163
ZIPPER	142
ZOONOOZ	183
ZYBAN	111

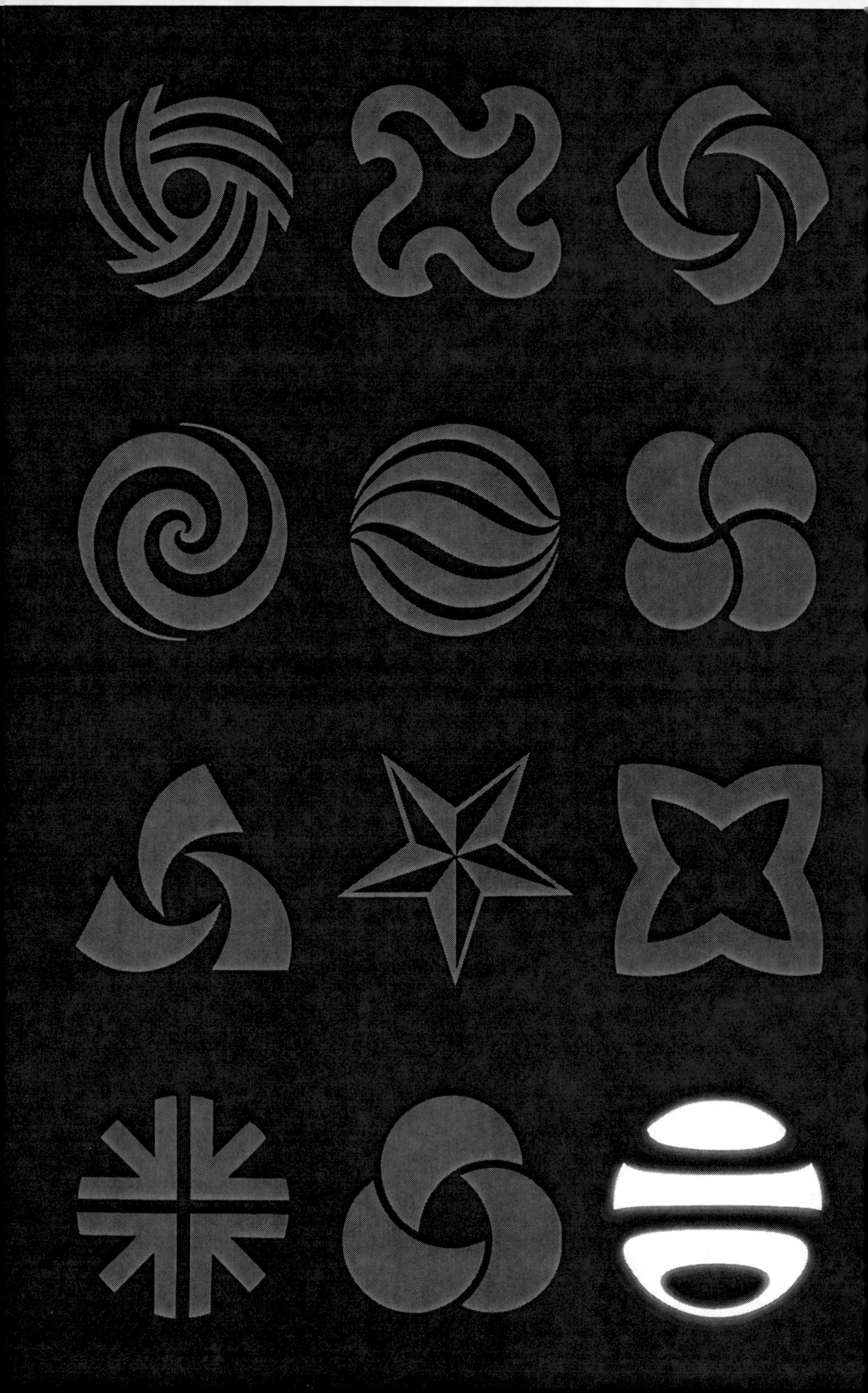

DESIGN MARKS AND OTHER NON-ALPHANUMERIC MARKS

XII Images

"He goes by the brand, yet imagines he goes by the flavor."

MARK TWAIN

The following images of design

marks and other non-alphanumeric marks cited in this work were extracted from the TARR database listings at the United States Patent & Trademark Office at www.uspto.gov/main/trademarks.htm.

FOR EACH MARK DEPICTED, the information provided is typically the registration number, registration date, any additional text describing the mark, and image of the mark. Not all additional descriptive text is necessarily included with each listing, and occasionally such descriptive text is edited in minor fashion, hopefully without materially changing its meaning. Just because a registered mark is mentioned in the text and its image depicted in this Section XII does not mean that the cited registration is active. Some registrations cited in the text, including those for *word marks* and for non-alphanumeric marks, are no longer active. Images of marks which appear in pending or abandoned applications at the time of assembling this work are shown first and identified by Serial Number.

Serial Number: 75205749;
Filing Date: 1996-11-29

Serial Number: 75216993;
Filing Date: 1996-12-23

Disclaimer: The representation of the material shown in dotted lines which serves to show the position of the mark.

Description of Mark: The mark consists of a live poinsettia plant configuration having certain features in the nature of incurved and puckered bracts and leaves, with the top of the plant having an overall round-like or bulbous appearance. The dotted lines outlining the stems and pot are not claimed as part of the mark.

Lining and Stippling: The lining, stippling and markings within the drawing do not represent color, but are features of the mark indicating the shape and texture of the plant.

Serial Number: 78909943;
Filing Date: 2006-06-16

Color(s) Claimed: The color(s) red, white, black and beige is/are claimed as a feature of the mark.

Description of Mark: The mark consists of the image of a man with a black bowtie and red apron in front of a red background.

Name Portrait Consent: The name(s), portrait(s), and/or signature(s) shown in the mark does not identify a particular living individual.

Reg. No. 147454;
Reg. Date: 1921-10-18

Description of Mark: The trade mark is the facsimile surname signature of Will K. Kellogg, president of applicant corporation.

Reg. No. 150620;
Reg. Date: 1922-01-03

Lining and Stippling: The star being in red and the "T" in green.

Reg. No. 192881;
Reg. Date: 1924-12-16

Disclaimer: No claim is made to the exclusive use of the representation of a rope apart from the trade mark as shown.

Description of Mark: The mark consists of an elongated lineal compound yarn, thread, twine or the like, formed of separate yarns of blue and yellow, incorporated in one of the threads of which the strands of the rope or cable are composed.

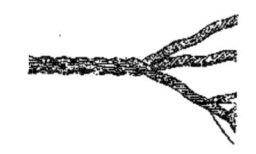

XII Images

Reg. No. 228220;
Reg. Date: 1927-05-24

Disclaimer: No claim is made to the exclusive use of the geographical term "Milano" apart from the mark shown in the drawing. No claim is made to a red cross or to a cross of any particular color.

Reg. No. 371803;
Reg. Date: 1939-10-10

Reg. No. 383644;
Reg. Date: 1940-12-17

Reg. No. 393492;
Reg. Date: 1942-02-17

Reg. No. 399245;
Reg. Date: 1942-12-22

Reg. No. 403487;
Reg. Date: 1943-09-28

Name Portrait Consent: The trademark consists of a facsimile of the signature of Mary Baker G. Eddy.

Reg. No. 403934;
Reg. Date: 1943-10-26

Description of Mark: The collective mark consists merely in the word Viyella.

Reg. No. 404248;
Reg. Date: 1943-11-16

Disclaimer: No claim is made to the exclusive use of the representation of a pair of overalls.

Description of Mark: The trademark consists of double arcuate designs of orange color displayed on the hip pockets of the overalls as shown on the drawing. The mark is applied to the overalls by stitching the double arcuate designs on the hip pockets with orange colored thread, or by painting the lines of said design on the hip pockets with orange colored paint.

Reg. No. 410701;
Reg. Date: 1944-12-12

XII Images

Reg. No. 426706;
Reg. Date: 1947-01-07

Lining and Stippling: the trade-mark comprises a facsimile signature of the founder of applicant, Domingo Ghirardelli.

Reg. No. 430729;
Reg. Date: 1947-06-24

Lining and Stippling: the seal forming the background of the word "Lee" is colored gold and the letters of the word as well as the ribbons projecting from beneath the seal are colored blue.

Reg. No. 542096;
Reg. Date: 1951-05-08

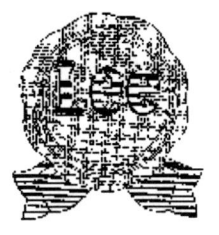

Reg. No. 543697;
Reg. Date: 1951-06-12

Disclaimer: No claim being made to the representation of a section of conductor cable or cord.

Description of Mark: The trade-mark consists of the characteristic arrangement of contrasting colors woven in the fabric covering of a conductor cable or cord, the ground color of the fabric being black and having woven therein two strands of red immediately adjacent each other at either side of which red strands and immediately adjacent thereto two strands of yellow or gold are disposed, the whole forming upon the background of the cable a spiral of red and yellow or gold dots arranged as described.

Lining and Sippling: The drawing is lined to show the said colors.

Reg. No. 557033;
Reg. Date: 1952-04-01

Name Portrait Consent: The service mark consists of a substantial facsimile of the signature of John Hancock (1737-1793), patriot of the American Revolution, as said signature appears on the Declaration of Independence.

Reg. No. 557412;
Reg. Date: 1952-04-08

Reg. No. 561629;
Reg. Date: 1952-07-15

Reg. No. 571798;
Reg. Date: 1953-03-10

Reg. No. 578653;
Reg. Date: 1953-08-11

(Words Only): PGA

XII Images

Reg. No. 589868;
Reg. Date: 1954-05-18
Disclaimer: The representation of a vehicle is disclaimed.
Description of Mark: The mark comprises a checkered band substantially encircling the vehicle near the upper edge of the main body portion where it joins the top portion.

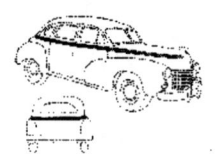

Reg. No. 592541;
Reg. Date: 1954-07-13
Disclaimer: The word "Inn" is disclaimed apart from the mark as shown.

Reg. No. 601864;
Reg. Date: 1955-02-08

Reg. No. 618932;
Reg. Date: 1956-01-10
Disclaimer: Applicant disclaims the word "Stuttgart" apart from the mark as shown.

Reg. No. 645541;
Reg. Date: 1957-05-14

Reg. No. 645893;
Reg. Date: 1957-05-21

Reg. No. 647962;
Reg. Date: 1957-07-02

Reg. No. 652995;
Reg. Date: 1957-10-15

Reg. No. 705081;
Reg. Date: 1960-09-27

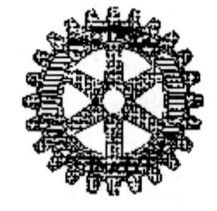

Reg. No. 720376;
Reg. Date: 1961-08-22
Description of Mark: The mark consists of a small white marker or tab affixed to the exterior of the garment at the hip pocket.

Reg. No. 739469;
Reg. Date: 1962-10-16
Lining and Stippling: The center scalloped edge medallion is lined for yellow and the background is lined for green in the drawing.

Reg. No. 741662:
Reg. Date: 1962-12-04

274

XII Images

Reg. No. 749915;
Reg. Date: 1963-05-21

Reg. No. 772552;
Reg. Date: 1964-06-30
Disclaimer: Applicant claims the exclusive right to "Hamburgers" and "Over 700 Million Served" as part of its service mark but not otherwise.

Reg. No. 787875;
Reg. Date: 1965-04-06

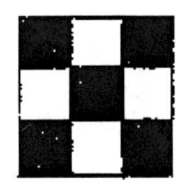

Reg. No. 790140;
Reg. Date: 1965-05-25

Reg. No. 800926;
Reg. Date: 1965-12-28

Reg. No. 804869;
Reg. Date: 1966-03-01

Reg. No. 806104;
Reg. Date: 1966-03-22

Reg. No. 862632;
Reg. Date: 1968-12-31

Reg. No. 877451;
Reg. Date: 1969-09-23
Lining and Stippling: The drawing is lined for the color gold.

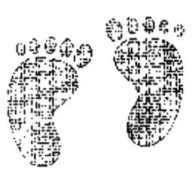

Reg. No. 887916;
Reg. Date: 1970-03-17

Reg. No. 888288;
Reg. Date: 1970-03-24

Reg. No. 902125;
Reg. Date: 1970-11-10
Disclaimer: No claim of exclusive right is made of the word "Toys" apart from the mark as shown.

275

XII Images

Reg. No. 907303;
Reg. Date: 1971-02-02

Disclaimer: The word "Donuts" is disclaimed apart from the mark as shown.

Reg. No. 911388;
Reg. Date: 1971-04-13

Reg. No. 916522;
Reg. Date: 1971-07-13

Description of Mark: The mark comprises a sequence of chime-like musical notes which are in the key of C and sound the notes G, E, C, the "G" being the one just below middle C, the "E" the one just above middle C, and the "C" being middle C, thereby to identify applicant's broadcasting service.

Mark : (Sensory Mark Only) ["NBC chimes"]

Reg. No. 930599;
Reg. Date: 1972-03-07

Reg. No. 941316;
Reg. Date: 1972-08-22

Description of Mark: The mark is a circular design showing a rotating wheel.

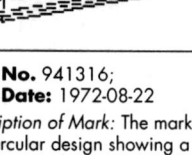

Reg. No. 945743;
Reg. Date: 1972-10-24

Description of Mark: The trademark comprises an arbitrary symbol of three stylized arrows radiating outwardly from a central point, the arrows being enclosed within a shield.

Reg. No. 947706;
Reg. Date: 1972-11-21

Description of Mark: The mark consists of an edge design consisting of serrations or indentations coupled with an irregular border colored brown.

Reg. No. 972082;
Reg. Date: 1973-10-30

Lining and Stippling: The drawing is lined for red, but color is not claimed as a feature of the mark.

Reg. No. 978340;
Reg. Date: 1974-02-05

Reg. No. 982182;
Reg. Date: 1974-04-16

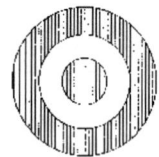

Reg. No. 983025;
Reg. Date: 1974-04-30

Description of Mark: The mark consists of stylized letters "BA" within a shield design.

Reg. No. 1023923;
Reg. Date: 1975-10-28

XII Images

Reg. No. 1057884;
Reg. Date: 1977-02-01
Description of Mark: The mark consists of the three-dimensional configuration of the distinctive bottle as shown.

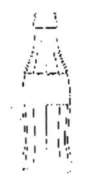

Reg. No. 1090231;
Reg. Date: 1978-05-02

Reg. No. 1094740;
Reg. Date: 1978-06-27
Lining and Stippling: The drawing is lined for the colors blue and orange.

Reg. No. 1112247;
Reg. Date: 1979-01-30

Reg. No. 1137391;
Reg. Date: 1980-07-01

Reg. No. 1145473;
Reg. Date: 1981-01-06
Description of Mark: The mark is comprised of a "Wing" design.

Reg. No. 1157769;
Reg. Date: 1981-06-16
Disclaimer: Applicant disclaims the representation of the goods apart from the mark as shown.
Description of Mark: The mark consists of a small marker or tab affixed to the exterior of the garment at the hip pocket.

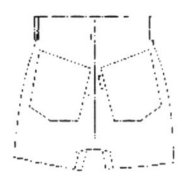

Reg. No. 1161313;
Reg. Date: 1981-07-14
Lining and Stippling: The drawing is lined for the color red which is claimed as a distinguishing feature of the mark.

Reg. No. 1161535;
Reg. Date: 1981-07-21

Reg. No. 1175337;
Reg. Date: 1981-10-27

Reg. No. 1181959;
Reg. Date: 1981-12-15

Reg. No. 1200407;
Reg. Date: 1982-07-06
Description of Mark: The mark consists of design of a tree.

XII Images

Reg. No. 1205090;
Reg. Date: 1982-08-17

Lining and Stippling: The lines shown on the drawing are a part of the mark and they are not intended to represent color.

Reg. No. 1234035;
Reg. Date: 1983-04-05

Reg. No. 1252912;
Reg. Date: 1983-10-04

Reg. No. 1255898;
Reg. Date: 1983-11-01

Description of Mark: The mark comprises the word "Extek" underscored and overlying an underscored mirror image thereof.

Reg. No. 1259406;
Reg. Date: 1983-11-29

Reg. No. 1260124;
Reg. Date: 1983-12-06

Reg. No. 1277688;
Reg. Date: 1984-05-15

Disclaimer: No claim is made to the exclusive right to use the shape of the container for the goods, apart from the mark as shown.

Description of Mark: The mark consists of the configuration of the container for the goods with wording and a design thereon. The mark consists of a rectangular bottle in which the cap merges with the bottle to make a rectangular configuration. The sides of the configuration are slightly bowed.

Lining and Stippling: The drawing is lined for the color silver, the cap is black with a silver and white top, and the color silver is also claimed for the words "Cristalle" and "Chanel", which could not be lined because of the small size of the letters. The remaining lines on the cap and the bottle are for the purpose of shading only.

Reg. No. 1278007;
Reg. Date: 1984-05-15

Reg. No. 1297161;
Reg. Date: 1984-09-18

Disclaimer: No claim is made to the exclusive right to use "Home", apart from the mark as shown.

XII Images

Reg. No. 1340720;
Reg. Date: 1985-06-11

Description of Mark: The mark consists of the word "Dior" in a repeating pattern.

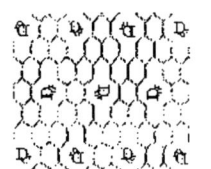

Reg. No. 1344589;
Reg. Date: 1985-06-25

Description of mark: the shoe outline shown in broken lines in the drawing forms no part of the mark, but is furnished to show the location of the mark in use.

Lining and Stippling: The stippling does not indicate color, but defines the extended saddle device.

Reg. No. 1395550;
Reg. Date: 1986-06-03

Description of Mark: The mark comprises a lion roaring.

Mark: (Sensory Mark Only)

Reg. No. 1399080;
Reg. Date: 1986-07-01

Reg. No. 1409041;
Reg. Date: 1986-09-09

Description of Mark: The collective membership mark is circular in shape consisting of a rimmed and gridlined globe with a Roman sword, point up, centered vertically on the globe and between the pans of a scale. Draped from the balance bar of the scalepans and in front of the sword is a blindfold. Surrounding the above is a circular scroll inscribed with "Legibus Armisque" above and "Devoti" below.

Lining and Stippling: The drawing is lined for the colors gold and dark blue.

Translation: The english translation of the words "Legibus Armisque Devoti" in the mark is "Devoted to Law and Arms".

Reg. No. 1413427;
Reg. Date: 1986-10-14

Description of Mark: The mark consists of a repeating raised pattern appearing on the surface of the fabric.

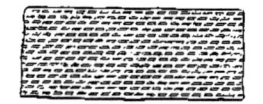

Reg. No. 1430705;
Reg. Date: 1987-02-24

Disclaimer: "100% Pure" and "Florida's Seal of Approval."

Reg. No. 1432152;
Reg. Date: 1987-03-10

Reg. No. 1439275;
Reg. Date: 1987-05-12

Disclaimer: "Founded 1906."

Description of mark: The mark consists of a medallion design with male and female heads and wreaths.

Section 2(f), in part, as to the words "National Collegiate Athletic Association".

XII Images

Reg. No. 1445475;
Reg. Date: 1987-06-30

Reg. No. 1461239;
Reg. Date: 1987-10-13
Disclaimer: "Light";
Description of Mark: The mark is comprised of the wordmark "Amstel" and the word "Light" in the innermost of a series of concentric circles, with a device incorporating a coat of arms above the wordmark "Amstel".

Reg. No. 1465556;
Reg. Date: 1987-11-17
Description of Mark: The mark consists of strips of ribbon of a color that contrasts with the rest of the shoe interwoven into the vamp of the shoe, running approximately parallel to each other and the longest axis of the shoe in the form shown.

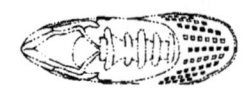

Reg. No. 1482342;
Reg. Date: 1988-03-2
Description of Mark: The mark is a sinusoidal curve having a repeating pattern of the word "permclip" in various shapes, and only four cycles of the sinusoidal curve are depicted on the drawing.

Reg. No. 1529006;
Reg. Date: 1989-03-07

Reg. No. 1531069;
Reg. Date: 1989-03-21
Description of Mark: The mark consists of the design characterized by cylindrical package wrap with pinched ends and brown center panel bordered on each end by white and orange/red strips.

Reg. No. 1539614;
Reg. Date: 1989-05-16
Disclaimer: "Mouse."
Description of Mark: The mark consists of designs and/or wording located on a motor vehicle as follows; mouse ears positioned on the roof; mouse nose and whiskers positioned on the hood; mouse tail positioned on the trunk; the design of a mouse face and tail and the wording "Truly Nolen" positioned on the doors; and the term "Mouse" positioned on the fender. The matter shown by dotted lines is not a part of the mark, and no claim is made to it. The dotted lines serve only to show the position of the mark.

Reg. No. 1542937;
Reg. Date: 1989-06-06

Reg. No. 1544679;
Reg. Date: 1989-06-20
(Words only): Campbell's;
Lining and stippling: The drawing is lined for the color red.

280

XII Images

Reg. No. 1552475;
Reg. Date: 1989-08-22
Disclaimer: The representation of a wire rope;
Description of Mark: The mark is used by painting two adjoining strands of wire, one yellow and one blue, which are wrapped around the core of the wire rope in a spiral fashion during the manufacture of the wire rope.
Lining and Stippling: The mark as shown in the drawing is lined for the colors blue and yellow.

Reg. No. 1569538;
Reg. Date: 1989-12-05
Description of Mark: The mark consists of a stylized "H" design within an ellipse design.

Reg. No. 1580456;
Reg. Date: 1990-01-30

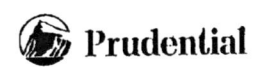

Reg. No. 1588960;
Reg. Date: 1990-03-27
Description of Mark: The mark consists of a three-dimensional sole of shoe design.
Lining and Stippling: The lining and stippling in the mark are features of the mark and are not intended to indicate color.

Reg. No. 1598941;
Reg. Date: 1990-05-29
Disclaimer: "Airlines"

Reg. No. 1605427;
Reg. Date: 1990-07-10
Description of Mark: The mark consists of a vehicle grille design comprising a diagonal slash. The matter shown in phantom outline, including the vertical lining in the grille section, is not part of the mark and serves only to indicate position.

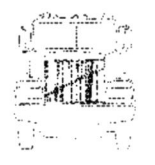

Reg. No. 1619755;
Reg. Date: 1990-10-30
Description of Mark: The trademark is a stylized letter "L" in an oval design.

Reg. No. 1623869;
Reg. Date: 1990-11-20
Description of Mark: The mark consists of an arcuate configuration of five flavors of ice cream, namely, chocolate, strawberry, palmer house (new york cherry with nuts), pistachio and orange sherbet, arranged from bottom to top, as it is sold on a cone.
Lining and Stippling: The mark shown on the drawing is lined for the colors brown, pink, white, green and orange, and color is claimed as a feature of the mark.

Reg. No. 1635681;
Reg. Date: 1991-02-19
Lining and Stippling: The lining shown on the drawing is a feature of the mark and does not indicate color.

XII Images

Reg. No. 1639128;
Reg. Date: 1991-03-26

Description of Mark: The mark is a high impact, fresh, floral fragrance reminiscent of plumeria blossoms.

Mark : (Sensory Mark Only)

Reg. No. 1654205;
Reg. Date: 1991-08-20

Description of Mark: The mark consists of a design of multiple human faces in silhouette and waves, generally within a circle.

Lining and Stippling: The lining shown in the drawing is a feature of the mark and not intended to indicate color.

Reg. No. 1665695;
Reg. Date: 1991-11-26

Description of Mark: The mark consists of the letters "DD" printed to depict a three-dimensional effect.

Reg. No. 1678597;
Reg. Date: 1992-03-10

Description of Mark: The mark consists of the depiction of a "Slippery When Wet" road sign.

Reg. No. 1688288;
Reg. Date: 1992-05-19

Description of Mark: The mark consists of a fanciful solid irregular circular design having a zig-zag line dividing the same and which may be read as an artistic representation of the letter "N" when viewed in one direction and of the letter "Z" when viewed in another direction.

Reg. No. 1691166;
Reg. Date: 1992-06-09

Description of Mark: The mark is comprised of the spiral design of applicant's goods. The features shown in dotted lines do not comprise part of the mark.

Reg. No. 1714499;
Reg. Date: 1992-09-08

Disclaimer: "Pets";

Description of Mark: The mark consists, in part, of a stylized representation of an individual in a wheelchair with a dog and cat.

Reg. No. 1732360;
Reg. Date: 1992-11-17

Reg. No. 1738756;
Reg. Date: 1992-12-08

Disclaimer: "Wellness";

Description of Mark: The mark consists in part of two "W"'s flanking a Roman "I" and three striped partial reflections of the design which suggest movement.

Lining and Stippling: The lining in the drawing is a feature of the mark and does not indicate color.

XII Images

Reg. No. 1740915;
Reg. Date: 1992-12-22

Description of Mark: The mark comprises a fiddle-shaped handle for a fork or spoon. The face has an oxidized finish, bordered and overlain with a floral ornamentation. There are cut-out portions on either side of the fiddle-shaped portion of the handle, creating a lace-like appearance. The rear of the fork or spoon has complimentary design features.

Reg. No. 1748360;
Reg. Date: 1993-01-26

Description of Mark: The mark consists of several marine signal flags and the word "Mares".

Lining and stippling: the signal flags in the mark are lined for the colors light blue, red and yellow, and the word "Mares" is lined for the color dark blue.

Reg. No. 1753026;
Reg. Date: 1993-02-16

Reg. No. 1785525;
Reg. Date: 1993-08-03

Reg. No. 1797716;
Reg. Date: 1993-10-12

Description of Mark: The mark consists of a stylized depiction of the letter "T".

Reg. No. 1803603;
Reg. Date: 1993-11-09

Reg. No. 1830915;
Reg. Date: 1994-04-12

Disclaimer: Top, handle and outline shape of the container.

Description of Mark: The mark consists of a plurality of angularly extending grooves formed in a container, the grooves being parallel but of decreasing length from bottom to top, the groove wrapping around the front portion of the container regardless of the container configuration.

Lining and Stippling: The lining in the drawing is a feature of the mark and not intended to indicate color.

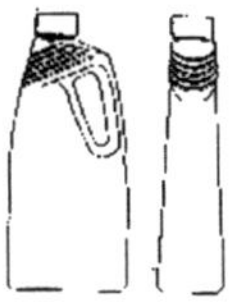

Reg. No. 1835705;
Reg. Date: 1994-05-10

Disclaimer: "Home."

Lining and Stippling: The drawing is lined for the color orange.

Reg. No. 1855918;
Reg. Date: 1994-09-27

Description of Mark: The mark consists of four M's in a cluster.

XII Images

Reg. No. 1860272;
Reg. Date: 1994-10-25

Reg. No. 1872759;
Reg. Date: 1995-01-10

Description of Mark: The mark comprises a three-dimensional, stand alone replica of a pyramid shaped building.

Lining and Stippling: The lining and stippling shown in the drawing are features of the mark and do not indicate color.

Reg. No. 190418;
Reg. Date: 1995-07-11

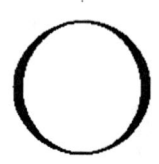

Reg. No. 1915975;
Reg. Date: 1995-09-05

Description of Mark: The mark consists of two stylized letters "T".

Lining and Stippling: The stippling in the drawing is used to show the mark's three-dimensional appearance as it is stamped on, burned into or welded onto the goods. The drawing is not lined for color, nor is color claimed as a feature of the mark.

Reg. No. 1917921;
Reg. Date: 1995-09-12

Reg. No. 1926947;
Reg. Date: 1995-10-17

Lining and Stippling: The drawing of the mark is lined for the color red, and applicant claims said color as a feature of the mark.

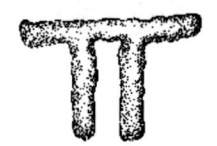

Reg. No. 1928424;
Reg. Date: 1995-10-17

(Words Only): 20th Century Fox

Description of Mark: The trademark is a computer generated sequence showing the central element from several angles as though a camera is moving around the structure. The drawing represents four "stills" from the sequence.

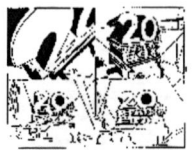

Reg. No. 1954583;
Reg. Date: 1996-02-06

Description of Mark: The mark consists of a fanciful representation of an infinity symbol.

Reg. No. 1959592;
Reg. Date: 1996-03-05

Description of Mark: The mark is composed of a hangtag attached to the goods at the back pocket in the form of a seed packet containing seeds. The dotted lines in the drawing show the placement of the packets.

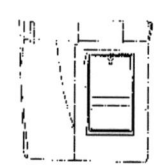

XII Images

Reg. No. 1970953;
Reg. Date: 1996-04-30

Reg. No. 1981233;
Reg. Date: 1996-06-18

Reg. No. 1986364;
Reg. Date: 1996-07-09

Description of Mark: The mark consists of an embossed butterfly design in a repetitive pattern.

Reg. No. 1987137;
Reg. Date: 1996-07-16

Reg. No. 2027054;
Reg. Date: 1996-12-31

Description of Mark: The mark consists of a stylized rotating light bulb.

Reg. No. 2032160;
Reg. Date: 1997-01-21

Description of Mark: The mark consists of a pair of heart shaped ventilation holes in the shield of a baby pacifier. The broken line matter in the drawing does not constitute part of the mark, but only serves to indicate the mark's position on the goods.

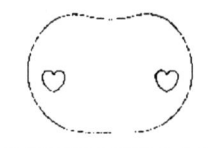

Reg. No. 2043809;
Reg. Date: 1997-03-11

Description of Mark: The mark consists of a stylized representation of a cat's paw print.

Reg. No. 2058985;
Reg. Date: 1997-05-06

Description of Mark: The mark consists of the markings on the aircraft and the wording "Delta". The dotted lines are not part of the mark and serve only to show the position of the mark upon the aircraft.

Reg. No. 2080375;
Reg. Date: 1997-07-15

Description of Mark: The mark consists of a configuration of an oval-shaped cut-out on the underside of a bicycle saddle.

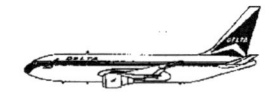

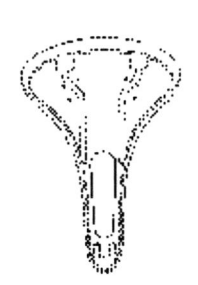

XII Images

Reg. No. 2093825;
Reg. Date: 1997-09-02

Description of Mark: The mark consists of the configuration of the body of a padlock with a roughened surface texture on the top, on the sides and on a bottom rim which surrounds a recessed, smooth surfaced, slightly convex bottom portion, and of the position of four dials on the bottom portion.

Lining and Stippling: The stippling represents the textured feature of the mark and does not indicate color. The dotted lines show the location of the mark and represent those features of the goods that are not claimed.

Reg. No. 2098781;
Reg. Date: 1997-09-23

Description of Mark: The mark consists of a portrait of a man and the terms "Choy Lee Fut-Wing Sing Tong" and the equivalent Chinese characters positioned above the design of a temple complex.

Reg. No. 2105501;
Reg. Date: 1997-10-14

Disclaimer: "Taco"

Reg. No. 2105546;
Reg. Date: 1997-10-14

Lining and Stippling: The drawing is lined for the following colors as defined with reference to the Pantone Standards:
Red – PMS 485; Blue – PMS 280; Yellow – PMS 116.

Reg. No. 2110368;
Reg. Date: 1997-11-04

Disclaimer: "Cleveland"

Description of Mark: The mark consists of a three dimensional costume worn by a performer.

Reg. No. 2130983;
Reg. Date: 1998-01-20

Description of Mark: The mark consists in part of a stylized representation of the Yin-Yang symbol.

Reg. No. 2131693;
Reg. Date: 1998-01-27

Description of Mark: The mark consists of the color brown applied to the vehicles used in performing the services.

Lining and Stippling: The drawing is lined for the color brown.

Reg. No. 2144136;
Reg. Date: 1998-03-17

Description of Mark: The mark is a design of a column of three parallel, symmetrical boat profiles having centerline transverse to the column with adjacent profiles being connected by a thickened vertical line and of another boat profile on either side of the column with centerlines parallel to the thickened vertical line.

Reg. No. 2144407;
Reg. Date: 1998-03-17

Description of Mark: The mark consists of a chevron type design in an ellipse or oval design.

XII Images

Reg. No. 2145378;
Reg. Date: 1998-03-17
Description of Mark: The mark is comprised of a stylized representation of a bicycle.

Reg. No. 2150616;
Reg. Date: 1998-04-14
Lining and Stippling: The drawing is lined for the colors red and blue.

Reg. No. 2159865;
Reg. Date: 1998-05-26
Description of Mark: The mark consists of the color brown which is applied to the clothing. The matter shown in the drawing in broken lines serves to show positioning of the mark and no claim is made to the configuration of the uniform.

Lining and Stippling: The drawing is lined for the color brown.

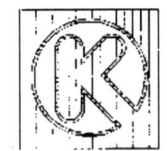

Reg. No. 2161779;
Reg. Date: 1998-06-02
Description of Mark: The mark consists of a grill for a motor vehicle comprising seven vertical slots with two round headlights. The dashed lines are meant to show the position of headlights and are not a feature of the mark.

Lining and Stippling: The dashed lines are meant to show the position of headlights and are not a feature of the mark.

Reg. No. 2163450;
Reg. Date: 1998-06-09
(Words Only): Budweiser King Of Beers Genuine

Disclaimer: "Inc." or "St. Louis, Mo."

Description of Mark: The mark consists, in part, of the following wording – "This is the Famous Budweiser Beer. We know of no brand produced by any other brewer which costs so much to brew and age. Our exclusive beechwood aging produces a taste, a smoothness and drinkability you will find in no other beer at any price".

Lining and stippling: The lining shown in the drawing is a feature of the mark and is not intended to indicate color.

Reg. No. 2165090;
Reg. Date: 1998-06-16
Description of Mark: The mark consists of a circular design of a kiosk unit having display racks and display cases topped by bridge containing multiple video displays terminals and a large disc gripped by a set of giant fingers.

Lining and Stippling: The lining shown in the drawing is a feature of the mark and is not intended to indicate color.

287

XII Images

Reg. No. 2172961;
Reg. Date: 1998-07-14

Description of Mark: The mark comprises distinctive trade dress consisting of the colors red, white and blue stacked in a horizontal striped pattern.

Lining and Stippling: The drawing is lined for red, white and blue, and color is claimed as a feature of the mark.

Reg. No. 2176030;
Reg. Date: 1998-07-28

(Words Only): IAMS Senior

Disclaimer: "Senior" and "Company."

Description of Mark: The mark consists of the trade dress characterizing packaging for applicant's goods.

Lining and Stippling: The drawing is lined for the color deep purple (PMS #512). Color is claimed as a feature of the mark.

Reg. No. 2176916;
Reg. Date: 1998-07-28

Description of Mark: The mark consists of a particular shade of the color blue, sometimes referred to as medium blue, applied to the entire surface of the goods. The dotted lines merely indicate the position of the mark on the goods and do not form part of the mark.

Lining and Stippling: The drawing is lined for blue and color is claimed as a feature of the mark.

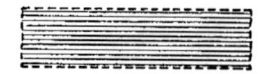

Reg. No. 2193387;
Reg. Date: 1998-10-06

Description of Mark: The mark includes a stylized representation of a peacock.

Lining and Stippling: The drawing has been lined for the colors yellow, orange, red, purple, blue and green, and color is claimed as part of the mark for which registration is sought here.

Reg. No. 2200332;
Reg. Date: 1998-10-27

Disclaimer: "Encircled PX Symbol For Christ."

Description of Mark: The mark consists of the Christian symbol for Christ, a depiction of a cross and a crown of thorns.

Lining and Stippling: The lining statement in the drawing is a feature of the mark and is not intended to indicate color.

Reg. No. 2205939;
Reg. Date: 1998-11-24

Description of Mark: The mark consists of the term "PP" shown in a stylized manner with one letter "P" upside down facing the other letter "P".

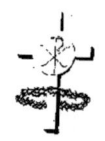

Reg. No. 2211951;
Reg. Date: 1998-12-15

Disclaimer: The representation of the shape of wire rope.

Description of Mark: The mark consists of adjacent orange and white strands that are wound as a part of wire rope as shown in the accompanying drawing.

Lining and Stippling: The mark is lined for the colors orange and gray.

Reg. No. 2212098;
Reg. Date: 1998-12-22

Description of Mark: The mark consists of the words "QUAKER STATE" in white and the roof line design in the colors green and gray.

Lining and Stippling: The drawing is lined for the colors green, gray, and white. The dotted lines in the drawing are intended to show the position of the mark on a building.

Reg. No. 2237052;
Reg. Date: 1999-04-06

Description of Mark: The mark is composed of a boomerang like shaped cut-out appearing on the body of the saw blade. The drawing of the saw blade appearing in dotted lines is for illustrative purposes to show the mark as used on the goods.

XII Images

Reg. No. 2248739;
Reg. Date: 1999-06-01
Description of Mark: The mark consists of an oval containing two symmetrical designs consisting of a series of angular lines and triangles.

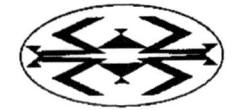

Reg. No. 2254662;
Reg. Date: 1999-06-22
Disclaimer: "Shoe", Lowest Prices" and "Name Brands."
Description of Mark: The mark comprises, inter alia, a microphone stand featuring games on the periphery, large shoe replicas, a center aisle leading to a center circle and the microphone stand, a checkered design with circles for signage, staggered display racks, seating pods, neon lighting on the signage featuring "circus" lettering with the wording "Shoe Carnival", "Family Fun", "Name Brands" and "Lowest Prices", and department signage in "bullhorn" style lettering.
Lining and Stippling: The lining shown in the drawing is a feature of the mark and is not intended to indicate color.

Reg. No. 2266269;
Reg. Date: 1999-08-03
Description of Mark: The words "Team Metal" inside an irregular shaped box with screw heads in each corner.

Reg. No. 2268107;
Reg. Date: 1999-08-10
Description of Mark: The mark consists of a configuration of a frame of a bicycle. The dotted lines show the position of the mark in relation to the goods.
Lining and Stippling: The dotted lines in the drawing do not indicate color and are not a feature of the mark.

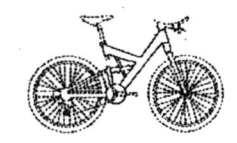

Reg. No. 2272458;
Reg. Date: 1999-08-24
Description of Mark: The mark consists, in part, of a stylized drawing of the letter "H".

Reg. No. 2273173;
Reg. Date: 1999-08-24
Description of Mark: The mark consists of the configuration and visual and tactile texture of a pot made from a fibrous material, such as coir (coconut husk fibers).
Lining and Stippling: The stippling in the oval area near the top of the drawing of the mark does not indicate color and is not a feature of the mark. The irregular lines on the surfaces of the pot also do not indicate color but are a feature of the mark.

Reg. No. 2288159;
Reg. Date: 1999-10-19
Description of Mark: The mark consists of a hologram which contains the word "Sebastian".

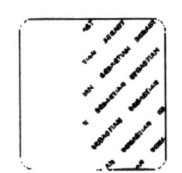

Reg. No. 2301660;
Reg. Date: 1999-12-21

Reg. No. 2312067;
Reg. Date: 2000-01-25
Description of Mark: The mark consists of an acorn and oak leaf, and in a square, tree branches with sun/moon behind, with partial ripple effect to branches.

XII Images

Reg. No. 2315036;
Reg. Date: 2000-02-01
Disclaimer: A realistic depiction of a brain.
Description of Mark: The mark is a computer-generated sequence showing the central element rotating. The drawing represents four "stills" from the sequence.

Reg. No. 2315261;
Reg. Date: 2000-02-08
Description of Mark: The mark consists of a five tone audio progression of the notes D Flat, D Flat, G, D FLAT and A Flat.
Mark: (Sensory Mark Only)

Reg. No. 2316631;
Reg. Date: 2000-02-08
Description of Mark: The mark consists of the shape and configuration of ready to eat breakfast cereal, having six arched sides, a hole in the center, and several holes surrounding the center hole connected by interlinking pieces of the cereal, resembling a cross-section in a "honeycomb."
Lining and Stippling: The stippling is a feature of the mark conveying the texture of the cereal.

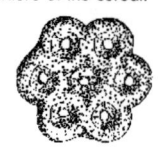

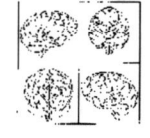

Reg. No. 2320497;
Reg. Date: 2000-02-22
Description of Mark: The mark consists of the configuration of a three-dimensional spiral shaped champagne glass stem with a cup portion composed of a glass with a crackled texture, represented by the lining on the surface of the cup. The dotted lines are drawn to show the location of the mark and are not part of the mark.
Lining and Stippling: The lining shown is a feature of the mark; it does not indicate color.

Reg. No. 2322919;
Reg. Date: 2000-02-29
Description of Mark: The mark consists of a stylized depiction of a wheelchair with a face.

Reg. No. 2323892;
Reg. Date: 2000-02-29
Description of Mark: The mark consists of a pre-programmed rotating sequence of a plurality of high intensity columns of light projected into the sky to locate a source at the base thereof.
Mark: (Sensory Mark Only)

Reg. No. 2324607;
Reg. Date: 2000-02-29
(Words Only): Aquafresh Triple Protection Whitening.
Disclaimer: Whitening.
Description of Mark: The silver color lining represents a silver foil hologram that reflects a spectrum of multiple colors.
Lining and Stippling: The mark on the drawing is lined for the colors red, blue, green/bluish-green and silver, and color is claimed as a feature of the mark.

Reg. No. 2334391;
Reg. Date: 2000-03-28
Description of Mark: The mark consists of a sun and the wording "Astropower" written upright and also written upside-down as a reflection.

Reg. No. 2339374;
Reg. Date: 2000-04-04
Description of Mark: The mark consists of a paisley-like shape for the sound hole of a guitar.

XII Images

Reg. No. 2352943;
Reg. Date: 2000-05-30

Description of Mark: The mark consists of a three-dimensional configuration, comprising a right facing smiling half moon design, set on a base having the outline design of the same half moon design.

Lining and Stippling: The lining is intended to show the three-dimensional nature of the mark and is not an indication of color.

Reg. No. 2352951;
Reg. Date: 2000-05-30

Description of Mark: The mark consists of a three-dimensional configuration, comprising a left facing frowning half moon design, set on a base having the outline/shadow design of the same left facing half moon design.

Lining and Stippling: The lining in the drawing is intended to show the three-dimensional nature of the mark and is not an indication of color.

Reg. No. 2357408;
Reg. Date: 2000-06-13

Description of Mark: The mark consists of the word "Chrysler" and a stylized depiction of an award ribbon flanked by two horizontally-extending wings.

Lining and Stippling: The stippling in its Chrysler & Design mark is a feature of the mark and is not intended to indicate color.

Reg. No. 2368337;
Reg. Date: 2000-07-18

Description of Mark: The mark consists of a stylized representation of the letter "W" within a darkened square design.

Reg. No. 2369787;
Reg. Date: 2000-07-25

Description of Mark: The mark consists of the melody notes E flat, F, B flat in octave below, B flat, followed by the spoken words "Breakthrough Medicines For Everyday Living" and a musical cord consisting of the melody notes E flat and E flat in two octaves.

Mark: (Sensory Mark Only)

Reg. No. 2380742;
Reg. Date: 2000-08-29

Description of Mark: The mark consists of the color pink as applied to the entirety of the goods. The dotted outline of the goods is intended to show the position of the mark and is not a part of the mark.

Lining and Stippling: The drawing is lined to indicate the color pink.

Reg. No. 2381564;
Reg. Date: 2000-08-29

Description of Mark: The mark consists of a stylized telescope on a tripod mount, topped by a solid sphere representing a heavenly body, with all elements of the design depicted in a calligraphic style.

Reg. No. 2385359;
Reg. Date: 2000-09-12

Disclaimer: "DIGITAL."

Description of Mark: The mark consists of a square with corners pointing to 45, 90, 135 and 180 degrees. Each side has the shape of a musical note carved out, the left an upright note, and the right is inverted.

DIGITAL POINT SOLUTIONS

Reg. No. 2386386;
Reg. Date: 2000-09-12

Disclaimer: "Frites."

Description of Mark: The mark consists of a bold capital letter "B" followed by a bold period, wherein the upper U-shaped opening in the "B" contains a dot in black or any other color, representing an eye, and the lower corresponding U-shaped opening in the "B" is filled in with any color, including the color white, thereby forming an open mouth, all of which create the representation of an animated character in the form of the letter "B." Each "B" and period is juxtaposed in proximity to the word "Frites", at various and irregular angles to the letter "B".

Translation: The English translation of "Frites" is "fried".

XII Images

Reg. No. 2387961;
Reg. Date: 2000-09-19

Reg. No. 2388016;
Reg. Date: 2000-09-19

Lining and Stippling: The stippling shown in the drawing is a feature of the mark and not intended to indicate color.

Reg. No. 2391140;
Reg. Date: 2000-10-03

Reg. No. 2410023;
Reg. Date: 2000-12-05

Lining and Stippling: The mark is lined for red, blue, yellow, green, purple, orange and brown.

Reg. No. 2413735;
Reg. Date: 2000-12-19

Disclaimer: "E".

Description of Mark: The mark consists of attached GIF: Triangle with a stylized letter "e".

Reg. No. 2417211;
Reg. Date: 2001-01-02

Disclaimer: "Business Organization & Occupation Service Training."

Description of Mark: The mark consists of the word 'Boost' in stylized letters enclosed on each end by numerous parallel vertical bars above the words "Business Organization & Occupation Service Training" described against a thin, dark, rectangular background.

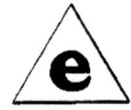

Reg. No. 2421618;
Reg. Date: 2001-01-16

Description of Mark: The mark consists of a checkered pattern of light and dark brown with an unusual contrast of weft and warp, and color is claimed as a feature of the mark. The pattern appears over substantially the entire surface of the goods. The lining constitutes a feature of the mark and itself does not indicate the colors described above. The matter shown in broken lines serves to show the positioning of the pattern on one of the goods, namely, a wallet.

Reg. No. 2427697;
Reg. Date: 2001-02-06

Disclaimer: The representation of the trigger bottle shape.

Description of Mark: The mark consists of a clear trigger bottle with a red cap and a red trigger handle, both attached to a white top, and with the neck of the bottle having a red upper section and a white section underneath, and the clear bottle containing a dual-layered liquid which appears through the clear bottle, with the two layers in the colors orange (top layer) and white (bottom layer). Color is claimed as a feature of the mark.

Reg. No. 2431472;
Reg. Date: 2001-02-27

Description of Mark: The mark consists of the sketch of a tree with the trunk transforming into a pencil.

XII Images

Reg. No. 2431546;
Reg. Date: 2001-02-27

Reg. No. 2436265;
Reg. Date: 2001-03-20

Disclaimer: "The design configuration of the goods."

Description of Mark: The mark consists of the configuration of a square, light blue bottle with rounded corners, having an eight sided conical top on which a stylized figure of an athlete appears, parallel ribs encircle the bottle which as a label and a darker blue cap.

Lining and Stippling: The lining on the bottle is intended to designated the color blue. The lining on the cap is intended to indicate the color blue and the lining on the label is intended to indicate the colors red and blue.

(Words Only): Vittel.

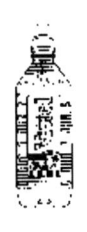

Reg. No. 2443841;
Reg. Date: 2001-04-17

Description of Mark: The mark consists of the signature of "Thomas A. Edison".

Reg. No. 2460550;
Reg. Date: 2001-06-12

Description of Mark: The mark consists of a depiction of three irregular lines created by crayons.

Lining and Stippling: The stippling in the drawing is a feature of the mark and does not indicate shading or color.

Reg. No. 2461532;
Reg. Date: 2001-06-19

Description of Mark: The mark consists of the word "Massengill" depicted in a stylized manner, specifically, the letter "M" is shown with a flower design appearing between the two peaks of the letter, within a ribbon design; under the ribbon design appears a panel showing a bathroom scene, featuring a bathtub with towel draped thereover and folded towels and washcloths and soaps in the background; to the right of the panel appear the words "Everyday Fresh" and a Seal Design with the same stylized "M" featured in the ribbon design described above.

(Words Only): Massengill Everyday Fresh M Trusted By More Women Since 1912

Reg. No. 2465306;
Reg. Date: 2001-07-03

Description of Mark: The mark consists of six rotating spheres. Applicant claims color as a feature of the mark. The six spheres are depicted in various colors, and these colors also appear between the spheres to reflect the rotation of the spheres around the perimeter of the circle. The colors of the spheres and in between the spheres are described with the corresponding Pantone Match system ("PMS") color as follows: Red (PMS 199u), Rubine (PMS 234u), Green (PMS 3295u), Blue (PMS 294u), Purple (PMS 527u) and Yellow (PMS 130u).

Lining and Stippling: The stippling in the mark is intended to reflect the shading of the mark, which depicts the rotation of the spheres. The stippling is not a feature of the mark.

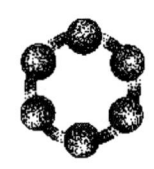

XII Images

Reg. No. 2494019;
Reg. Date: 2001-10-02
Lining and Stippling: The mark is lined for the colors purple and gray.

Reg. No. 2494399;
Reg. Date: 2001-10-02
Description of Mark: The mark consists of a stylized eagle.

Reg. No. 2495311;
Reg. Date: 2001-10-09
Description of Mark: The mark consists of a trash can design, with sides having a pebbly texture, and having a smooth plastic frame with corners on the diagonal to the sides.
Lining and Stippling: Color is not a feature of the mark.

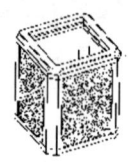

Reg. No. 2503242;
Reg. Date: 2001-10-30
Description of Mark: The mark consists of the color blue (Pantone Matching System No. 280) below the elliptical line design, the color teal (Pantone Matching System No. 3005) as the horizon immediately above the elliptical line design, and the color blue (Pantone Matching System 280) above the horizon, which is imprinted on silver metallic foil that comprises a toothpaste or tooth gel tube. The dotted outline of the cap of the tube and the tube are not part of the mark but is merely intended to show the position of the mark.
Lining and Stippling: The mark is lined for shades of blue, and color is a feature of the mark.

Reg. No. 2523590;
Reg. Date: 2001-12-25
Description of Mark: The mark consists of a series of dashes intended to represent a bag composed of see-through material (though certain portions will be obscured by printing on the bag) filled with mushroom spawn having bright orange particles interspersed throughout. The orange particles in the drawing are magnified. Magnification was necessary to allow for lining. The actual orange particles are smaller in size than the remaining particulate and are visible due to their coloration rather than size.
Lining and Stippling: The stippling is a feature of the mark and does not indicate color.

Reg. No. 2524075;
Reg. Date: 2002-01-01
Description of Mark: The mark consists of two seeds of the universe rotating counter clockwise to each other, each seed depicted in contrasting colors and separated from each other by another contrasting color.

Reg. No. 2524859;
Reg. Date: 2002-01-01
Description of Mark: The mark consists of a silhouette of a lamp.

Reg. No. 2526447;
Reg. Date: 2002-01-08
Description of Mark: The mark consists of a design generally circular shaped, made up of a number of elements, each are crescent in shape and overlap.

Reg. No. 2533131;
Reg. Date: 2002-01-22
Description of Mark: The mark consists of the design of interlinked diamond shapes used as a watermark.

XII Images

Reg. No. 2535181;
Reg. Date: 2002-02-05

Description of Mark: The mark consist of a formation of light beams resembling the conical framework of a tipi emanating from a circular source of light.

Reg. No. 2538512;
Reg. Date: 2002-02-12

Description of Mark: The mark comprises the overall design of a circle featuring the ancient swastika symbol derived from the Sanskrit word meaning "being fortunate" at the center. The symbol is encircled further by various depictions of the Yin-Yang symbols.

Lining and Stippling: The lining shown in the mark is merely to indicate shading

Reg. No. 2539168;
Reg. Date: 2002-02-19

Disclaimer: "Discount Auto Parts."

Description of Mark: The mark consists in part of a building configuration.

Lining and Stippling: The lining is a feature of the mark and does not indicate color.

Reg. No. 2539549;
Reg. Date: 2002-02-19

Description of Mark: The mark consists of the total impression of a multitude of small tablets in the colors blue and white. The colors, blue and white, are claimed as features of the mark.

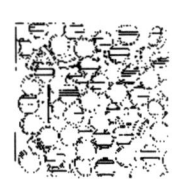

Reg. No. 2560030;
Reg. Date: 2002-04-09

Description of Mark: The mark consists of a stylized representation of a warehouse building seen from a ground level perspective. The five shapes on the left side of the mark represent loading dock doors receding in the distance. The large shape on the right represents an outside wall of the building bathed in sunlight.

Reg. No. 2564873;
Reg. Date: 2002-04-30

Description of Mark: The mark consists of a part circle or globe incorporating stripes extending partially from left to right as a means of portraying rotation.

Reg. No. 2567799;
Reg. Date: 2002-05-07

Disclaimer: "10, 20, 30" and "40."

Description of Mark: The mark consists, in part, of stylized tablets in the colors pink, green, yellow and blue.

Lining and Stippling: The drawing is lined for the colors pink, green, yellow, blue and red.

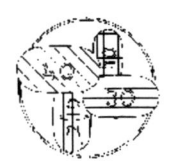

Reg. No. 2567941;
Reg. Date: 2002-05-07

Description of Mark: The mark consists of a six-petal floral design. The dotted lines shown on the borders of the drawing are not a part of the mark. The stippling shown in the drawing is a feature of the mark and is not intended to indicate color.

Reg. No. 2568512;
Reg. Date: 2002-05-07

Description of Mark: The mark consists of the grape scent of the goods.

Mark: (Sensory Mark Only)

XII Images

Reg. No. 2568837;
Reg. Date: 2002-05-14

Description of Mark: The mark consists of the configuration of a cylindrical bottle with a red cap and a decorative wave pattern, there is also a raised design of mountains with the word "Arrowhead" above the mountains. Applicant makes no claim to the cylindrical shape of the bottle or the cap, it is shown in the drawing only to indicate the application of the mark to a container.

Lining and Stippling: The lining on the bottle shows features of the bottle and is not intended to designate color. The lining on the cap is intended to indicate the color red.

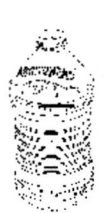

Reg. No. 2569635;
Reg. Date: 2002-05-14

Description of Mark: The mark consists of the configuration of numerous lollipops wrapped together in a transparent film with a band of securing material surrounding the pops along the stick portion. The packaged pops have the appearance of a bouquet.

Reg. No. 2571610;
Reg. Date: 2002-05-21

Description of Mark: The mark consists of a styled infinity symbol, with the middle crossing in a form of a styled letter "X". Both sides of the infinity symbol are half-opened, forming a double-sided arrow.

Reg. No. 2573116;
Reg. Date: 2002-05-28

Description of Mark: The mark consists of a stylized human figure inside a square, which partially contains a circle. The figure in the foreground (wearing a patterned tie), with arms outstretched at a 90 degree angle and feet together, is rendered in heavy lines (the "Foreground Figure"). Behind the foreground figure are stylized representations of another pair of legs, and two pairs of arms (the "Background Figure"). Clockwise from the top left, the Background Figure is shown holding - compact discs, papers, a briefcase and a telephone handset. The Background Figure is intended to create a sense of motion with reference to the Foreground Figure.

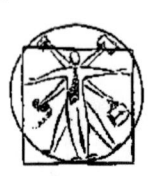

Reg. No. 2580468;
Reg. Date: 2002-06-11

Description of Mark: The mark is comprised of the configuration of a vehicle body which has a pair of wing-shaped grills with metallic veining on either vertical side of a generally triangular shaped hood, teardrop shaped fenders, narrow side and rear windows, and rounded, continuous pickup bed sides and tailgate.

Lining and Stippling: The lining shown in the mark, excluding the design of the grills, is merely to indicate shadowing.

Reg. No. 2583984;
Reg. Date: 2002-06-18

Description of Mark: The mark consists of a gel which is viscous, but still liquid. The gel is colored light blue and contains blue speckles. The colors, various shades of blue, are claimed as features of the mark.

Lining and Stippling: The drawing is lined for the color(s) blue.

296

XII Images

Reg. No. 2594558;
Reg. Date: 2002-07-16

Description of Mark: The mark consists of a modified pentagon shape tablet with a smaller raised pentagon shape at the top on both sides of the tablet.

Lining and Stippling: The stippling show on the drawing is for shading purposes only and does not signify color.

Reg. No. 2600861;
Reg. Date: 2002-07-30

Description of Mark: The mark consists in part of a three-leaf design.

Reg. No. 2614008;
Reg. Date: 2002-09-03

Description of Mark: The mark is comprised of a diamond-shaped black outline containing two (2) two-dimensional right-angled "L" shapes, one red and one black, with the red shape inverted and reversed and joined with the black shape to create a red and black diamond with red and black extensions at top left and lower right, respectively; a three-dimensional black sphere is superimposed over the center portion of the black and red diamond.

Lining and Stippling: The drawing is lined for the colors red. The stippling in the drawing is for shading purposes only.

Reg. No. 2616736;
Reg. Date: 2002-09-10

Lining and Stippling: The drawing is lined for the color red. The drawing is in black and red, and color is claimed as a feature of the mark.

Reg. No. 2617369;
Reg. Date: 2002-09-10

Description of Mark: The mark consists of a design of a horse facing left, overlaying a circle divided by a horizontal diameter.

Reg. No. 2621742;
Reg. Date: 2002-09-17

Description of Mark: The mark consists of the universal Om symbol.

XII Images

Reg. No. 2629751;
Reg. Date: 2002-10-08

Description of Mark: The mark consists of a miscellaneous design of slightly irregular rectangular shape with rounded sides and edges. A white square shape is the center of the design. Surrounding the square is a series of odd shapes resulting from bisecting lines within the rectangle. Each shape contains a different color. The upper portion of the left side is yellowish green, the left side of the interior portion of the top is light green, the exterior portion of the top is purple, the upper right corner is violet, the interior portion of the right side is magenta, the exterior portion of the right side is red, the interior portion of the lower right side is dark red, the exterior portion of the bottom is dark bluish green, the left side of the interior portion of the bottom is bluish green, the lower left corner is dark green, and the interior portion of the left side is green.

Lining and Stippling: The mark is lined for the colors green, yellow, green, purple, violet, magenta, red, dark red, dark bluish green, bluish green, dark green and green, and said colors are claimed as features of the mark.

Reg. No. 2630709;
Reg. Date: 2002-10-08

Description of Mark: The mark consists of a design of a horse facing right, overlaying a circle divided by a horizontal diameter.

Reg. No. 2638403;
Reg. Date: 2002-10-22

Reg. No. 2651962;
Reg. Date: 2002-11-19

Reg. No. 2681747;
Reg. Date: 2003-01-28

Description of Mark: The mark consists, in part, of a stylized drawing of a triangular-shaped measuring square in motion.

Lining and Stippling: The stippling is a feature of the mark and does not indicate color.

Reg. No. 2684917;
Reg. Date: 2003-02-04

Description of Mark: The mark consists in part of the configuration of the goods consisting of a dosage tablet in an almond shape, characterized by one end being narrower than the other.

Lining and Stippling: The stippling on the drawing is used to indicate shading and is not used to designate color.

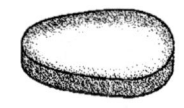

XII Images

Reg. No. 2737196;
Reg. Date: 2003-07-15
Description of Mark: The mark consists of the shape of a container for the goods in the shape of a female torso.

Reg. No. 2737383;
Reg. Date: 2003-07-15
Description of Mark: The mark consists of a design which represents the letters "GG" and also forms the shape of a butterfly.

Reg. No. 2738105;
Reg. Date: 2003-07-15
Description of Mark: The mark consists of a diamond shape. The upper left and lower right quarters of the diamond are inward pointing "V" shapes. The upper right and lower left quarters of the diamond each include two trapezoidal shapes.

Reg. No. 2752236;
Reg. Date: 2003-08-19

Reg. No. 2767075;
Reg. Date: 2003-09-23
Description of Mark: The mark consists of a stylized clockwise spiral with 13 short rays surrounding the outside of the spiral.

Reg. No. 2778472;
Reg. Date: 2003-10-28

Reg. No. 2781800;
Reg. Date: 2003-11-11

Reg. No. 2782146;
Reg. Date: 2003-11-11

Reg. No. 2783750;
Reg. Date: 2003-11-18

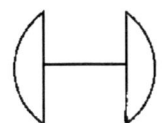

XII Images

Reg. No. 2795999;
Reg. Date: 2003-12-16

Description of Mark: The mark consists of a butterfly design. The upper portion of the left wing of the butterfly is blue, the center portion dark green, and the lower portion is light green. The upper portion of the right wing of the butterfly is red, the middle portion is orange and the lower portion is yellow. The body of the butterfly is purple. Color is claimed as part of the mark.

Reg. No. 2901090;
Reg. Date: 2004-11-09

Description of Mark: The mark consists of the color chocolate brown, which is the approximate equivalent of Pantone Matching System 462C, as applied to the entire surface of vehicles and uniforms. The mark consists of the color brown alone. The broken lines indicate the position of the mark and do not form part of the mark.

Lining and Stippling: The drawing is lined for the color brown.

Reg. No. 2914546;
Reg. Date: 2004-12-28

Description of Mark: The mark consists of a star-like design having six slightly curved arms radiating from a central point, accompanied by several smaller star designs.

Lining and Stippling: The stippling is a feature of the mark.

Reg. No. 2934291;
Reg. Date: 2005-03-22

Description of Mark: The mark consists of configuration of a prenatal vitamin tablet in the shape of a heart.

Reg. No. 3012841;
Reg. Date: 2005-11-08

Description of Mark: The mark consists of the ornamental design of a lid for a package which includes several corn ear designs.

Reg. No. 3017593;
Reg. Date: 2005-11-22

Disclaimer: "Adrenaline Sports";

Description of Mark: The mark consists of Two adjacent oppositely directed angular shaped designs overlaid with the word Extreme.

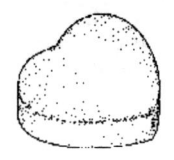

Reg. No. 3022077;
Reg. Date: 2005-11-29

Description of Mark: The mark consists of stylized design of a three-dimensional box.

Reg. No. 3029125;
Reg. Date: 2005-12-13

Description of Mark: The mark consists of the word Revel reading forward and the word Level reading like a mirror reflection of the word Revel, so that the letters in Lever appear backwards.

XII Images

Reg. No. 3061548;
Reg. Date: 2006-02-28

Description of Mark: The mark consists of design elements and color combinations appearing on uniforms worn by letter carriers when providing delivery and mail services. Specifically, the mark consists of a bluish-black stripe down each outer seam of the pants, a red over silvery-white stripe on each front pocket, a horizontal red over silvery-white stripe in the center of the back of the uniform jacket, and an eagle logo (subject of U.S. Reg. No. 1917921) over the mark "United States Postal Service" placed on the jacket's left chest and the front of a baseball style hat. Color is claimed as a feature of the mark.

Lining and Stippling: The broken lines along the outline of the uniform are not part of the mark but are merely intended to show the position of the mark and no claim is made to the configuration of the uniform itself.

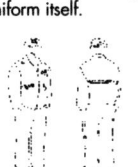

Reg. No. 3073740;
Reg. Date: 2006-03-28

Description of Mark: The mark consists of a stylized ram's head design.

Reg. No. 3075822;
Reg. Date: 2006-04-04

Description of Mark: The mark consists of a stylized "Y" stitching design on the pockets of the goods. The dotted lines serve to show the placement of the mark on the goods.

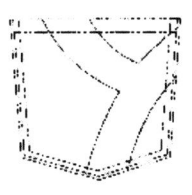

Reg. No. 3076949;
Reg. Date: 2006-04-04

Color(s) Claimed: The color(s) green, yellow, white is/are claimed as a feature of the mark.

Description of Mark and Any Color Part(s): The mark consist of the design element of a horizontal strip running along the edge of the canopy of a vehicle service with green, yellow and white device in the centre of the horizontal portion of the canopy fascia. The color green appears on the canopy fascia; the colors green, yellow and white appear on the circular decal in the centre of the horizontal portion of the canopy fascia.

Reg. No. 3081473;
Reg. Date: 2006-04-18

Description of Mark: The mark is the stylized letters IB forming a butterfly like shape.

Reg. No. 3114470;
Reg. Date: 2006-07-11

Color(s) Claimed: The color(s) gold, yellow and black is/are claimed as a feature of the mark.

Description of Color Part(s): The color gold appears in the bottle top. The color yellow appears in the center of the bottle. The color black appears in the etched wording Yves Saint Laurent.

Description of Mark: The mark consists of a configuration of a bottle for the goods featuring on one side horizontal grooves and letters engraved vertically in the material in variation of the wording Yves Saint Laurent.

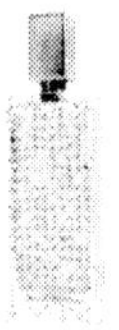

XII Images

Reg. No. 3141398;
Reg. Date: 2006-09-12

Description of Mark: The mark is a sound mark which consists of approximately an 8 to 10 second musical phrase. The time signature of the phrase is 4/4 and the approximate tempo is 112 to 116 bpm. The first measure of the phrase starts with a forte fanfare-like 6 note brass motive consisting of the notes C3,D3,EB3,D3,C3,G3 with a rhythm of (1/8 note rest) 16th note, 16th note, 8th note, 16th note, 16th note, half note. Then on beat 4 there is a low C minor forte sustained chordal hit played by percussion and lower brass and a "filter swept" synthesizer sound. In the second measure there is an "answering" forte fanfare-like 6 note brass motive starting on an upbeat consisting of the notes C3, D3, Eb3, D3, C3, Ab3 with a rhythm of (1/8 note rest) 16th note, 16th note, 8th note, 16th note, 16th note, half note. Then on beat 4 there is a low Ab major with a C in the bass forte sustained chordal hit played by percussion and lower brass. This is followed by a repeat of the first measures melodic content. On beat 4 of the third measure is a series of chords played by high brass (trumpets) . The sequence of chords is, starting on bar 3 beat 3 second 1/8 note, an 1/8 note C minor , then 1/4 notes F minor, Eb major and, in a half note rhythm, G major. The melodic content of this chord sequence is an 1/8th note F4, then in quarter notes, G4, Ab4, Bb4 and in a half note rhythm, B4. This then resolves to a chordal hit of a C minor chord with a C5 as the melody note. Last melody note is doubled on electric lead guitar processed with a "tap delay" that regenerates to fade out".

Mark: (Sensory Mark Only)

Reg. No. 3143735;
Reg. Date: 2006-09-12

Description of Mark: The mark consists of a vanilla scent or fragrance.

Mark: (Sensory Mark Only)

Reg. No. 3151994;
Reg. Date: 2006-10-03

XII Images

Reg. No. 3153559;
Reg. Date: 2006-10-10

Color(s) Claimed: The color(s) blue, black, and white is/are claimed as a feature of the mark.

Description of Mark and Any Color Part(s): The mark consists of the stylized letters C and D, in blue color, forming the shape of a heart, with a gray shadow extending from the letters. The color white is found in the background and as the insides of the heart designs.

Reg. No. 3183905;
Reg. Date: 2006-12-12

Reg. No. 3216067;
Reg. Date: 2007-03-06

Color(s) Claimed: The color(s) pale blue (272c by Pantone), orange (144c by Pantone) and lime green (369c by Pantone) is/are claimed as a feature of the mark.

Description of Mark and Any Color Part(s): The mark consists of three curved lines; the color pale blue appears in the left curved line, the color orange appears in the middle curved line and the color lime green appears in the right curved line of the mark.

Reg. No. 3221551;
Reg. Date: 2007-03-27

Reg. No. 3238974;
Reg. Date: 2007-05-08

Description of Mark: The mark consists of the configuration of a point of sale display comprising eight live Clydesdale horses hitched to a full-size beer wagon carrying cases of beer with uniformed human drivers and a dog.

Reg. No. 3259981;
Reg. Date: 2007-07-10

Description of Mark: The mark consists of a cylindrical beverage container with a cylindrical lid.

Reg. No. 3271576;
Reg. Date: 2007-07-31

303

ABOUT THE AUTHOR

Peter H. Karlen, founder of NEONYM Naming & Trademark Service and its principal naming professional, practiced intellectual property law for over 25 years, including art, literary, and entertainment law, and the law of trademarks, copyrights, and moral rights, with a specialty in trademark law. As a lawyer he was "AV" rated by Martindale-Hubbell. He was also concurrently active for 18 years in law school teaching both in the USA and UK, where he taught courses on art, entertainment, and intellectual property law.

Mr. Karlen is the author of over 325 trade and academic publications in the areas of aesthetics and art, publishing, and intellectual property law. In 1991 he began compiling the book that later became THE ART OF NAMING: NEONYM CREATIVE GUIDE TO SELECTING NAMES AND TRADEMARKS. In 2001 he began offering NEONYM naming and trademark selection services, and today he is dedicated exclusively to the creative side of the naming business.

Mr. Karlen has served clients in a wide range of industries, trades, and professions, including publishing, entertainment, art, apparel, nutrition, health/medical, physical fitness, personal development, spiritual disciplines, education, computer software, and other technical fields. He has been listed in numerous editions of *Who's Who in American Law* and *Who's Who in American Art*. He lives and works in La Jolla, California and can be contacted via the Contact Us page at **www.neonym.com**.